RMS QUEEN ELIZABETH
THE UNRUFFLED CUNARDER

RINGO VARISCO

Ferry
Publications

DEDICATION

This book is dedicated to the Late Harold Ernest Philpot who, aside from any one of the *Queen Elizabeth*'s captains or Chief Engineers, probably knew more about the workings of the ship than anybody else. His affection for the "Lizzie" was second to none. This book is also for Filomela – my number one fan, critic and motivator.

Published by Ferry Publications
(A trading name of Lily Publications IOM Ltd)
Copyright © 2015. All rights reserved.
ISBN 978-1-906608-95-8

The rights of Ringo Varisco to be identified as the author of this work have been asserted in accordance with the Copyright Act 1991.

No part of this publication may be reproduced, stored in a retrieval system or transmitted in any form or by any means, electronic, mechanical, photocopying, recording or otherwise, without prior permission in writing from the publisher.
Produced in the Isle of Man by Lily Publications Ltd.

Contents

Foreword 4

Introduction 6

Chapter 1
The Noble Ship: Coming to Life... Off to War 8

Chapter 2
The Working Ship 38

Chapter 3
Southampton – Cherbourg – New York: Earning Her Keep 56

Chapter 4
Adornment of the North Atlantic: A Nicer Shade of 'Grey' 76

Chapter 5
The Sixties and Beyond: A Difficult Time for an Ageing 'Queen' 112

Chapter 6
Hong Kong: A 'Queen' Dies 150

Chapter 7
Preserved for Posterity 178

Appendix 1: Chronology and Statistics 185

Appendix 2: Masters of The Queen Elizabeth 186

Appendix 3: RMS Queen Elizabeth Cruises 191

Acknowledgments 192

Bibliography 192

Foreword

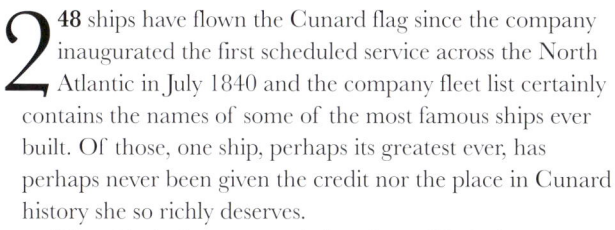

248 ships have flown the Cunard flag since the company inaugurated the first scheduled service across the North Atlantic in July 1840 and the company fleet list certainly contains the names of some of the most famous ships ever built. Of those, one ship, perhaps its greatest ever, has perhaps never been given the credit nor the place in Cunard history she so richly deserves.

That ship is the company's first *Queen Elizabeth*.

She was the first of three to carry what has probably become Cunard's most revered name.

History could have been so very different if hostilities had not erupted in September 1939 and it is not too difficult to wonder just what an introduction, what newspaper headlines and what acclaim the *Queen Elizabeth* would have received if she had entered service in 1940 as planned. What better way for Cunard to celebrate the centenary of its revolutionary service and the first permanent link between the Old and New Worlds than introduce the largest, greatest and – most probably – the fastest Atlantic liner the world had seen?

Cunard's new flagship would surely have dazzled the same old and new worlds the little *Britannia* had connected in 1840 and the same *Queen Mary 2* links today.

Whenever she was allowed to shine the *Queen Elizabeth* did so magnificently – a true masterpiece in the Atlantic tradition. She performed her war duties and passenger service with great style and flare despite being in the shadow of the *Queen Mary*, her elder, more famous and more dowdy sister. Perhaps even Cunard knew they had treated their masterpiece in an unbefitting way when her former owners became 'involved' with her again after she had left Atlantic service for a promised retirement in the sun.

The story of the *Queen Elizabeth* and her legacy lives on in this magnificent book by Ringo Varisco whose love of all things *Queen Elizabeth* is evident for all to see. Ringo has captured the spirit of the ship and, for the first time, completes her story with such a detailed account of the years the *Queen Elizabeth* bore another name and another livery – the white and yellow *Seawise University*.

But for many she will always remain the *Queen Elizabeth*.

It was an honour to be asked to write the foreword for such a special book and I would like to express my thanks to Ringo for ensuring the *Queen Elizabeth*'s continued place in Cunard, maritime and world history.

Michael Gallagher
Cunard Public Relations Manager and Historian,
January 2016

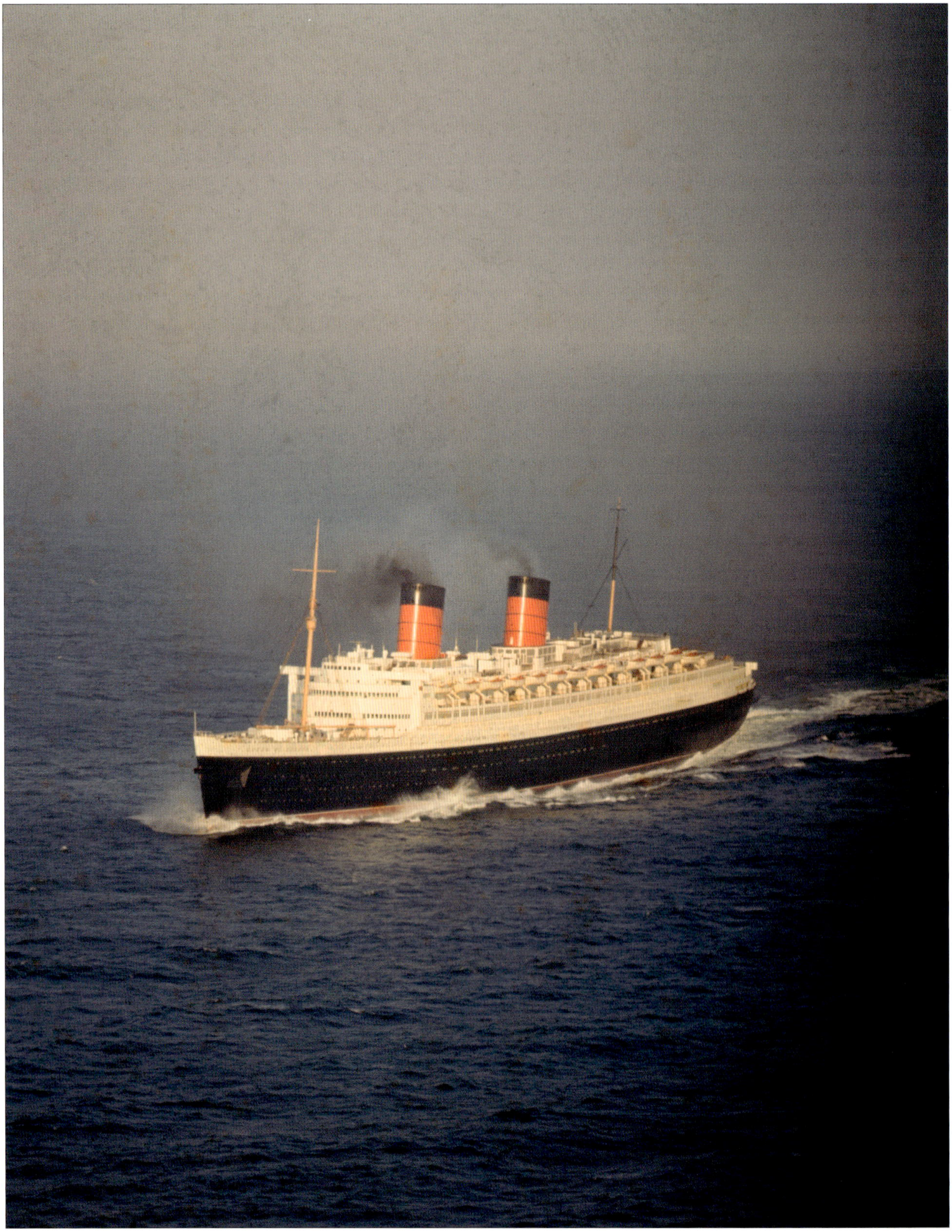

RMS Queen Elizabeth: the Unruffled Cunarder

Introduction

More than forty years have elapsed since the *RMS Queen Elizabeth*, re-named the *Seawise University*, was destroyed by fire and was broken-up in Hong Kong Harbour. This is a much longer time than the 34 years she was in existence, from 1938 to 1972.

Her hull was launched into the River Clyde in Scotland 77 years ago as the largest vessel in the world. Upon completion, she was the world's largest passenger ship, remaining so throughout her entire service life, into her retirement years, and long after her death at the hand of arsonists – a period of 58 years, from 1938 to 1996. No ship since has surpassed this record and it is likely no ship ever will, given the fast rate at which modern cruise ships supersede each other in dimension.

The face of a "Queen": The liner looks as solid as a mountain against the rolling white-caps of the blue, North Atlantic in the background. (Philpot/QEHS Collection)

Much has been said about this long-gone ship which many consider to be less desirable than her near-sister and more-famous running-mate the *RMS Queen Mary*. However, after so many years, time has not allowed her to be forgotten.

The noble and now iconic name *"Queen Elizabeth"* has, with the passing of time, become synonymous with that of Cunard – so much so that it has, once again been emblazoned along the bow of the most recent Cunarder. This gesture alone is the greatest tribute that could be bestowed on the *RMS Queen Elizabeth*, which was, bar none,

the most successful liner on the North Atlantic run for many years. It is an honour which has rekindled for ship buffs new and old alike, a refreshed interest in the original "Lizzie". She now becomes the only passenger liner, of this longest-surviving of all passenger ship lines, to lend her name to two worthy successors – the *Queen Elizabeth 2* (1969) and the M/v *Queen Elizabeth* (2010).

Despite having to work within size-restraints in regard to how much detail can realistically be included in a single volume, this work fills-in important gaps that exist regarding the life of the ship and those around her. It shines new light to a ship which has, in many respects, remained somewhat of an enigma. This is achieved both through the inclusion of many previously unpublished photographs and behind-the-scene details contributed by those involved.

Much inside information has been extracted from an archive of nearly 200 letters written between the ship's last English Master, Commodore Geoffrey Thrippleton Marr, and his good friend Harold Philpot.

An entire chapter is dedicated to the designing of the ship's décor and interior layout (a topic which until now has only superficially been covered), described by the Interior Architect himself – Grey Wornum – taken from his recently-unearthed and as-yet -unpublished biography.

To assist further with the re-discovery of this historic vessel, a complimentary CD is included with this book, containing various sound recordings as well as the phenomenal and unparalleled set of documentary drawings of the entire ship, that were expertly hand-drawn by Harold Philpot (Late). Harold was the founder of the *RMS Queen Elizabeth Historical Society* and the inspiration for producing this volume.

It is hoped, that by delving into this book, the current generation of cruise passenger and ship-lover in general, comes to appreciate just what fine ancestry and lineage the passenger ships of today have emerged from. Equally as important, the intention for this production is that it contributes to purging the "Lizzie", once and for all, from the unwarranted label as the "Forgotten Queen".

To her loyal fans – and there are a lot more than most have been led to believe – the *RMS Queen Elizabeth* is the most perfect, paradigmatic ocean liner, the quintessential "Queen", the consummate Cunarder; and – as will be confirmed in the following pages – the "Masterpiece of British Shipbuilding."

Allow yourself, as I have during my research and writing, to be transported back in time, and travel on a ship which had plenty of class and a tangible soul. Enjoy the journey for it is there that half the fun is had. Godspeed!

Ringo Varisco – April 2016

The three Queen Elizabeths: sharing an iconic name that is now synonymous with that of Cunard.

Chapter 1

The Noble Ship: Coming to Life… Off to War

Due to the ravages of World War I, Britain's passenger ship fleet was severely depleted by the second half of the 1920s, and those ships that had survived were noticeably aged. This, coupled with ever-increasing competition from other European sea-faring nations, was the stimuli the British shipping companies needed to replenish fleets and push harder at retaining their share of the very lucrative transatlantic passenger trade. The plans for building larger and more advanced British passenger ships were once again in place, only now, fast approaching the 1930s, there existed a whole new range of specifications, standards, and innovations.

Since its formation in 1840, the Cunard Line played a major role in influencing the size and speed, as well as the internal and external appearance, of the Ocean Liner. Cunard realised from early on that a ship's chances of commercial success depended largely on its ability to win-over public appraisal and satisfy passengers in all areas. Cunard was also wise in the knowledge that the designing of a successful ocean liner — a colossal and complex task — must involve the harmonious and combined efforts of naval architects, marine engineers, interior designers and artists. Successive new ship designs evolved partly due to ever-changing trends and fashions, but more so from the urgent need for more economically efficient liners.

Two Distinct Liners

Samuel Cunard's company had, in earlier times, used four ships to sustain the express passenger and mail service to New York from Liverpool, but by 1914, thanks to major advancements in maritime technology, the number of ships was reduced to three. Ongoing ship propulsion betterment, coupled with continual pressure to stay competitive and operate more economically, meant that by the mid 1920s, Cunard realised the need for a simultaneous ferry service in both directions, linking Europe with North America, using but two liners.

This "two-ship-policy", as it has become known, was the ambition and brainchild of visionary Cunard Chairman Sir Percy Bates. Bates' vision meant that for every week of the year, except for short periods of annual winter overhaul, one Cunarder would depart Southampton and the other New York. The two liners entrusted with the task were the *RMS Queen Mary* and the *RMS Queen Elizabeth*. Both were destined to become the most celebrated ships in the world.

In 1934, thanks mainly to Sir Percy's clever and timely negotiations, Cunard and the financially-crippled White Star Line, formed The Cunard White Star Limited. His foresight and brave decision-making saved both companies from going under as a result of the World Financial Crisis which, by 1930, had devastated businesses world-wide.

RMS Queen Elizabeth: the Unruffled Cunarder

Overnight the company's fleet grew to 25 ships — 15 from Cunard and 10 from the White Star Line. Not to lose time after the successful introduction to service of the beloved the *Queen Mary* in 1936, Cunard were now focused on building the next flagship of line: the *Queen Elizabeth*. That very same year, the naval architect and his team, began work on penning technical drawings to hull 534's successor and running mate — hull "552".

John Brown Gets the Job

Despite invitations to tender also given to shipbuilders Swan Hunter & Wigham Richardson, Cammell Laird, and Vickers Armstrong, it was somewhat of a foregone conclusion, following the completion of the *Queen Mary*, that the contract to build the second ship would fall in the hands of Messrs. John Brown of Clydebank. Nonetheless, it was officially made public in the House of Commons on the afternoon of 29th July 1935:

"The Chancellor has received specific proposals from the Cunard White Star Co., and has now agreed that advances shall be made, under the provision of The North Atlantic Shipping Act, for the building of a sister ship to the *Queen Mary*. The company have supplied evidence showing clearly that technical and commercial considerations oblige the Cunard White Star Company to give the order to John Brown and Co. Ltd."

On 6th October 1936 the official build contract for job 552 was signed, but not before British Prime Minister Neville Chamberlain first gave his approval.

Designing an Icon

The brilliant Sir James McFadyen McNeill (1892-1964) was John Brown & Co.'s principal naval architect and technical manager. McNeil had been with the Upper Clyde Shipbuilder since 1908, beginning as an apprentice draughtsman. As Sir Percy Bates' creative collaborator, McNeil completed the design specifications for the two ships needed to economically maintain the profitable, yet cut-throat, North Atlantic run — two, 1,000-foot-plus, fast "super-liners". The first, the *RMS Queen Mary*, was already hugely successful and twice holder the Blue Riband as

He planned Clydebank's "Queen" for and aft,
And now she's done her due
He whets his wits upon the draft
For Britains 552

Above: Sir James McFadyen McNeill (Philpot collection)
Left: Friday 4th December 1936: The laying of the *Queen Elizabeth*'s first keel plates. The beginnings of the largest ship the world had ever seen. (©SCOTLANDIMAGES.COM - The National Archives of Scotland)

The Noble Ship: Coming to Life, Off to War...

Sir James McFadyen McNeill: The brilliant Naval Architect responsible for designing both the Queens - *Mary* and *Elizabeth*. McNeill was knighted in 1950 and in 1954 he completed the design of The Royal Yacht Britannia. With his passing in 1964 the world lost one of the greatest naval architects of all time. (Philpot collection)

the world's fastest ship. McNeill and the John Brown yard had a big challenge ahead, to create an even better liner with job 552.

Responsibility for the details of 552's construction and lay-out rested with McNeill. He had the incomparable advantage of having been most active in his work at a time when passenger ship development was at its most progressive stage. He brought with him a wealth of indispensable experience through his work on previous ships which included the Canadian Pacific liner the *Empress of Britain* and culminating with his biggest project yet, the *Queen Mary*. He was, in the eyes of those who mattered most, the best choice for designer of Cunard's newest ship.

Testament to McNeill's skill and judgment was his prediction, to within inches, of just how far following its launch into the Clyde, the hull of the *Queen Mary* would travel in the water before coming to a complete halt within the confined space of the river. This extremely vital calculation is made that more difficult to solve due to indeterminable and unpredictable wind and tidal fluctuations, as well as the variation in resistance on the moving hull caused by an undulating river bed. His calculations predicted that the distance the *Mary's* hull would travel before stopping would be 1,196 feet. Quite remarkably, his estimation came to within 24 inches of what actually took place: the hull travelling 1,194 feet. It was vital that the Cunard White Star Line take full advantage McNeill's invaluable experience and proven competence, for it would render the construction of the next and very large job far less formidable.

Every ship owes a great deal to her predecessors and so it was that the major influence to the *Queen Elizabeth's* external appearance was the *RMS Queen Mary*. Her design was also influenced, although to a much lesser extent, by the *Aquitania* and the *Empress of Britain*. Job 552's overall design was, to a degree, a rule of thumb, with lineage progressing from these three earlier Clyde-built passenger liners. Not so widely known however, is that much inspiration for the *Queen Elizabeth's* hull design also came from two other famous hulls that emerged from the John Brown and Co. yard at Clydebank – the *HMS Hood* and the *HMS Repulse* which were, for a long time, the world's largest and fastest warships.

John Brown & Co. possessed experience in building very large, very fast ships — certainly the best of any British yard and possibly in the world. Historically, in British shipyards, hull form had always developed along fairly conservative lines. Moreover, the nation's shipbuilders were successful companies, made up of steadfast, parochial men with an inexorable attitude of: *why should we copy what other nations are doing when we are the leaders in ship design and always have been?*

Shipbuilder John Brown & Co. was fully aware of the latest foreign hull innovations, curiously observing the

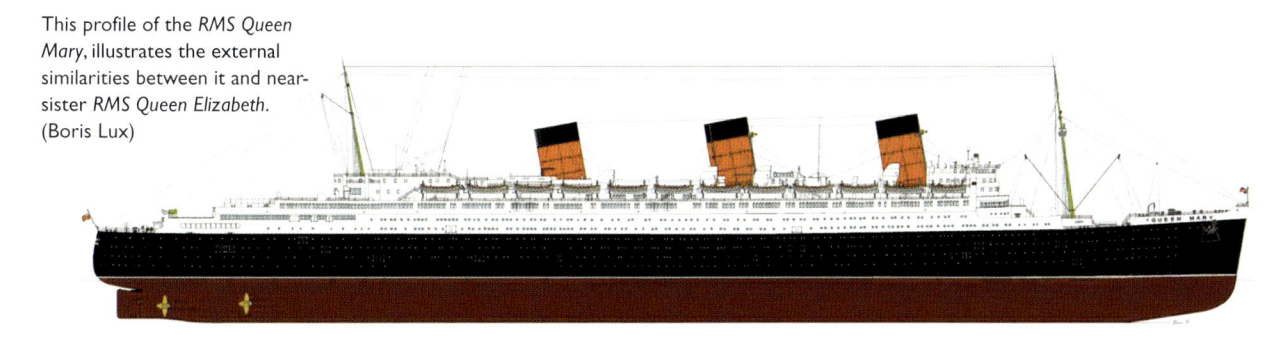

This profile of the *RMS Queen Mary*, illustrates the external similarities between it and near-sister *RMS Queen Elizabeth*. (Boris Lux)

RMS Queen Elizabeth: the Unruffled Cunarder

radical shapes that were emerging from nations across The Channel, namely Germany, France and Italy. But whether or not they would choose to break away from building their traditional trademark hull and imitate that which was being built overseas, was always going to be questionable. The Clydebank yard would, however, acknowledge the continental hulls a certain degree of worthiness, by stooping to performing tank-test experiments in order to determine once and for all if there was truth to the claim that the more streamlined foreign hulls performed more favourably in comparison to the Clydebank firm's well-established hulls.

In the months prior to the construction of job 552, Chairman Sir Percy Bates was put under pressure to consider adopting a more modern hull form on the upcoming Cunarder – something more innovative than the one adopted on the *Queen Mary*. It was even suggested under total secrecy that the *Normandie's* designer Vladimir Yourkevitch be given the task of designing 552's hull.

A complete and thorough study was made on the performance of job 552's French rival the *Normandie* in the John Brown yard's testing tank. At the conclusion of this study, Sir Percy Bates announced that: 'Partly as a result of this testing, the model of "552" will differ from that of "534", but will still not be of such an extreme type as that of the *Normandie*'. He also confirmed what builder John Brown had confirmed, that the *Queen Elizabeth* would be at least half a knot faster than the *Queen Mary*, due to changes that would be incorporated into the new liner's hull. Sir Percy did concede in a written statement that the *Normandie's* hull was: "an easier model to propel, but only in smooth water, with waves not exceeding three feet". "Beyond that", he said, "*Normandie's* model becomes a disadvantage – the Atlantic is rarely smooth enough to make the *Normandie's* hull form worthwhile month in and month out."

The *Queen Elizabeth* was ultimately built with slightly more 'tweaked' propulsive machinery compared to the

The 'Queens' advocate: A Stunning painting of Sir Percy Bates, Cunard's legendary Chairman from 1930 until his death in 1946. (©National Museums Liverpool, artist unknown)

A tough bunch: It was stalwart and spirited Scotsmen like these who put the *RMS Queen Elizabeth* together, but that's probably as far as their connection with the ship would go, unlikely to form part of the social class of people who would travel on her. (QEHS collection)

Above: March 24th 1937. The triangular-shaped brackets seen here indicate the 'Hull Crown', where the hull begins its curve upward at the level of the tank tops. The double-bottom is now complete and will be plated over. Most of the people in this photo are boys with a minimum age of fifteen. They were employed as apprentices by the shipyard. The minimum apprenticeship age was raised to sixteen in later years. (©SCOTLANDIMAGES.COM - The National Archives of Scotland)

Above: 1937: Men had to work in increasingly confined spaces as the double-bottom framework nears completion. Although hard to believe, there exists more than one instance of a worker being entombed, accidentally or otherwise within the hull, during a ship's construction. The poor fellow's skeleton only discovered when the ship was broken up many years later. (Cunard - supplied by Open Agency Ltd.)

Right: June 12 1937: Visible in this view looking forward, is the four foot wide and six feet tall round topped pipe and escape tunnel, located on the forward tank tops – tanks used for domestic fresh water and drinking water. (Philpot Collection)

RMS Queen Elizabeth: the Unruffled Cunarder

Deep Inside the hull, shut-off from external light, workmen fasten the deck plates with hydraulic riveting hammers. This work created a booming percussion of metal on metal which reverberated and recoiled in all directions within the hull.
(©SCOTLANDIMAGES.COM - The National Archives of Scotland)

The Noble Ship: Coming to Life, Off to War...

22 April 1938: The men building '552' were content in the knowing that they had secured work for themselves and for their families and proud to know they were building the biggest ship in the world - a great national achievement. (Philpot/QEHS Collection)

Queen Mary, but any major speed advantage would still have to come mainly from developments in her hull design. There were two major alterations made to job 552 which would, under normal circumstances, enable her to go slightly faster than the *Queen Mary*. These were firstly, a

June 6th 1938. This panoramic view, taken three and a half months before the ship's launch, shows work progressing at the stern on A-Deck. Here will be installed motorised mooring equipment, bollards and capstans. The opening on the deck is the steering gear casing which would later be covered over with a skylight.
(©SCOTLANDIMAGES.COM - The National Archives of Scotland)

larger water-plane area at the after-end of the hull, enabling improvements to be made to the lines of the propeller shaft casings and brackets. This had the effect of minimising the turbulent reaction between the outer propellers and hull. Secondly, a complete fairing, using a rubber-based cement, of the entire hull surface below the water line, at the areas where shell plates overlapped one another — the so-called called Butt Straps. This experimental technique allowed the *Queen Elizabeth's* hull to be move slightly faster through the water by reducing skin frictional resistance or drag.

What many people still ask today is, *was the Queen Elizabeth's speed ever proven to be consistently faster than the Queen Mary's?* One would think so, however, despite the "Lizzie's" officers and engineers continually saying she was the faster of the two, there is a lack of official evidence to support the claim. Either the *Queen Elizabeth* didn't live up to expectations or, perhaps more plausibly, those in charge at Cunard wouldn't allow unnecessary competition to develop between her and the *Queen Mary*. Record-breaking was outside their policy but regularity of service and safety was not. Further, seeing that the *Queen Elizabeth's* speed was at least comparable to that of the *Queen Mary's*, they instructed their crew to be content in the knowledge that they had secured the Blue Riband with the fastest passenger ship in the world, and now, with the *Queen Elizabeth*, they also had the biggest.

Job 552 Takes Shape

Lacking all commemoration, with just two officials in black suits and bowler hats as the only on-lookers, the *Queen Elizabeth's* first, 6x15-foot keel plates were very gently lowered onto the blocks on Slipway Number 4. That was Friday the 4th December 1936, and from that day on hull 552 went ahead in a no-nonsense and unpretentious manner.

In the first months of the ship's construction, she was coming to life at an impressive pace. Then without warning, from July 1937, progress on the *Queen Elizabeth* became seriously affected by a shortage of steel supplies and delays

RMS Queen Elizabeth: the Unruffled Cunarder

Tuesday September 27th, 1938 – launch day: Basking in the early morning Clydebank sunshine, is the future "Queen" of the seas. Later that day and in a counter-amphibious way, the hull would venture from the land, whence it came into being and complete its evolution in the water, becoming the largest passenger liner the world had ever seen. (Philpot Collection)

in the delivery of materials required for construction of both her hull and machinery. The setback was so serious that even the Director of the Clydebank Yard, Mr Stephen J. Pigott, later revealed at a post-launch gathering that: "In one respect, progress with the construction of the *Queen Elizabeth*, up until her launch, had been far more difficult than in the building of the *Queen Mary*."

The shortage of steel and delays in deliveries was caused by the increasing number of naval vessels and military machinery being constructed at that time. Things became so critical that grave fears emerged for meeting the scheduled launch deadline. It was, for a while, thought that her launch would have to be indefinitely postponed. Thanks only to the considerate cooperation and timely aid forthcoming from the suppliers of the various building materials; the predicament of delaying the launch was eventually averted.

The industrial empire which was the John Brown Works, with its engineering and machine shops, forges, smelting and milling sheds, would self-produce a great deal of the steel structures used in constructing the ship, including

This ticket permitted the bearer a view of the *Queen Elizabeth's* launching from the fields of Inchinian, directly across the River from the slipway. An estimated 150,000 spectators witnessed the launching from this area. 40,000 people viewed the launch from within the John Brown yard, and several hundred VIP's, including the Royal Party, were seated in the specially constructed viewing platform right next to the ship's bow. (Philpot Collection)

The Noble Ship: Coming to Life, Off to War...

Above: September 26th 1938, the day prior to launching: The impressive raked bow looms high above the Royal Box below. Some workmen found time to gather on the fo'c'sle' for a few moments, chatting or just leaning against the ship's rails, taking in the sights of the shipyard and Clydebank in the background. (Philpot/QEHS Collection)

Left: She's moving! Cunard White Star Chairman Sir Percy Bates points up at the departing hull. By good fortune, Her Majesty Queen Elizabeth was one of the first persons aware of the ship's premature, off-cue movement and just in time managed to name the ship, baptizing her with a decorated bottle of Australian wine. Judging by the photo, stiff necks were the order of the day.
(Courtesy of Ian Johnston, Glasgow)

much of the machinery for the two main engine rooms and the twelve, enormous Yarrow-Type boilers.

Draughtsmen in the yard's drawing offices produced many hundreds of drawings that documented each and every single part of the ship. These were utilised in an enormous shed called the Mould Loft, where one of the most skilled jobs in shipbuilding, known as 'Lofting', took place. The shipwright, using a piece of white chalk, transferred onto the enormous floor expanse of this otherwise featureless room, the master lines from the plans to create exact moulds for each individual plate, frame or other part, in their full-scale.

The yard's steel mills delivered a rough-shaped plate or bar to the forges and plating sheds, which was then cut,

RMS Queen Elizabeth: the Unruffled Cunarder

The huge crowd went wild, cheering Britain's latest and greatest shipbuilding triumph. The launching cradles on the bows support the hull and the piles of drag chains will soon come into play, arresting the vessel's reverse motion once fully immersed in the Clyde. (Philpot Collection)

sheared, stamped and pounded by machines into its unique curve and shape, previously patterned to precision in the Mould Loft. Each completed and numbered plate, beam and bracket was then, either by locomotive or horse-drawn cart depending on its size, carried out to the waiting cranes at the appropriate part of the ship to be installed.

Her Majesty Queen Elizabeth Lends Her Name

On 27th September 1938, the 1,031 foot-long hull, weighing 39,400 tons, was ready for launching into the River Clyde. Her Majesty Queen Elizabeth, accompanied by her two young daughters Princess Margaret and Elizabeth, travelled to Clydebank to perform hull 552's naming ceremony and release the newly-baptised hull into its element. The Queen's husband, His Majesty King George VI, had also planned to travel to Scotland and stand beside his wife as she launched the ship bearing her name but at the request of the British Prime Minister, cancelled the trip the evening before due to the political turmoil which began three weeks earlier, on the 3rd September, when Britain and France declared war on Germany.

Prior to the launch, Sir Percy Bates in the Royal Box, spoke:

"May it please Your Majesty; I am speaking for all who have combined to build this ship when I say I wish to express our deep regret that his Majesty the King is unable to be present as planned. I hope that in his Majesty's absence my address of welcome will be acceptable to your Majesty. I desire to offer sincere thanks for your Majesty's gracious presence here to-day.

Left: Damming the Clyde: For a moment, the *Queen Elizabeth's* hull became like a huge cork, plugging the entire breadth of the River. (Philpot Collection)

Above: On the 5th of August 1939, the two-and-a-half foot tall brass letters were screwed into place, providing the ship with one of her most important and recognisable features - her name. The letters, spelling out "Queen Elizabeth", occupied a length sixty-seven feet along both sides of her bow. (©SCOTLANDIMAGES.COM - The National Archives of Scotland)

Critical point: At this precise moment of the launch, the stern is afloat while the bows are still are still land locked. It was the job of the two forward launching poppets or cradles to relieve the enormous stresses and strains on the unsupported middle-section of the hull, thus preventing the keel and decks above from buckling and sagging. (Philpot Collection)

The newly-launched hull being towed to the fitting-out basin. Once there, one of the first tasks was the installation of her propelling machinery. The boilers and main engines, due to their extraordinary size and weight, were handled in sections and re-assembled in their appropriate spaces within the hull. (©SCOTLANDIMAGES.COM - The National Archives of Scotland)

Mid-1939: A dramatic image which gives the impression that the *Queen Elizabeth's* nose is pressing right up against of the wall of the factory building that houses the engine shop (right) and foundry, directly opposite the prow. (Philpot Collection)

The Noble Ship: Coming to Life, Off to War...

"...Thanks to his Majesty's Government, this ship's progress has been smoothed, and, therefore, I call her fortunate. But she is doubly fortunate in having secured your Majesty's name for her own. It is reserved for your Majesty to set us on the last lap of the road to success, and we shall all strive to be worthy of your grace to-day."

Following a poignant speech by Her Majesty, there was a short pause in which the optimum high tide for the launch was awaited. This would occur at precisely 15:30. Just seconds after the half hour, and totally unexpectedly, the precariously-balanced hull, with most of the log shores supporting it, pulled away and began of its own accord to creep down the slipway still un-named. Job 552 had moved

Above: 21 August 1939: The raising of the foremast. The forward funnel is virtually complete and dons Cunard livery. Clydebank's historic Titan crane is seen in the background keeping an eye on procedures. (©SCOTLANDIMAGES.COM - The National Archives of Scotland)

Below: 28 August 1939: Squeezed-in tight within the fitting out basin, next to the single-funnelled *Queen Elizabeth*, are left to light, the Federal Steam Navigation Company's cargo ship, *M.V. Suffolk*, and Crown Colony-Class light Cruiser *H.M.S Fiji*. The Fiji is seen here being fitted-out after being launched at the John Brown yard in May 1939. She would be sunk by enemy planes off Crete two years later, with a loss of 241 souls of the 764 on board. (©SCOTLANDIMAGES.COM - The National Archives of Scotland)

RMS Queen Elizabeth: the Unruffled Cunarder

a short distance down the ways before most people in the stands had become aware of the runaway hull; however, Her Majesty was immediately aware of the situation, perhaps being alerted by a loud shout from below – "She's moving!" Her Majesty swiftly yet very calmly, reached for the ceremonial scissors and cut the ribbon, at the same time speaking the following words into a switched-off microphone: "I name this ship *Queen Elizabeth* and wish success to her and all who sail in her."

Following these now famous words, audible only to those in Her Majesty's immediate vicinity, a specially decorated bottle of premium, Australian red wine only just managed to catch the departing hull, smashing and spilling its contents onto the bow. Despite the glitches, the launch was a

Right: Skilled hands: Carpenters are applying some of the beautiful wood veneer that was found throughout the interior of the ship. In this instance, an attractive burled-maple veneer along one of the *Queen Elizabeth's* plethora of corridors. (Philpot Collection)

Below: The highly-polished, inner starboard propeller has been fitted to its shaft and is being fine-tuned. (Philpot Collection)

The Noble Ship: Coming to Life, Off to War...

Above: A montage of two photographs taken from the crows nest in February 1940, just a few days before her secret escape to New York. A metal plate armour which, bends downward at the bridge windows, has been laid on 'Monkey Island' to shield the bridge below it from possible bomb and bullet damage. Bullet-proof cabins have been fitted to the ends of both bridge wings. (©SCOTLANDIMAGES.COM - The National Archives of Scotland)

Below: In this photo, taken from the west crane, workers suspending a degaussing girdle or coil. This new invention, which girthed the entire ship, had the effect of demagnetising the statically-charged hull so that floating mines would not be attracted to it. Later on in the war, a larger, more secure coil would be fitted further down the hull. These were the days shortly before her departure in February 1940 and the final work into getting the ship seaworthy and capable of moving under her own power proceeded at a frantic pace. The entrance to the bridge is fully armoured and all windows are painted over. She is almost ready to go to war. (©SCOTLANDIMAGES.COM - The National Archives of Scotland)

resounding success. It took 60 seconds for the hull to be completely waterborne, with a top speed reached of 15 miles per hour reached just before entering the water.

Once the *Queen Elizabeth* had come to a stop, feet from the opposite bank, tugs took hold and were busy for one hour, manoeuvring the behemoth into its berth within the fitting-out basin, a man-made estuary located immediately adjacent the slipway. From there, the next and final phase of her construction would begin — the installation of the propelling and navigating machinery, building of the superstructure, and completion of her interior furnishings and fittings.

In approximately one year's time, the *Queen Elizabeth* would be handed over to Cunard White Star, but not before a series of sea trials to test her engines and seaworthiness. That was the normal procedure for a newly built ship, but the start of World War II would see to it that "normal procedures" when it came to the passenger liner the *RMS Queen Elizabeth*, would be waivered for the next six years.

HMT *Queen Elizabeth* -The Grey Years

By late 1939, with the *Queen Elizabeth* nearing completion, some loud critics in British parliament accused her of being a 'white elephant' and it was strongly suggested she would better serve the Empire if she was scrapped on the spot and her steel used to build ships for the Admiralty instead. There was now a frantic and exponential demand for vessels of war and for steel with which to build them — not for passenger ships. Most liners were now being requisitioned or laid up in what few neutral ports existed around the world for safe keeping.

A topic of much concern was the position in which the huge ship now found itself, well upstream, in a narrow river that was dotted with vital shipbuilding yards. Many opponents saw the ship as a sitting duck, a dangerous liability to the country, and called for her immediate dismantling. Adolf Hitler had already offered an Iron Cross to the Luftwaffe Pilot, battleship or U-boat Captain who sank her. For her own safety and for the security of John Brown's and the other shipbuilding yards along the Clyde that were so crucial to building warships, the *Queen Elizabeth* had to be removed from the Clyde a soon as possible.

On 2nd November 1939, the Lord of the Admiralty, Winston Churchill, finally made the decision which, for all intents and purposes, saved the *Queen Elizabeth* from being converted into an aircraft carrier or from the cutters torch for scrapping. Churchill saw the virtue of using her as a troop transporter in combination with the *Queen Mary*. Because of their great size and speed, both ships would encumber enemy advances world-wide by disembarking huge numbers of allied soldiers in a short time, indeed entire divisions wherever needed, thus out-numbering the enemy and giving the Allies the upper hand. Two days after Churchill's announcement, the *Queen Elizabeth* was painted over in a cheerless slate-grey.

Extra hands were immediately employed to hasten the essential work which would get her ready for sea, to take on her revised trooping role. The work had to be done quickly, as 26th February 1940 would provide the next king or flood-

Above right: 26th of February 1940: The Grey-clad, *RMS Queen Elizabeth*, finally leaves Clydebank to start her maiden voyage. Thankfully, an equally grey-clad security blanket cloud cover was in place that morning, offering Nazi bombers no view whatsoever of what was taking place below. To reduce her draught, only four of her twenty six lifeboats were left on board for the short journey to the Tail O the Bank. (©SCOTLANDIMAGES.COM - The National Archives of Scotland)

Right: Safe harbour: On March 7th 1940, the *Queen Elizabeth* arrived into New York Harbour, triumphantly completing her clandestine maiden voyage. (Philpot Collection)

The Noble Ship: Coming to Life, Off to War...

tide, creating water deep enough to allow the *Queen Elizabeth's* keel plates to clear the river bed and let the ship to move unobstructed down the narrow, shallow-in-parts, river. There were but two such high tides per year and if missed, the next opportunity wouldn't exist until six months later. It was imperative she left on time.

All work relating to the passenger living areas was discontinued. Most staterooms and public spaces would remain incomplete, with none of the intended lavish fittings or cosy furniture added to them. The crucial tasks now included work on her plumbing system and power plant, the navigational and mooring equipment, lifeboats and the teak decking. Work also included the blacking-out of all windows and portholes, and the suspension of a degaussing girdle or coil, hung from large hooks which encircled the entire hull at the level atop A-Deck, de-magnetising the liner's statically-charged hull so that floating mines would not be attracted to it. In the first few days of 1940, following the brief and successful testing of her propulsion machinery, the still-unfinished liner was declared as "capable of putting to sea".

An Inconspicuous Start

Following registration at Custom House in Liverpool, the *Queen Elizabeth* was given the official number of 166290 and her official call sign, GBSS. She was fuelled and stocked with provisions and her tanks filled with fresh water. On 22nd February her crew boarded, and in just four days the *Queen Elizabeth* would finally be leaving home for a secret destination.

In the months prior to her departure, high-flying German reconnaissance planes flew almost daily over Glaswegian skies, checking the progress of the *Queen Elizabeth*. As the morning of 26th February 1940 dawned, it thankfully revealed a dark, drizzly day. The overcast sky would deny spy planes any clue as to what was unfolding underneath the protective cloud-blanket at the Clydebank yard. Nevertheless, everyone was tense, the day of the ship's flight from Clydebank would be one of the most dangerous she would ever face.

It took just under five hours for the *Queen Elizabeth* to reach her anchorage at the Tail O the Bank, arriving at

Near-sisters, *Queen Elizabeth* and *Queen Mary*, meet and greet each other for the first time, with a dipping of their respective Red Ensigns. The grandiose Gaul, *Normandie*, was nearby to witness this historic British get-together. For two weeks, in February of 1940, New York was treated to the spectacle of having the three largest, longest, fastest, costliest, most beautiful ships in the world, berthed side by side. The *Queen Mary* was the first to depart, followed by *Queen Elizabeth* eight months later while *Normandie*, sadly, would never leave…intact that is. (Richard Weiss collection)

Above: 7th March 1940. Good work Jack! Photographed on the Captain's Open Bridge, Captain J.C. Townley looks relieved at having safely guided the *Queen Elizabeth* into New York for the first time. He casually described the daring and secret maiden crossing on an untested ship, as being: "just a lovely cruise", adding, with a touch more seriousness: "we're just glad that she's safe." Similar sentiments were shared by Her Majesty Queen Elizabeth who sent a telegram to the ship reading: "I send you my heartfelt congratulations on the safe arrival of the *Queen Elizabeth* in New York. Please convey to Captain Townley my compliments on the safe conclusion of her hazardous maiden voyage." Another telegram, from the missus back home in Hampshire, simply read: "good work Jack!" (Philpot Collection)

Above: Extra protection: Two motorcycle cops are on the job of patrolling the area between Piers 90 and 92, underneath the raised West Side Highway. The *Queen Elizabeth* was well guarded against any possible subversive or mischievous behaviour during her time in New York, especially from Nazi advocates who may have had their headquarters in the city. Extra fire lookouts were posted all over the ship and at night she was kept well floodlit. It wasn't sabotage, rather negligence on the part of a worker, which caused the liner *Normandie* to catch fire and eventually capsize on the 9th of February 1942. (Jessica Barrios)

Below: With the *Queen Mary* now on her way to embark Australian troops in Sydney, Hobart, and Fremantle, the *Queen Elizabeth* remained as the sole companion to a melancholy *Normandie*. This rare colour photograph was taken late in March of 1940. (Richard Weiss collection)

25

The *Queen Elizabeth* was eventually moved to the south side of Pier 90, taking the *Queen Mary*'s berth alongside *Normandie*. The 'Lizzie' was manned, provisioned and ready to sail at a moment's notice and notice came soon enough - on the 12th of November 1940. The 'Lizzie's' instructions were to sail for Singapore for dry-docking and the continuation of her troopship conversion. (Philpot Collection)

RMS Queen Elizabeth: the Unruffled Cunarder

17:15. She picked up the rest of her lifeboats and the remainder of her crew, which now totalled a complement of some 500 persons, the majority of these coming chiefly from Cunarder the *Aquitania*.

After a brief ceremony in the Third Class dining room, the following morning, the new ship was officially handed over to the Cunard White Star. Records showed she was indeed a Cunarder, but for an unforeseeable length of time she would have to perform war duties as His Majesty's Troop Ship. This was probably the first time ever that an uncompleted ship was handed over to her owners lacking full-scale testing and sea trials, but her builders had great faith in her, and there simply was no other way it could be done.

Much contemplation and planning went into deciding what deceptive tactics should be used in getting the *Queen Elizabeth* to a safe, neutral port. Certainly none existed anywhere in the British Isles. Paranoia, propaganda, scepticism and fear – each was running rampant and caused largely by the knowledge that the Germans were actively searching, desperately wanting to sink her. One negligent slip of the tongue and the *Queen Elizabeth's* contribution to World War II would be over before it started.

Because nobody could be trusted, an audacious and adventurous bluff was thought up. It would fool not only the Germans, but also any Brit who did not need to know the truth about the whereabouts of the liner once it left the shipyard. The ploy was to make the whole world believe that the *Queen Elizabeth*, once having left Clydebank, was on its way to dry-docking in Southampton. If the ship was to have any chance of escaping to safety, it was imperative that the enemy was looking the wrong way. The name Southampton was publicly yet very subtly dropped so as not to make it too obvious that the Nazis were being duped.

At Southampton's Ocean Dock warehouses, many large crates began arriving by train from Clydebank, containing all the paraphernalia that was to be fitted into the *Queen Elizabeth* had she not been requisitioned for war duty. Further to this, the King George V Dry Dock was reserved so that the ship could have her rudder and propellers inspected, and many hotel rooms were booked around the docks area to supposedly accommodate all the workers that would be carrying out the continuation of the ship's fitting-out. One final, convincing touch was to get Southampton Pilot, Captain Duncan Cameron, to board the ship whilst she was still in the Clyde Estuary – a clever ploy, further

The First-Class Lounge is filled with attentive troops, during a briefing on one of the *Queen Elizabeth's* wartime voyages. (Philpot Collection)

Above: 11th of April 1941 - At anchor shortly before her first departure from Sydney: On board are 5,333 Aussie and Kiwi diggers, made up of army air force and naval personnel, on their way to the Red Sea. Evident is the 6-inch gun mounted on her aft mooring-deck and less conspicuous is a 3-inch AA Gun on the raised Boat-Deck, one of three installed in the Singapore drydocking, where the ship's hull was also repainted black. This unusual colour scheme lasted only until mid-May in 1941, after which the hull was repainted grey once more. (Australian War Memorial)

Below: June 1941: An in-coming H.M.T *Queen Elizabeth* and an out-going H.M.T. *Queen Mary*, meet off Sydney Heads during the early stages of WW2 when both ships carried Australian and New Zealand troops to the stages of war. Both ships met at sea for the first time on the 9th of April 1941, in an almost identical position to this, just outside Sydney Harbour. (Australian War Memorial)

Left: 'Forenoon Watch' - painted in 1943 by Australian maritime artist Oswald Brett. Brett served as Able Seaman on the 'Lizzie' during WW2, from 1941 to 1945. This picture of the port bridge wing of HMT *Queen Elizabeth* was sketched by Brett in the spring of 1943, during his watch in the crows nest, on a westbound North Atlantic crossing. (Oswald Brett)

Below: *Sunrise at Suez:* The original sketch was drawn on location, by Oswald Brett during breakfast hour break (8-9a.m.) on Monday 24th November 1941, looking west towards the Egyptian Hills. The painting shows HMT *Queen Elizabeth* approaching anchorage at Port Tewfik, Egypt with the last detachment of Australian troops (A.I.F.) to the Middle-East. The oil painting now hangs in the Australian War Memorial Museum Collection, Canberra. It (Oswald Brett)

Above: With barely sufficient clearance on both sides and in one of the very few dry docks around the world which could accommodate her, the *Queen Elizabeth* receives a protective coat of grey paint in Esquimalt, BC, Canada, in 1942. Inside, the ship also received a much-needed fumigation and on her foredeck, 3-inch guns were mounted. Initial work to lower the position of her degaussing cable is evident in the form of a row of small brackets along the length of the hull. (Cunard Archives)

Right: Flt. Lt. Fitzjohn in his B24 'V' Victor Liberator snaps a wonderful stern-view of an ocean-slicing *Queen Elizabeth*, carrying close to eight thousand men to the war zones of Europe. There were occasions when enemy subs managed to get sightings of the *Queen Elizabeth* and there were reports of torpedoes actually fired. On November 12th 1942, a dispatch from Germany's high command stated that the *Queen Elizabeth* had been torpedoed by *U-704* in the North Atlantic and was badly damaged. Dispatches from Germany often contained misleading and false statements intended for propaganda purposes. (Graham Fitzjohn. Photo: Frank Fitzjohn)

The Noble Ship: Coming to Life, Off to War...

20th of August 1945 - The *Queen Elizabeth's* maiden call into Southampton. When the ship was finally secured at Ocean Dock, the Mayor J.C Dyas went aboard to welcome Captain Fall and personally thank him for bringing 'Southampton's baby safely home'. (Philpot Collection)

signalling the intention that the *Queen Elizabeth* was headed for Southampton.

The earliest conceivable date in which the *Queen Elizabeth* could arrive into Southampton would be on the 3rd March 1940. By coincidence or not, on that very same day, several Luftwaffe planes were spotted high above the city and also for the next few days to follow. The feint had worked. By the time the enemy realised that they had been made fools of, the *HMS Queen Elizabeth*, under the experienced Command of Captain Jack Townley, was already knuckling down, one day out into the North Atlantic, headed for New York, zigzagging westward under total ship black-out and keeping well away from regular shipping lanes.

The Maiden Voyage

The *Queen Elizabeth's* maiden voyage was also her first mission of the war: to get over to the other side as quickly as

RMS Queen Elizabeth: the Unruffled Cunarder

possible without being torpedoed. This daring voyage has been described in every book on the subject as a "secret dash", but her entire wartime service was made up of one clandestine dash after the other. Every mission and destination, every one of her movements throughout the duration of the war was top secret and carried out under complete black-out and mostly radio silence. Any photograph taken of her during this time was highly-classified government information and subject to stringent censorship.

For the next five days, the radio-silenced liner was

20 February 1946: The *Queen Elizabeth* is joyously welcomed into New York Harbour repatriating a boat load of troops who had fought in Europe. (Philpot Collection)

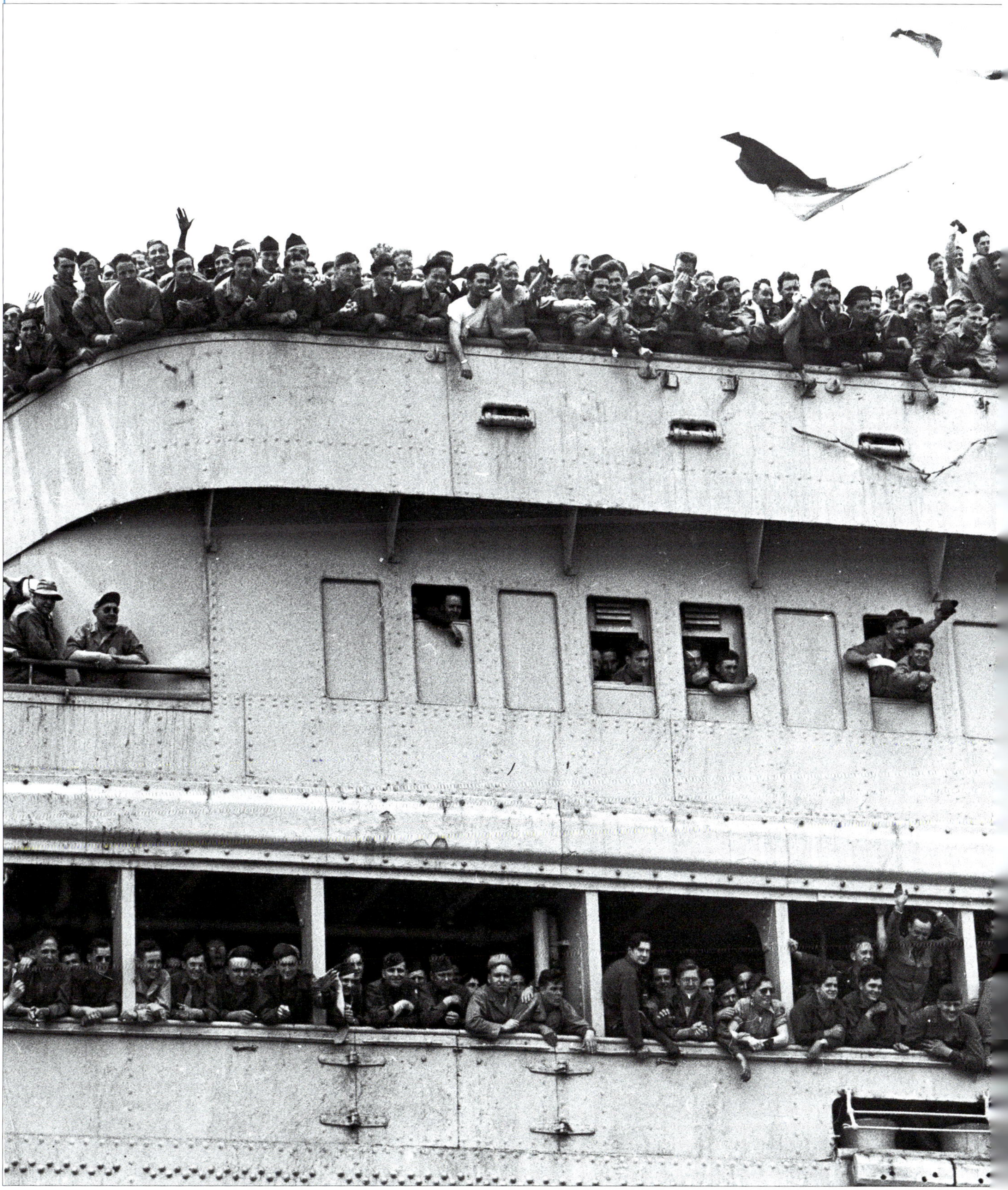

The Noble Ship: Coming to Life, Off to War...

RMS Queen Elizabeth: the Unruffled Cunarder

Above: A rare colour slide of the *Queen Elizabeth* in 1946, bringing American servicemen and women home. The liner is passing Pier 7 on Battery Place, Lower Manhattan, which was at the time owned by the Unifruit Banana Steamship Service and like all piers in that part of town it has long since been torn down. (Michael Lindsay Slide Collection)

Left: On this 20 February 1946 arrival into New York, the ship was carrying 12,214 Canadian troops and 879 crew members – a total of 13,093 souls on what was officially known as Voyage Number 66. (Philpot Collection)

pushed to the maximum revs possible without putting too much strain on her brand-new engines. This translated to a very respectable average speed of 24 ¼ knots for most of the 3,127 miles trip to New York. On occasion she was allowed to do 27 ½ knots — by no means considered her maximum speed. She responded superbly with all twelve boilers in use, leaving Chief Engineer William Sutcliffe adamant that she would prove to be faster than her future running mate the *Queen Mary*.

The combined trial trip/maiden voyage was later described as "just a lovely cruise" by Skipper Townley and as "almost boring" by Technical Assistant Robert Stein. Most of the four hundred or so crew on board seemed "utterly lost," said Stein, who had the impression of being on a "phantom ship steered by phantom hands." He elaborated by adding; "the voyage was an eerie experience and it was strange to wander for miles along deserted corridors and darkened decks, feeling as if we were on a ghost ship." Cables were trailing all over the place within the uncompleted ship and the only illumination, within the empty, echoing vastness, was from bare bulbs hanging from their electrical wires.

The inhabitants of the ship, for the duration of the voyage, were kept mentally preoccupied with the continual concern of being torpedoed. Despite this foreboding, the crew were outwardly cheerful and an affiliation was soon established between them. The typically British stiff-upper-lip-attitude and ability to maintain high spirits in times of despair and worry, was illustrated no better than during the maiden voyage with the forming of an honorary club known as *The Unruffled Elizabethans*. "Honi soit qui mal y

The *Queen Elizabeth* being nudged into her ice-filled, Hudson River berth on the 28 February 1946 for what was the last of her repatriation voyages of North American troops. Her post war refit on the Clyde would soon follow. (Philpot Collection)

RMS Queen Elizabeth: the Unruffled Cunarder

The *Queen Elizabeth* arrives at Southampton on March 6th 1946, ending six years of war service. The very next day, workers began removing all war-related, temporary fixtures from within the ship, including lavatories, wash basins and non-permanent bulkheads. She remained in Southampton until the 30th of March, steaming to Gourock to shed the remainder her soiled war clothes including her grey dress. (Southern Daily Echo)

pense", was the club's motto, or "Evil be to him who evil thinks." The Club was the idea of the ship's Purser, and Captain Townley was elected President. The objective of the club was to demonstrate the premise that, "True Twentieth Century Elizabethans are able to remain, under all conditions, completely unruffled." The conditions of war which they now found themselves in would provide the members of the club a good opportunity to put this premise to the test.

On the morning of 7th March 1940, a news plane carrying a group of reporters spotted a huge, grey ship sailing at high speed, heading for New York. With an as-yet unrecognizable profile and her name not clearly distinguishable due to being painted grey like the rest of the hull, it was at first thought that this mystery ship was under threat and rushing for shelter in New York. It didn't take too long for her true identity to be established. The *Queen Elizabeth's* hushed-up inaugural voyage came to its conclusion and she took the city by surprise. Her unexpected arrival was the news of the day: "The strangest maiden voyage in maritime history," exclaimed one New York daily journal, a sentiment confirmed by Captain Townley who jokingly quipped to one reporter, "It was virtually like leaving on a trial voyage and suddenly finding yourself in New York." The "Lizzie" berthed on the opposite side of the pier to the *Queen Mary* which was sharing her slip with France's the *Normandie*. This created a rare and spectacular gathering of the world's three largest ships.

Fitting for War

On the 21st March, the *Queen Elizabeth* was moved into the slip vacated by the *Queen Mary* which left for Australia. During the eight months the *Queen Elizabeth* remained in New York, her war refitting would be resumed. Decks were caulked, lighting and electrical

The Noble Ship: Coming to Life, Off to War...

wiring added, remaining navigational equipment was installed, as was ventilation, heating, water, and sanitary services. On the 12th November 1940, the *Queen Elizabeth* bid the *Normandie* and New York farewell and sailed for Singapore, where she would be dry-docked for further refitting into a trooper.

The *Queen Elizabeth*, sporting the unusual livery of a black hull and drab grey upper-works, arrived in Sydney on the 21st February 1941. Work on the ship was carried out at the Cockatoo Island Dockyard, including converting the First and Tourist Class restaurants into mess halls that would feed over 2,000 men per sitting. Hospital wards were set up in the First Class dance salon as well as in the two smoking rooms and garden lounges. The Turkish baths were converted into an X-Ray room, with the large squash court used as a storage area. The ship's First Class lounge was used for gatherings and as an entertainment area which sometimes saw the troops putting on impromptu shows for one another. All beds from the ship's incomplete staterooms were landed and replaced with bunks.

On 9th April 1941, the *Queen Elizabeth* and the *Queen Mary* had their very first sea-encounter, passing each other just off Sydney Heads. The *Elizabeth* was returning to Sydney after embarking diggers in Hobart, and the outbound *Mary* was headed for Jervis bay to load more troops. Two days later, the *Queen Elizabeth* was sailed out of the harbour-city carrying well over 5,000 Australian and New Zealand troops headed for the Red Sea and the coast of Egypt. She would rendezvous at Jervis Bay with the *Queen Mary* and other famous liners, the *Ile de France*, the *Nieuw Amsterdam*, the *Aquitania* and the second *Mauretania*, forming what was known as Convoy US 10.

The *Queen Elizabeth* made three further round trips to the Middle East from Sydney, arriving at Port Tewfik with her last detachment of Australian troops for the Middle East on 24th November 1941. She returned to Sydney on the 16th December 1941 to a harbour crowded with mostly US vessels, as WWII had drastically altered: America was no longer neutral, but a major participant in the war. From that moment, the Admiralty ordered a change of plans for the "Queens", both were to be utilised for shuttling thousands of US forces to the threatened Pacific region.

The *Queen Elizabeth* picked up her first batch of American troops bound for the Pacific, from San Francisco, arriving there for the first and only time on 13th March 1942. With 8,000 souls aboard, she headed Down Under once more, arriving in Sydney on 6th April. Off Sydney Heads, the *Queen Elizabeth* met once more her future Cunard running mate, the *Queen Mary*. This became a familiar Aussie-rendezvous point for the two ships; for despite Sydney having a large harbour, the ships' more than 1,000 foot length meant that it was too dangerous, in terms of swinging on the tides and manoeuvring, for them to be there simultaneously. This, and that the enemy would have found two sitting-duck "Queens" confined in the harbour too irresistible not to act upon.

When the *Queen Elizabeth* entered Sydney Harbour with her first load of American troops, Woolloomooloo was crammed with cargo vessels discharging war material. The busy times saw to a critical shortage of longshore labour. Thankfully Sydney's wharfies agreed to allow a specified number of the *Queen Elizabeth's* crew to work her own cargo which consisted mainly of the soldiers' baggage. The agreement stipulated that the crew work throughout the night and be free the following day, with the added bonus of some extra money. Naturally the set up was seen as a good deal and many shipmates volunteered to unload the ship. Troops worked down in the hatch, loading the gear into the cargo nets which were hove up by winches operated by the "Lizzie's" crew, who then swung them over the side of the ship into lighters alongside. It required three full nights to completely discharge all the 8,000 men's baggage, but when the work was completed, the "Lizzie's" crew went ashore and could be seen making merry in the harbour city for the next three days.

European Expeditions

The *Queen Elizabeth* left Sydney for the last time on 19th April 1942. It was an emotional departure because the ship had won the hearts of Sydney-siders with her frequent calls over the past two years. The Admiralty had decided that the ship would now be needed for transporting British troops to the Middle-East and sending US troops to fight the enemy in Europe. The *Queen Elizabeth* headed back to Europe via Freemantle, Simonstown, Rio de Janeiro, with a stop in New York, where she embarked her very first contingent of American soldiers for Europe, before finally arriving at Gourock on 9th June 1942.

With the ship in home waters once again, her crew had a chance to take some well-earned shore leave. The few days of absence would pass by quickly and very soon they, along with over 10,000 British soldiers, would be embarking the ship for a trip to the Red Sea. There the troops would be deployed in the North African desert as reinforcements to the British army which was having a tough time against the Germans.

After serious consideration was given to converting the *Queen Elizabeth* into an Aircraft Carrier at the end of 1942, it was decided that she should continue in her already successful role. The *Queen Elizabeth's* very significant worth to

the war effort was now clearly in evidence to both sides. She could move huge numbers of fighting men in quick time to any battle field around the world and thus both "Queens" were major catalysts for the war turning in favour of the allies.

The liberation of Europe was now within sight for the Allies, but in order to make it a foregone conclusion, close to one million soldiers would have to be brought over from America to the United Kingdom. Ferrying the troops across on the *Queen Elizabeth* would be the quickest way to achieve this. For the next three-and-a-half years of her life, the ship would depart New York or Halifax and head for Europe with an average load of no less than 15,000 troops during the summer months and 12,000 during the winter months. With so many people on board at one time, the stability of the ship was a serious concern and calculations were taken daily to ensure the liner was as balanced as possible in the water. This apprehension led to fewer troops being carried during the winter months across a typically unsettled North Atlantic Ocean.

In a book published in 1956 titled *Merchant Shipping and the Demands of War*, by C.B.A. Beherens, one of the *Queen Elizabeth's* wartime captains recalls that when the ship heeled due to ocean swells, he could sense something unusual and disconcerting in the feel of the giant hull. The explanation lay with the tremendous human cargo distributed throughout the vessel. Inert cargo would stay put when the ship rolled but vast numbers of men, unaccustomed to the sea, would lurch with the rolling motion. On a ship of such breadth as the *Queen Elizabeth*, an eighteen degree roll seemed twice that.

A Lucky Escape

On the final leg of the *Queen Elizabeth's* wartime North Atlantic crossings, while still several hundred miles from either the east coast of America or the Irish coast, she would be met by naval escorts and shadowed by Liberator aircraft on the lookout for U-boats which tended to proliferate close to both shores. Many allied ships were sunk by German torpedoes along the coastlines of both continents, and many U-boat "kills" were made by USAF and RAF planes in these parts as well.

In the winter of 1942/43, the *Queen Elizabeth* was speeding through the bleak North Atlantic and, unbeknown to her officers, a U-boat lay directly in her path. An opportunity the German navy had desperately been waiting for had at last presented itself. Occasionally U-boat officers had fleeting glances of the *Queen Elizabeth* as she sped elusively across the sea, zig-zagging and outstripping any attempts to catch her. But this time it was different. The U-boat was in position, waiting silently to launch torpedoes.

The sea was calm, conditions perfect. Suddenly, out of the darkness, dove a B24 Liberator under the command of Flt Lt. Harold Kerrigan of Westmount Quebec. It was one of the first times in which searchlights were used to hunt submarines, and it proved relatively successful. Kerrigan missed the U-boat on his first run, but he found the raider when it started to hurl flak at him. He made another run, but the slippery U-boat had submerged. Meanwhile the *Queen Elizabeth*, warned of the danger, altered course and put safe miles between herself and the U-boat.

Peace at Last

As the war gradually came to its conclusion, an ever-increasing number of sick and injured servicemen were being transported back home on the *Queen Elizabeth*, sometimes as many as 4,000 veterans at a time. More than 3,000 wounded men were aboard the "Lizzie" on the 7th April 1945 for her final wartime voyage to New York, departing from The Clyde as part of Convoy TA 200. When she arrived on the 14th, waiting to greet her was the *Queen Mary* at her Pier 90 berth. Both ships remained in port until after VE Day, celebrating the end of the European part of World War II, on the 8th May 1945. After several more crossings, the *Queen Elizabeth* finally made her maiden call into Southampton on the 20th August. She became, at that time, the biggest ship ever to enter Southampton Docks.

For the remainder of 1945 until March 1946, the *Queen Elizabeth* repatriated the many thousands of American GIs, nurses and civilians still waiting in Europe. The first of these emotional and much welcomed post-war arrivals into New York happened on the 29th June 1945, when she made a spectacular entry up the Hudson River. She was fully dressed and carrying over 13,000 passengers, filling her outside decks completely. All of her arrivals into New York with returning US servicemen were spectacles to behold, and huge crowds were always waiting on Pier 90 to welcome home the joyous men aboard.

When World War II was over, the *Queen Elizabeth* could finally sail without her position and movements kept a secret. She could travel in a straight line for great lengths and with windows and portholes fully opened. During World War II, the "Lizzie" made 48 voyages, safely delivering close to one million troops around the world.

The *Queen Elizabeth's* wartime duties ended on the 6th March 1946, when she arrived back in Southampton. Compared to the numbers she had recently been carrying, she was virtually an empty ship with only 1,709 passengers and a crew of 814 aboard. The *Queen Elizabeth* and the *Queen Mary* were indispensable and lion-hearted contributors to the Allied success. Their combined work will forever be remembered as a benefaction of utmost significance.

Chapter 2

The Working Ship

Speaking tubes, seen in front of the officer, enabled voice communication between the flying bridge and the wheelhouse. The large instrument on the left is called a Pelorus Compass. A powerful search light, behind the officer, was controlled from the open Upper Bridge, or 'Monkey Island'. The *Queen Elizabeth*'s navigating bridge was 125 feet across, from wing tip to wing tip. (Philpot/QEHS Collection)

With World War II over, Cunard decided that the *Queen Elizabeth* would be the first of their passenger ships to re-establish the Company's transatlantic passenger service. The decision to choose her in preference to their other liners, including the very popular *Queen Mary*, boiled down to the *Queen Elizabeth* being the Flagship of the line, the biggest liner in the world and the most modern of their ships.

To ready the *Queen Elizabeth*, she would have to be comprehensively reconditioned, refurbished and to a degree, rebuilt inside and out. The transformation was an enormous task, but when completed, she would emerge a virtually brand-new ship.

Upon arriving at Southampton, on 6th March 1946, work commenced immediately, removing the temporary lavatories, washbasins and the non-permanent bulkheads that were erected to protect the beautiful wood panelling aboard. All troop-related fittings, as well as many miles of temporary wiring and piping that ran throughout the ship, were landed in Southampton, as too was all furniture in need of upholstering and repair.

On the 31st March, the ship left for Gourock, where the heavy structural refurbishment would take place, including the overhaul and repair of the main engines, turbines and boilers. The most conspicuous, most awaited part of her overhaul was the change from drab grey to the shiny colours of Cunard's livery. It was an arduous two and a half months of complicated work, made all the more difficult with the ship being at anchor in the Clyde Estuary and by the impressionable amount of wear and tear to all parts of the ship which had remained unchecked during her hard-pushed trooping days. She may have just turned six, but she had aged to the equivalent condition of a 25 year old ship.

The "Lizzie" returned to Southampton once more on the 16th June, so that the finishing touches could be made to her interiors. A bee hive of activity prevailed. Everywhere on board, carpet and linoleum was being laid, curtains were hung, and lighting fixtures installed. Everything was shined,

Opposite top: June 16th 1946. After six long years, the *Queen Elizabeth*, finally dressed in her Cunard colours, having just arrived back at Southampton from Gourock where the first part of her post-war refit was carried out. Standing next to the freshly-painted ship is a happy gathering of just some of the workers who made the trip down from Scotland to perform the final finishing touches to the ship's public spaces and staterooms. (© The Southern Daily Echo Archives)

Opposite bottom: From April 1st until June 15th 1946, the *Queen Elizabeth* remained anchored in the Clyde Estuary off Gourock undergoing post-war transformation. The propulsive equipment was overhauled, the air conditioning, refrigeration, electrical and plumbing systems were made good and new teak was laid. In the public rooms, many fittings were removed from their bulkheads to be reconditioned then later reinstalled in Southampton along with the rest of her interiors. (Philpot Collection)

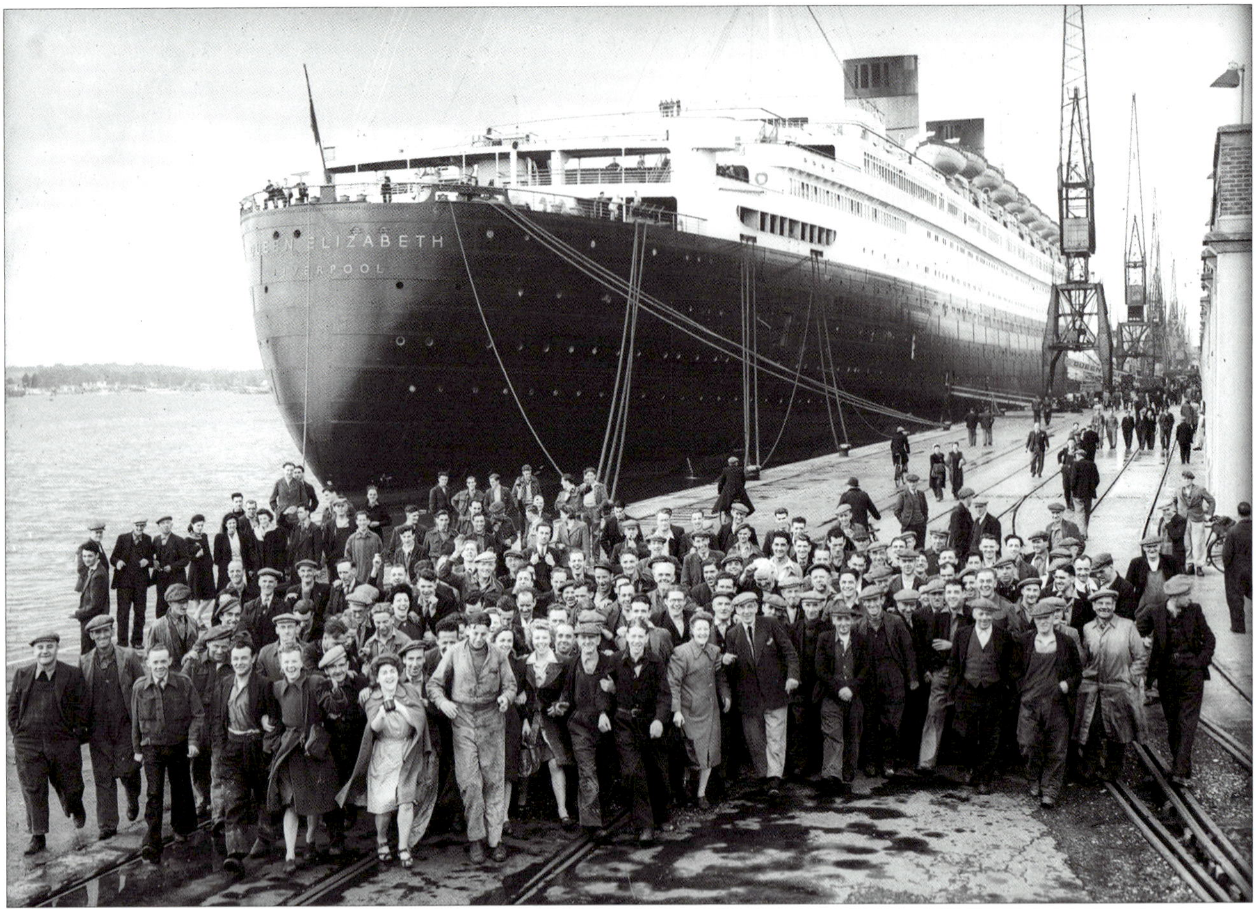

RMS Queen Elizabeth: the Unruffled Cunarder

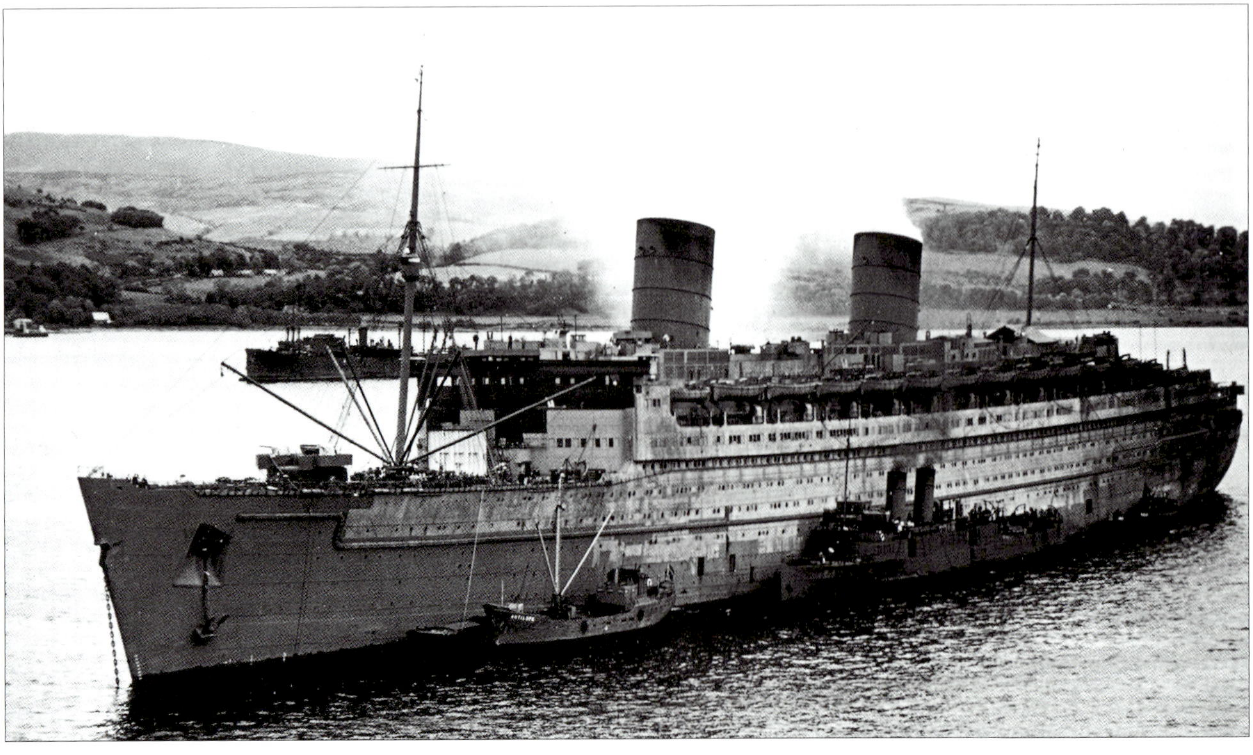

The Working Ship

Above: The entire first class swimming pool area was redone during the post-war refit.
(© The Southern Daily Echo Archives)

Right: August 22nd 1946: France's contribution to the restoration of 'Le Reine Elizabeth' was a group of female French-polishers who, with much elbow grease - and shellac, polished furniture and other woodwork back to life. Merci beaucoup Femmes.
(© The Southern Daily Echo Archives)

RMS Queen Elizabeth: the Unruffled Cunarder

oiled, polished and rejuvenated, with furniture and artworks that were landed in various ports at the beginning of the war restored, finished and finally installed. Hundreds of trade workers arrived from Clydebank, and over a hundred French-polishers from France. On the 26th June, she entered the King George V Dry Dock, where the entire underwater part of the hull was scraped free of barnacles and her teak decks were refreshed.

The *Queen Elizabeth's* long-overdue official sea trials were held in the Firth of Clyde, off the Isle of Arran on the 8th October 1946, under the Royal presence of the ship's Godmother, HM Queen Elizabeth and her two, now grown up, daughters Elizabeth and Margaret Rose – all travelling on the liner for the first time. The Commodore, under specific instructions from Sir Percy Bates not to drive his ship to maximum speed, guided the vessel on the first mile northwards to 29.71 knots and on the second mile to 29.75 knots. The Southward run, according to some reports, was not recorded accurately, as the low and very bright sun obscured the position of the starting mark, but some of those present later confirmed that the ship did in fact climb to the anticipated 30 knots.

When the official trials were completed, Her Majesty Queen Elizabeth took the helm for a few minutes and with her eyes fixed ahead, she spun the wheel and steadied her on course – naturally carried out under the wings of Commodore Bisset. "She was so easy to handle, I was surprised," commented The Queen on Cunard's 'Queen'. Commodore Bissett then took the liner back to Southampton in readiness for the much-awaited commercial maiden voyage as Cunard's very own, the very wonderful *RMS Queen Elizabeth*.

Thirsty work: Cabinet makers are busy making the First class Library resplendent. Judging by the little hint the worker at the extreme right is giving us, a no-alcohol policy must have been in place aboard - If one looks closely 'NO BEER' can be seen written on the top pane where he is cleaning. (© The Southern Daily Echo Archives)

The *Queen Elizabeth's* sea trials would check, among other things, her manoeuvrability, compass settings and that hotly-disputed topic, her speed. Chairman Sir Percy Bates reminded Commodore Bisset to tow the company line and not attempt any speed records on either the sea trials or on the maiden voyage. Referring to the liner's speed, Bisset went on record to say after the trials were over: 'we had some more up our sleeve'. (Philpot Collection)

The Working Ship

Maiden Voyage… Take Two

« BON VOYAGE »
At last, young giant, infant of the fleet,
Your medals on, you sail down Civvy street:
And may you serve the peaceful folk you bring
As well, as nobly, as you served the King!
Here come your passengers; but who will check
The ghosts of soldiers crowding on your deck?
~ Sir A.P. Herbert ~

Left: A not-so-secret dash. The *Queen Elizabeth* is seen here nudging 30 knots during official sea trials on the 8th of October 1946. Aboard were HM Queen Elizabeth and her daughters, travelling on the liner for the first time. The Queen even took a spell at turning the wheel, and was amazed at how light and responsive the big ship was. (Philpot/QEHS Collection)

Below: After having successfully completed sea trials, the *Queen Elizabeth* heads home to Southampton, where in a few days, she would begin her first commercial voyage to New York. During a crew lifeboat drill, Commodore Bisset keeps check on things from the bridge wing, still sporting the wartime bullet-proof roof at its end. The seven-feet-tall wire mesh fence along the sports deck would eventually be replaced by a regular ship railing and the lifeboats were covered for the maiden peacetime crossing. (Philpot/QEHS Collection)

It is said that, "tragedy is never far from festivity" and the sad event which took place on the eve of the maiden voyage gave further credence to this expression. On the 14th October, two days day before sailing, Sir Percy collapsed in his office in Liverpool following a stroke, passing away two days later, hours before his conception embarked on her first transatlantic crossing for Cunard.

And so, at 14:00 on 16th October 1946, after six years of steaming and clocking over half a million sea miles, the *Queen Elizabeth* cast-off her moorings to commence her maiden commercial voyage. For some of the more than 2,200 passengers making the trip, this day took an especially long time in coming. They had made their reservations ten years earlier, a few months before the ship's keel was laid in December 1936, only to see her whisked away to war upon completion at the beginning of 1940. In all, some 7,000 applications were made for the opportunity to sail on the maiden voyage.

Despite the shadow of sadness cast by Sir Percy Bates' death, the mood on board the *Queen Elizabeth* on departure day was generally high spirited. In the public rooms and everywhere along her wide corridors, a holiday atmosphere prevailed with boisterous visitors and passengers milling about, in scenes resembling crowds found in Piccadilly Circus on New Year's Eve. Sir Percy Bates would have wanted it no other way.

The *Queen Elizabeth* leisurely cast off from her berth to a rousing rendition of "Rule Britannia". Along the entire length of Ocean Terminal and at all vantage points along the waterfront, a large crowd of people took in the wondrous sight of the newly reborn liner commencing the life she was designed for. As she took to the open sea, her bows lifted slightly with her first surge of power. At that point the pleasure craft gradually dropped back, and the liner, crammed with excited passengers, gradually settled down and did what she had done so well over the last six years.

On board the ship were 797 First Class, 655 Cabin Class and 797 Tourist Class passengers. The ship's company totalled 1,275, twelve of whom belonged to a group of the youngest members of staff, aged between 14 and 18. Known as the busboys or Bellboys, they were recent graduates from a six-week course in seamanship and personal service where they learned how to serve, lay tables, make beds and respond to discipline.

The Bellboys were under the instructions of the ship's catering officials and performed duties such as paging passengers, manning the doors to public rooms, delivering messages, walking dogs kept in the kennels, and collecting offerings during the ship's church service on Sundays. The smallest Bellboy on the maiden voyage was 4ft.10in, Master William Bath of Southampton, just 14 years of age. Despite their small stature and tender age, these boys were not shy.

The Maiden voyage certificate, signed by Commodore James Bisset. (Philpot Collection)

They took full advantage of their cuteness and young age for gaining passenger sympathies and excellent tips.

While signing the beautiful maiden voyage certificates, which were given to each passenger aboard, Commodore Bissett told prying reporters who were asking about a possible fast crossing, that he had no intention of trying a record-breaking run. He appeased them by stating that the ship was known to be capable of doing more than 32 knots, and that in four and a half days she was scheduled to dock in New York, hopefully before noon. It was a perfect crossing, made under mostly moderate weather and at 07:39 on Monday 21st October, the *Queen Elizabeth* tied-up ahead of schedule. The crossing, measured from Nab Tower to Ambrose Light, took 4 days, 16 hours and 18 minutes, with the ship travelling at an average speed of 27.99 knots.

The Working Ship

October 16, 1946: Tugs pull the liner stern first from her berth. Some of those travelling to New York had reserved their place for this historic maiden commercial voyage back in 1936. (Philpot Collection)

Despite the flowing champagne, cigar smoke and partying, some American passengers found the maiden voyage a low-key affair. One man, interviewed by reporters as the ship lay anchored at quarantine, described the trip as "pleasant but unexciting." When reporters passed this on to a company official, he replied: "Well, we could have brought half a dozen or so glamour girls along to brighten things up a bit if we wanted to, but we are emphasising security, comfort and service. This ship bears the name of the Queen of England and the Queen has held her wheel. Don't forget that!"

With passengers gradually being discharged over the course of the morning, a great deal of commotion developed within the Pier. New York customs officials had their hands full but seemed to be enjoying themselves. "Gee, this is just like old times," one was overheard saying, referring to the hustle and bustle of the pre-war days on the piers.

During the ship's four-day stopover in New York, a number of luncheons and receptions were held on board for invited guests. Then on Friday 25th October, she sailed once more for home, taking five hours longer than the westbound leg and, to many a surprise, with two stowaways on board.

The fully-dressed liner leaves Southampton behind as she heads towards The Solent at the start of her maiden peacetime voyage. (Philpot Collection)

A wonderful aerial image of the *Queen Elizabeth* arriving into New York for the first time in Cunard dress, on the 21st of October 1946. This would be the only time her lifeboats were covered throughout her peacetime career. (Philpot Collection)

The Working Ship

Ship's Company – Taking Care of Business

"A big ship is a big business," as Commodore Thelwell pointed out, and they didn't get any bigger than the "Lizzie". Formally, her business was to carry the Royal Mail, as indicated by the definition of the acronym R.M.S. – Royal Mail Ship. Her bread and butter, however, was the scheduled ferrying of passengers back and forth across the North Atlantic.

Transatlantic ocean liners were, first and foremost, working ships and as such had to earn their keep. The "Lizzie" was no exception. On the contrary, she was the forerunner, setting example for all the rest on the North Atlantic. In 1947, just one year after entering service, she became the greatest money spinner ever to have sailed on the North Atlantic, singly netting Cunard a profit of almost $5 million. The *Queen Elizabeth's* most lucrative years were from the period of her commercial maiden voyage until the end of 1957, a good ten years, spurred on by the world-wide boom in business and trade.

The *RMS Queen Elizabeth*, like all large passenger vessels, was a complex island. She was a multifarious floating municipality, a luxurious floating hotel – the sustaining of which required a huge and concerted effort on the part of all the men and women whose livelihood depended on the ship's existence. The smooth running of such a large and complex enterprise like the *Queen Elizabeth* stemmed chiefly from the perpetuation of a Cunard custom, namely optimal crew-training, loyalty, professionalism and discipline. Nowhere was this more evident than in the conduct and attitude of the officers aboard. Each officer on the bridge, from the Captain to Junior Third Officer, had a Master Mariners Certificate. All Cunard officers had to work their way up through the lowest grades, to be tried and tested for many years, until finally manufactured to the highest standard into a fully-fledged captain. Not even Noah, according to American author and humourist, Mark Twain, could deviate from this route should he wish to command a Cunarder.

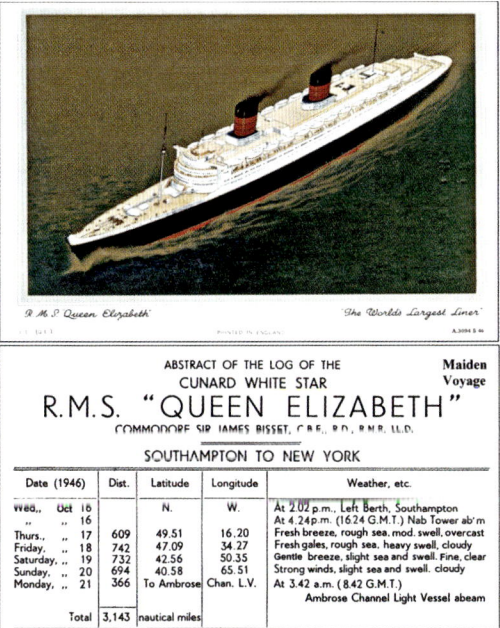

To the Captain or Master went all-authority, as well as all-answerability. Despite delegating much of his power, the ship and the human cargo it contained was ultimately his responsibility.

The Captain, in his own way, had to be something of an ambassador, demonstrating diplomatic qualities to both his passengers and crew. On-call 24 hours a day, the burden of accountability and leadership, at times, must have weighed heavily on him. However, on the *Queen Elizabeth* this load

Top left: Although only two were necessary, a total of eight tugs arrived to push on her port side bows in order to line the ship up with her berth following her triumphant maiden peacetime arrival into New York. (Philpot Collection)

Left: Maiden voyage log abstracts.

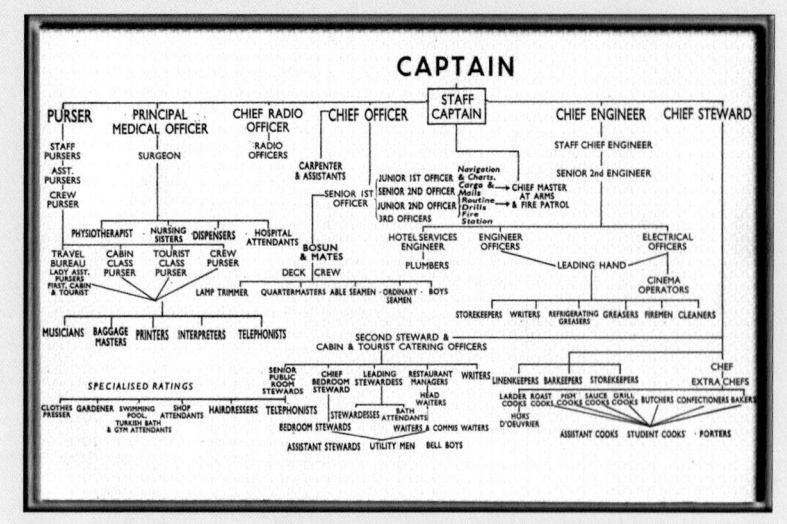

RMS Queen Elizabeth: the Unruffled Cunarder

Left: Ship's Company Hierarchical Tree.

Below: A Detailed drawing of the Bridge by Harold Philpot - from a series of hand-drawn documentary drawings of the entire ship. (QEHS Collection)

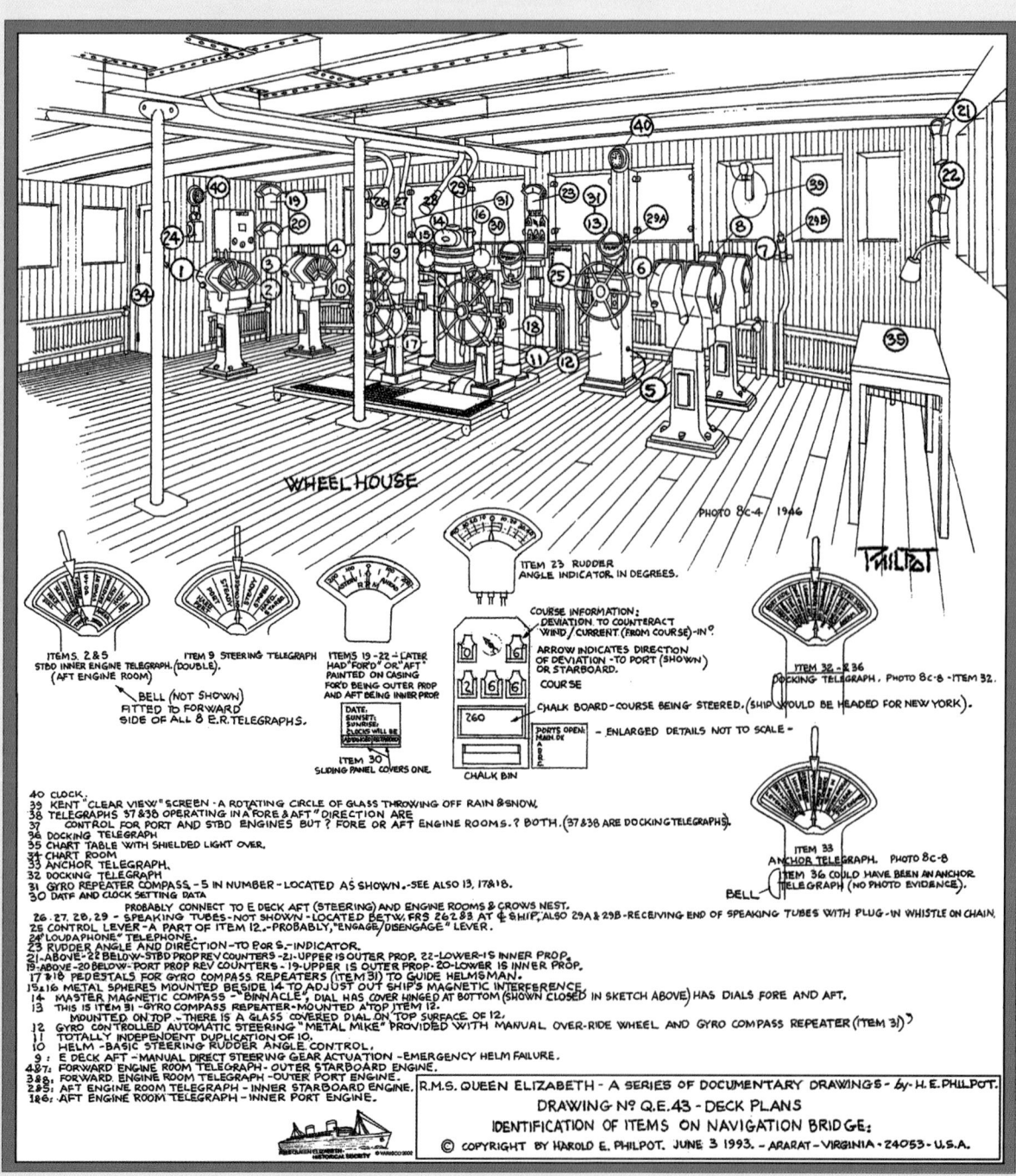

The Working Ship

Above: A wide view of the *Queen Elizabeth's* bridge in 1946. (Philpot Collection)

Left: Never without a face at the window: A senior officer, perhaps the Staff Captain, looks out the wheelhouse windows as the Helmsman, just visible to the left, keeps the ship on course. 1965. (Philpot Collection)

would have been lightened in the knowledge that he was ably supported by a close-knit team of officers, crew and staff, widely regarded by those who served on her as the finest to be had – better than on any other liner in service at the time – including the *Queen Mary*.

The Staff Captain was the Captain's deputy, a role created to ease the workload of the master. He was a buffer and load carrier, without any navigational duties, in charge of the internal administration of all departments within the ship and much more besides. One of the *Queen Elizabeth's* former masters, Commodore Thelwell, described the Staff Captain as the ship's "Handyman", while another captain described him as a kind of "general manager" who runs the entire crew. The larger part of the meeting and greeting of VIP's on board was an exhaustive and time-consuming duty that was performed by the Staff Captain.

The builders of the *Queen Elizabeth* supplied her with a set of calculation tables which enabled the Chief Officer to determine the changes in the ship's draught on each day of the voyage, as she steadily consumed fuel and water from her tanks. The tables covered stability and righting lever, detailing ballasting fore, aft and the ship's metacentric height (the distance between the centre of gravity and the metacentre). As the ship continued to consume both oil and water from her tanks during an Atlantic crossing, it was not a big problem to work out her expected draught (the depth of the loaded hull under the waterline) upon arrival to Southampton or New York. Knowing the exact draught and the specific gravity of the water from which the ship sailed, (at certain states of the tide in New York the water can be nearly fresh) the estimated arrival draught was correct to plus or minus one inch.

It was the Chief Officer's job to sit down, at 09:00 daily, with the soundings of the water tanks supplied by the ship's carpenter and of the oil tanks by the Chief Engineer, and work out the draught of the ship for noon that day. Just

before noon, he would present the Captain a list, indicating which tanks should be used during the next 24 hours to maintain an even keel and what her estimated draught would be upon arrival. This procedure became a fairly routine job on the transatlantic crossing at those times when the ship sailed with all of her oil tanks full. However, this was not always so.

Bunker "C" oil was much cheaper in New York, therefore the *Queen Elizabeth's* owners purchased only sufficient oil in Southampton to allow the ship to reach New York, leaving enough in reserve for just one day's steaming, a practice which was cause for much worry when the ship encountered adverse weather en-route, consuming more fuel than predicted. Moreover, because of this usage, some oil tanks had to be filled with fresh water in Southampton to provide overall stability and trim for the voyage over to New York. As the ship neared her destination, the ballast water, which now contained a small amount of oil from being stored in the oil tanks, had to be pumped out through separators before the ship came to 100 miles off the US Coast, to prevent fouling of American beaches. This jettisoning of ballast water from the ship meant that she was sailing with reduced stability into New York. This was not normally a problem because the ship was already in sheltered waters. However, in the days when she was carrying many thousands of returning GI's all wanting to be on the starboard side of the upper decks to wave to their friends as the ship steamed up the Hudson, it gave her a noticeable list and the MP's had to use force to drive many of them below and others to the port side to get the ship upright for docking.

The Chief Officer and Senior First Officer – assisted by the Senior Second Officer – were also responsible for the stability of the ship. This is referred to as the ship's trim, and it is greatly influenced by the way the liner is loaded. Under their direction, all cargo, baggage, stores, mail and specie, including gold and silver bars, was loaded in such a way as to keep the ship properly trimmed and floating evenly.

The maintenance of the ship's navigational apparatus including charts, compasses, chronometers and signalling devices was the responsibility of the Junior First Officer or 'navigator'. The Junior Second and Third Officers both assisted the Senior First Officer with routine ship drills and alternated weekly schedules to patrol the ship at night with the head of security on board, the Chief Master at Arms.

The Senior First Officer was the officer in charge of assigning duties to the deck crew on watch, including ship's Bosun, Quartermasters, and able seamen. Both the a.m. and p.m. daily watches were 12 to 4, 4 to 8 and 8 to 12 – a 'three-watch-system', meaning that three officers shared two watches a day. The officers of the watch along with a junior officer shared the wheelhouse with other helmsmen – usually quartermasters.

A Quartermaster's First-hand Account

Peter Gerald West served on the *Queen Elizabeth* from February 1956 until the spring of 1959, joining her as a 20 year old deck hand and finishing three years later a quartermaster. Peter recalls his time on the ship:

"As a regular crew member, one would do five two-week trips then have a trip off on full pay. You should understand that in the main we, as quartermasters, almost led the lives of hermits. There were only six of us – two on each of the three watches or shifts. We were classed as petty officers so, in terms of rank or standing, we were between the 'deck' rating, i.e. deckhands and able seamen and the navigating officers with whom we worked. One of the several privileges we, as petty officers, enjoyed was that we were allowed to view the tourist class cinema – not, I hasten to emphasise, from the normal viewing seats, but behind the screen, squat on stools, so of course everything was mirror-imaged. One didn't notice too much difference until you watched the film later in a cinema ashore, the right way round, when it looked then, rather strange.

February 1956, New York: Twenty year-old Peter West is photographed during his very first trip on the Queen Elizabeth: 'I was an 'EDH' – Efficient Deck Hand and one rating below able seaman. I am sitting on the forward bollard of the fore deck. It is 'coffee-break' and as you will see, my coffee is in a beer glass. That was the fashion then – don't ask me why, please! By the state of my jeans I have been doing a dirty job, probably greasing those wire cables you see on the deck' (Peter Gerald West)

The Working Ship

"As I mentioned, there were two quartermasters to each four-hour watch plus two 'Boy' ratings known as Bridge Boys. Each watch had its own navigating officers – both a senior and a junior. By tradition, the third officer usually being quite young, was given the 08:00 to noon and the 20:00 to midnight shifts, with a junior fourth as his assistant as, during these hours, it was most probable that the captain himself would be present in the wheelhouse to keep check on things.

"To the chief officer, who had overall command of the deck department, was assigned the most desirable watch, the 4 to 8 shift, together with a junior officer. At 07:00 the night officer, who was on duty internally from 21:00 to 06:00 would relieve the chief officer momentarily so he could have his bath and once again at 19:00 to allow him to dress for dinner. The Senior Second Officer, with a junior, had the middle-watch of Noon to 16:00 and Midnight to 04:00. daily.

"Whilst at sea, each quartermaster would take a two-hour "trick" (strange name I know) at the wheel and two hours standing-by in the wheelhouse either supervising the bridge boys or watching the radar screen etc. The Bridge Boy on watch was also required to keep the brass in the wheelhouse spotlessly clean. The ship's wheel is attached to the Tele-motor which had to be kept well-lubricated by topping up with viscous glycerine. Often, however, this horrible sticky substance was used for purposes not intended. It was a useful form of punishment for Bridge Boys if they had misbehaved in any way. We would smear it liberally all over their gleaming brass, guaranteeing it would take the remainder of the watch for them to remove it — cruel? You bet!

"Most of the time, meaning when the ship was out of sight of land, the ship was automatically steered by a device called the gyro pilot, which pointed true-north. It was nicknamed 'Iron-Man' or 'Metal-Mike'. However, in rough

June 1958: Driving the largest ship in the world at just 22: Peter West has been promoted to quartermaster - the youngest ever at Cunard until then. 'Here I am during my two-hour 'trick' at the wheel. I have the 'Lizzie' by the reigns at 'full-ahead', black hair, and my mother's double-chin! The cone-shaped speaking tube in front of my head terminates on 'Monkey Island', the open bridge directly above the wheel house. Very occasionally, when docking, the Pilot or Navigating Officer would negotiate the procedure from up there as it gave a better all-round view. He could communicate with the quartermaster on the wheel by shouting down the tube, 'HARD-TO-PORT', or whatever. These days it's of course all done with wireless technology. How times have changed.' (Peter Gerald West)

On each bridge wing was an instrument called a Pelorus which, in appearance and use, is similar to a compass and is used to take relative bearings. (Philpot Collection)

weather or fog, both hazards very common in the western North Atlantic, 'Iron Mike' would be switched off and we would be steered manually and of course, always in the presence of the 'Old Man' himself!

"Whilst steaming through fog, the ship would deliberately veer first 10 degrees to port then 10 degrees to starboard every 15 minutes. This was because the radar scanner was located on the open area above the bridge called 'Monkey Island' (another odd name) which was positioned directly behind the foremast. The constant change of direction ensured that there were no blind spots.

"There were two identical helms or tele-motors in the wheelhouse a few feet apart from each other. They were totally independent and of course, used only one at a time; the other was there in case of emergency, for example one of them failing. In between and immediately in front of the two tele-motors, is the large brass binnacle which housed a magnetic compass. It was hardly used, only there for emergency in the rare event that the ship's gyro-controlled, automatic steering, 'Iron-Mike', broke down or there was a power failure. If this occurred, the magnetic course was chalked-up on a board directly below the rudder angle indicator, on the wheelhouse's front bulkhead. If the course had to be adjusted for leeway or drift due to tides and currents, then the course deviation amount and direction was shown in frames directly above the chalk board. I can only remember one occasion when this occurred on my watch. Steering by a magnetic compass is completely different of course – nowhere near as precise and by comparison, tricky."

A Vast Crew

While the work of the majority of the ship's crew was there for all to see, as long as the propellers kept turning, it was only mechanically minded passengers who ever stopped to appreciate the labours of those below decks. The chief engineer on the *Queen Elizabeth* and his two immediate subordinates not only had to worry about the maintenance and a continual proper working of the propelling engines, the 4,000 miles of electrical wiring, the huge air conditioning, and refrigeration plants, they also had to supervise close to 100 engineers, making sure they were all doing their part in preventing or solving disasters. Fire, flooding and breakdowns on their floating city were constantly on these men's minds – a big responsibility indeed.

The Chief Steward was high up the hierarchical tree; responsible for overseeing the numerous employees within the catering department. He was assisted by the Second Steward as well as a Cabin and a Tourist Catering Officer, and between them they shared the responsibility for staff employed in bedroom and cabin service, the kitchens,

Top: Two of the *Queen Elizabeth's* able seamen take time out from duties to pose for a photograph taken by a passenger during a 1950's crossing. (Philpot Collection)

Above: Deck crew attend to the hawser which is being taught by the revolving 36-ton capstan, drawing the ship closer to her berth. The hawsers were a 9-inch circumference Manila Fibre. Each of these ropes was 120 fathoms in length, weighed 18 cwt (about 9000kg) and had a breaking strain of 31.5 tons. The capstan is being controlled by the crew member at the extreme right of the photo who has his hand on the capstan's speed and direction controller. (Bob Malinowski)

dining rooms, restaurants and bars, the bakery, shops, pools, baths, gymnasium and the food and drink stores. On cruises, the Chief Steward's responsibilities increased. At the beginning of the cruise all refrigerators were crammed full with basic foodstuff, but each time the ship reached a port he, along with the Head Chef, would go ashore to the markets and buy local produce to supplement their stores.

The catering department was staffed by well over 800 persons, making it the most represented group within the ship's company and often the most difficult to run due to its diversity and complexities.

In the late 1960's, a restructuring of various staff positions aboard passenger ships was introduced, along with

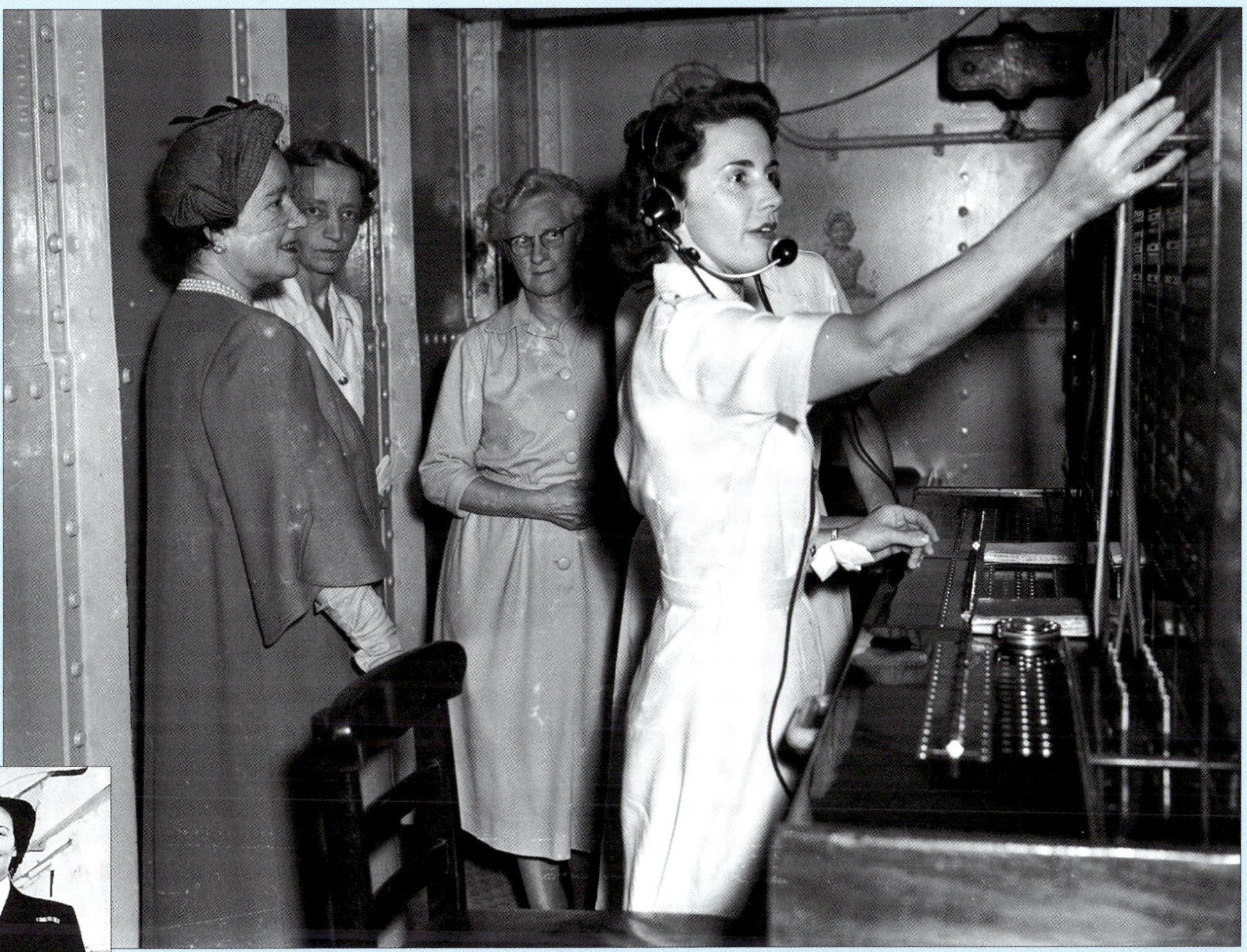

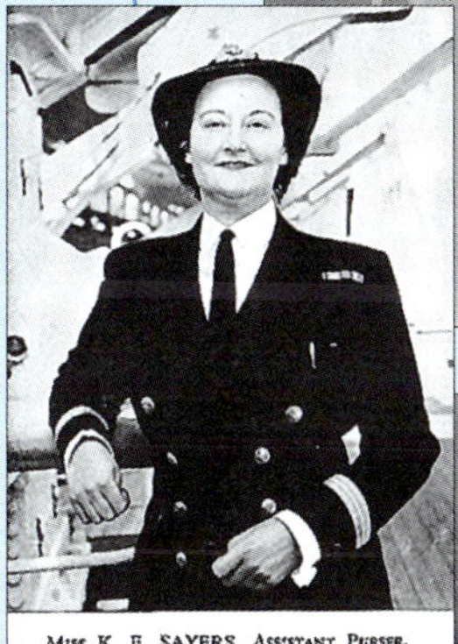

Miss K. E. SAYERS, Assistant Purser,
"QUEEN ELIZABETH"

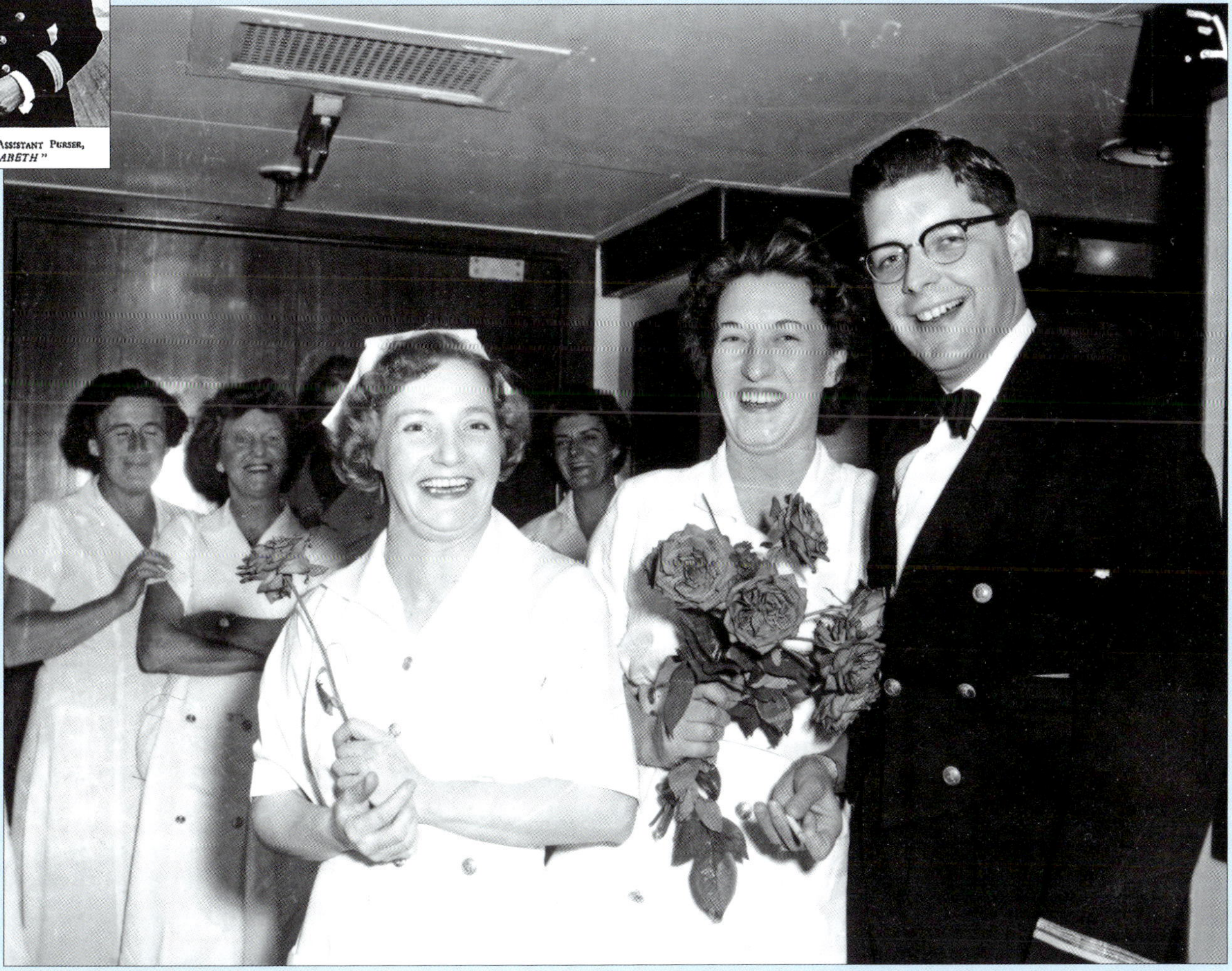

Opposite top: Her Majesty Queen Elizabeth is seen visiting one of the auxiliary telephone switchboard rooms, during her July 1948 crossing - a department manned almost exclusively by women. Whenever on board, she was always anxious to meet a wide cross-section of the ship's company going about their various duties. (Cunard)

Opposite centre: Women may have played a role back then, but only in very small numbers: In 1953, from a crew of 1,280 on the *Queen Elizabeth*, just over seventy - or 5% - were women. The highest female ranking then was Assistant Purser. In 2012, the percentage of female crew on Cunard ships had risen to the vicinity of 30% - still low in comparison to males despite the passing of more than sixty years. Captain Ingrid Olsen, however, has become the first female Master in Cunard's long history. (Cunard/Open Agency Ltd.)

Opposite bottom: The *Queen Elizabeth's* Purser seen celebrating with a group of nurses for the occasion of one of the nurse's birthday -1958. Female nurses were first employed aboard passenger ships during World War One when ocean liners were used as hospital ships. As it was not uncommon for shipboard births taking place during voyages, especially in third-class, nurses working on Cunard ships were required to have a midwifes certificate and all were State approved. (Phil G: Forder)

Above: In this picture we see four of the *Queen Elizabeth's* compliment of nine bakers in the process of making the bread that would accompany each of the three main meals served daily in all the restaurants aboard – including for the crew's mess' and for afternoon tea. (©SCOTLANDIMAGES.COM - The National Archives of Scotland)

Right: The *Queen Elizabeth's* team of five, highly-skilled confectioners, were responsible for the making of petit fours, pralines, brittles, and other sweets that were served at the end of a meal and also the ornamental and highly-decorated cakes that were created for children's birthday parties, buffets and special gala events. (Cunard/Open Agency Ltd.)

The Working Ship

Even today aboard Cunard ships, during the presentation of the senior staff to passengers, at the captain's cocktail gathering, the Head Chef is introduced as 'the most important person on the ship': In this 1948 image, the Maître d' introduces the Head Chef of the Verandah Grill – the most exclusive restaurant aboard – to British screen legends, Michael Wilcox and Anna Neagle. (Cunard Line Hunter Cox Archive)

changes in the way things were run on board, especially in the catering and Purser's departments. Prior to the *Queen Elizabeth 2* coming into service, in 1969, Cunard introduced the title of Hotel Manager, who performed a similar role to that of a general manager of a land-based hotel. Hierarchically, the role came in above both the Chief Purser and the Chief Steward with the latter renamed the Food and Beverage Manager later on. Today, the old name of catering staff has been changed to Hotel Staff and along with the whole of the hotel operation aboard, is ruled by the Hotel Manager via five main reports; the Senior Doctor, the Entertainment Director, the Food and Beverage Manager, the Executive Housekeeper, and the Chief Purser.

The Hon. Mrs. W.W. Astor was ever faithful to the *Queen Elizabeth* and when she was asked the reason why, she replied without hesitation: "Oh well, I always use the *Queen Elizabeth* because the Purser's so sweet to me."

In the days of the two "Queens", it was an accepted fact that a ship of such great size was only as good as her Purser. Passengers expected the Purser to be knowledgeable, tactful, presentable, good tempered, hardworking and fair minded.

Summer of 1952: Afternoon tea was always eagerly awaited by passengers during a crossing. Punctually, at 4p.m daily, the waiters served tea or coffee with sandwiches, cupcakes and scones. The waiters on the *Queen Elizabeth* covered great distances in a days work and many complained of having 'Cunard feet' by the end of the day. 'I cun'ardly walk', they would lament. (Philpot Collection)

The after mooring deck is crowded with kitchen and catering staff during one of the *Queen Elizabeth*'s final voyages in 1968. This staff-only area of the ship was a popular place for those who otherwise spent most of the day below-decks, to come up during breaks and get some fresh sea air. (Bob Malinowski)

RMS Queen Elizabeth: the Unruffled Cunarder

With a good head for the ship's business, it was essential that he or she understand people as well. During a typical voyage the Purser was bombarded with a barrage of questions and enquiries about accommodation, entertainment, safe deposits, money, clerical assistance, mail and telegrams, bookings, and ship-board etiquette. It began the moment the first passenger walked aboard until long after the gangway had been lowered at voyage end.

Traditionally, the Staff Purser was the clerk of the ship, who kept the ship's accounts from all sales on board and also acted as paymaster. The Assistant Purser was responsible for all passenger entertainment and games. The ship's musicians and various entertainers, telephonists, shop attendants, pool and gymnasium attendants, printers and gardeners, were all overseen by the pursers department. On today's cruise ships, a single purser's desk is located, in most instances, in or near the mid-ship lobby and looks after all these matters. The *Queen Elizabeth* had a purser's office located in each of the three classes sections in the ship, dealing with all 'front-of-house' matters such as lost property, complaints, passenger accounts, travel arrangements, tours, and preparing immigration manifests for customs officials at the liner's three terminal ports: Southampton Cherbourg and New York.

A partial view of the *Queen Elizabeth*'s starting platform in the aft engine room. From here, the engineering officers controlled the ship's propulsion by turning the ahead or astern manoeuvring valves, regulating steam reaching each of the propelling machinery units. (Philpot/QEHS Collection)

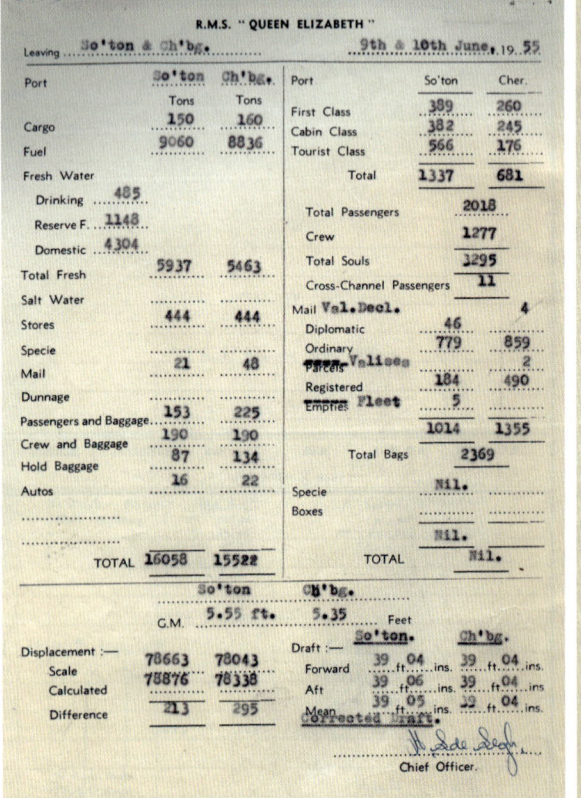

Log Book report for both the Southampton and New York departures, for Voyage 178, 7th-21st June, 1955, with Captain Thelwell in command. Both the stability and the draught of the ship were the responsibility of the Chief Officer and were determined by the figures on this report.

Chapter 3

Southampton – Cherbourg – New York: Earning Her Keep

The *Queen Elizabeth* seen in the Solent in the early 1960's. The image was taken by David Ward's father during a family outing to the Isle of Wight – David recollects: 'I can see and feel this now, the launch bobbing around in relatively calm water while this huge ship passes by, then turning into the bow wave, which was quite enormous - we rode over two or three separate waves. To a 12 year old this was a sight indelibly etched on my memory'. (David Ward)

CUNARD

Southampton Water possesses a double tide daily, two flooding and two ebbing. For most shipping to and from the port, this phenomenon was a convenience. However for a ship the size of the *Queen Elizabeth*, with an overall length of 1,031 feet and a 40-foot draught, the time frame within which she could enter and leave Southampton Water was strictly limited — Southampton Water being the stretch of water five miles long from Southampton's docks to Calshot. The Captains of both "Queens" were under orders not to enter Calshot Channel at times when there would be less than two feet of water under the keel.

Occasionally, after crossing the English Channel from Cherbourg, the *Queen Elizabeth* would arrive too early off the Nab Tower to coincide with the tidal condition that provided the minimum clearance required between seabed and ship bottom. This meant she had to drop anchor in St. Helens Roads, to the east of the Isle of Wight, and wait a couple of hours until the flooding tide rose to provide sufficient clearance. The trick used by some captains to avoid a lingering at anchor was to carefully adjust the cross-channel speed from Cherbourg, so as to pass the Nab Tower at the optimal time for entering the Solent.

Steaming past Spithead and after passing Cowes, the *Queen Elizabeth* – like all large ships to this day – had to navigate a series of tight turns to clear a challenging underwater obstacle known as The Brambles.

The Brambles is an arrowhead-shaped sandbank which lies just off Cowes, at the most northern point of the Isle of Wight and immediately to the south east of Calshot Spit. The *Queen Elizabeth* firmly embedded her bows in the infamous sandbank on 14th April 1947, after failing to take the hard-a-starboard turn to bring her around it. Only after jettisoning several thousands of tons water, transferring her remaining fuel, and the arrival of a high tide, was she finally afloat again – some 26 hours after grounding. Even so, she required the assistance of 16 tugboats to move her into deeper water.

Passing Calshot Castle and with Brambles Bank safely

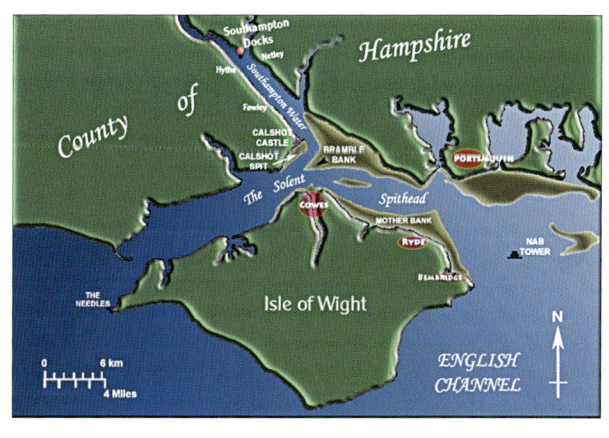

Top: Southampton map.

behind, the *Queen Elizabeth* travelled the final, relatively straight, five-mile stretch to her berth at Ocean Dock. Her speed was about 7 knots, with a minimum clearance under her keel of just 18 inches in places. This was regarded as ample by her captains. On the final approach to the docks, the ship was guided by two navigational aids – a lozenge atop a pylon on the old Royal Pier, and a triangle at the end of Town Quay. These were a clear sight as she approached the swinging basin just off the entrance to Ocean Dock.

Notwithstanding the advantage of Southampton's more frequent tidal movement, the actual high tide on which the ship left her berth at Ocean Dock at the start of her voyage gave the Captain a little more than one hour's grace to make his exit. Frequently, there was a race between time and tide.

If there was, for any reason, a delay in casting off on time, the ship had to fight against a whirlpool which forms just off the rear of her berth as she reversed out of it. The power of this swirling water – caused by the moving tide as it began to fall – was strong enough to thwart even a large ship like the *Queen Elizabeth*, thrusting her back towards the dock and preventing her from entering the stream of Southampton Water – despite the assistance of tugs.

Finally, sailing gracefully down the main-channel of Southampton Water, the huge liner must keep going. Reducing speed too much would render the rudder useless, leaving the ship at the mercy of the current and certain grounding. For this reason, it is obligatory that when a large ship is scheduled to sail down Southampton Water, the channel be kept clear of obstructions, particularly from other large vessels.

A big ship, the narrow channel, Brambles Bank hazard and the Solent's complex tidal pattern, meant that the *Queen Elizabeth* required the assistance of a Company Pilot to guide her to the Nab Tower. Steaming the short distance across the English Channel to Cherbourg was the next leg of the voyage.

Cherbourg

After 64 miles, roughly five hours steaming from Southampton, the *Queen Elizabeth* would arrive at the ancient French sea port of Cherbourg. She would first slip through the outer breakwater, past the Fort de l'Ouest, to enter the Grande Rade, then, if winds permitted, through the inner breakwater to enter the Petite Rade, and finally tie-up alongside the passenger terminal – le Gare Maritime.

The "Queens" were not restricted, as such, from entering the harbour by the tides, rather by strong winds. On occasion, strong gales were cause for much concern and ultimately forced the Captain to anchor his ship just inside the harbour away from the quay, where tenders would come out to the ship to bring passengers, baggage and cargo

Top: Passengers proceed through embarkation inside the Ocean Terminal building which was built in 1950. It was demolished in 1983. (Michael Lindsay Collection)

Above: The *Queen Elizabeth* is bunkering in Ocean Dock's 43/44 berth beside the old Ocean Terminal which was replaced in 1966 by The Queen Elizabeth II Terminal at berth 38/39 - out of picture to the right. (Michael Lindsay Collection)

ashore – a time consuming and difficult job.

The Cherbourg Pilot would board the approaching liner from a small launch, three and a half miles from the harbour entrance. Once aboard, his first job was to get the vessel through the outer breakwater's western opening, passing very close to Fort de l'Ouest: an 1840-built circular stone construction. Although the gap was more than wide enough to accommodate the *Queen Elizabeth*, it always appeared to passengers, high up on the outer decks, that she would barely make it through.

Once inside the Grande Rade, four tugboats met the *Queen Elizabeth* and were quickly made fast to her bow. After guiding the ship into the Petite Rade, the French pilot's concern was

Southampton – Cherbourg – New York: Earning Her Keep

Above: Overlooking the *Queen Elizabeth*'s fo'c's'le, on a busy day at Ocean Dock in 1966. To the left, at 46 Berth, is Cunard's 1954-built *Ivernia*, shown remodelled as *Franconia*. Ahead at 45 Berth, where *Titanic* berthed in 1912 - is a Battle Class Destroyer, probably H.M.S. Sluys and on the right, two Alexander tugs. The *Queen Elizabeth* is moored at 43/44 Berth. (Alan Richardson)

to keep the huge liner parallel with the docking quay, made all the more difficult by the persistent, stiff westerly wind that blows across the harbour. Two tugs kept pressure on the ship until she was safe in the lee offered to her from the large terminal building. Now protected from the wind, the ship was drawn to the dockside and into final position.

The Cherbourg stop-over would last around one hour. In that time, passengers boarded – arriving in special trains from Paris – and baggage, mail and cargo was lowered into the ship's hold. The French Pilot remained on board throughout the stopover. When all was finished and officers and crew were all back at their stations, the Captain ordered his ship be released. Gangways were landed, the lines were cast off and the ship's whistle was blown. The Pilot had his tugs pull the stern out into the Petite Rade, as the ship's engines rung out – "dead-slow astern", backing the ship slowly away from the quay.

The wind – earlier a foe, was now used to help swing the stern to port across the quay. When the bow was clear of the end of the dock, two tugs on the port bow would push the stem all the way around to the north until the westerly wind would once again provide amicable service by catching the port bow and help to spin the ship around clockwise, until she was lined up with the opening to the inner breakwater.

The "Lizzie" then moved off under her own power, exiting first the smaller, then the larger confines of the port's double harbour – New York bound.

New York

For two days of each week, there would be one "Queen" or other berthed at Cunard Line's Pier 90, which jutted into the Hudson River at the end of W50th Street.

Right up until the end in 1968, after 28 years of calling

Above: Founder of the RMS Queen Elizabeth Historical Society, Harold Philpot took this image naming it, 'The last time I saw her, she was at home'. The date was June 22 1964, having just crossed from New York. His wife Beverley, waiting in the car, knew Harold was in no hurry to leave. (Philpot Collection)

Right: The docks and tugs are left behind and the ship slowly moves down the river, accompanied by a pleasure craft full of sightseers. (Michael Lindsay Collection)

Below: September 11 1968 off Netley, possibly the closest ever passing of the RMS Queen Elizabeth with her rival, the SS United States. (Michael Lindsay Collection)

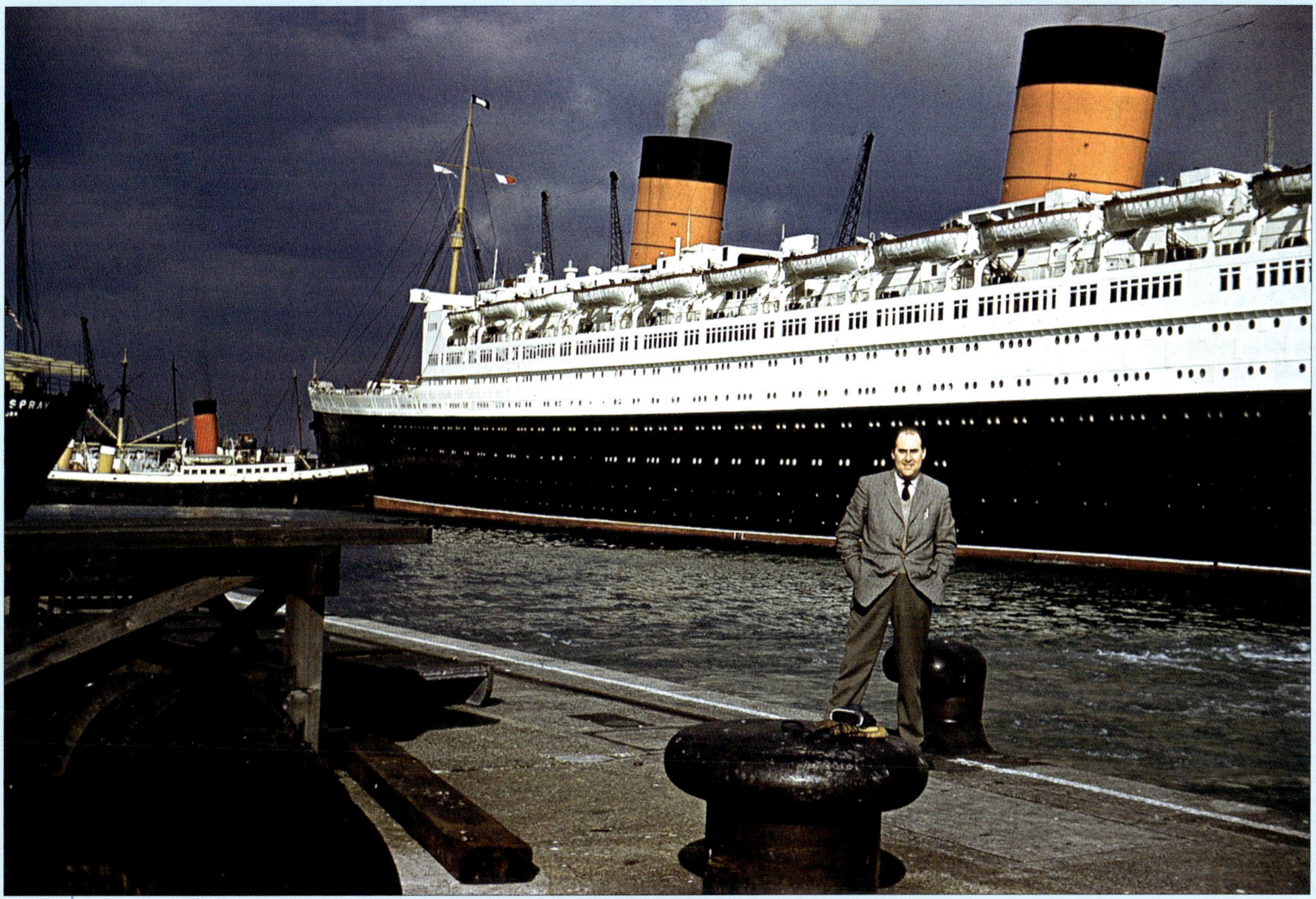
SPRAY

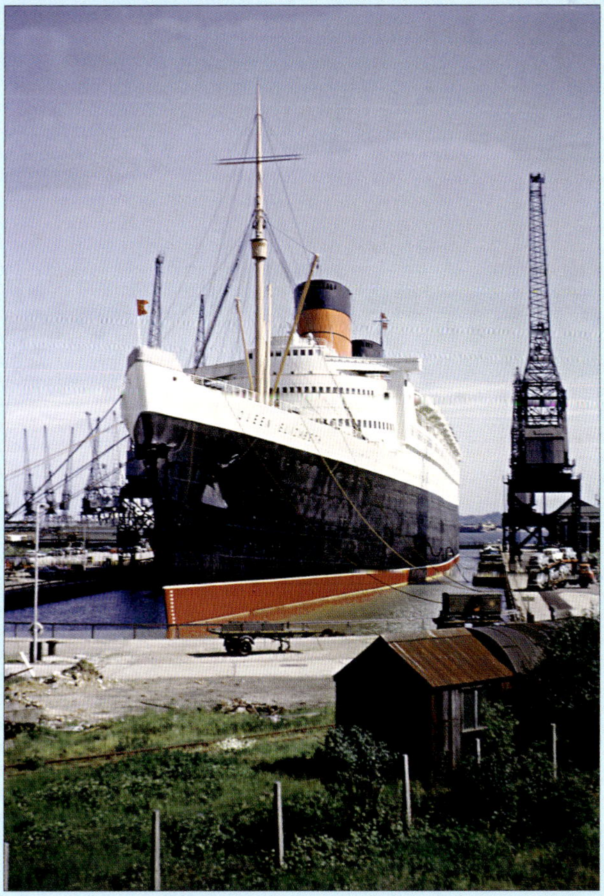

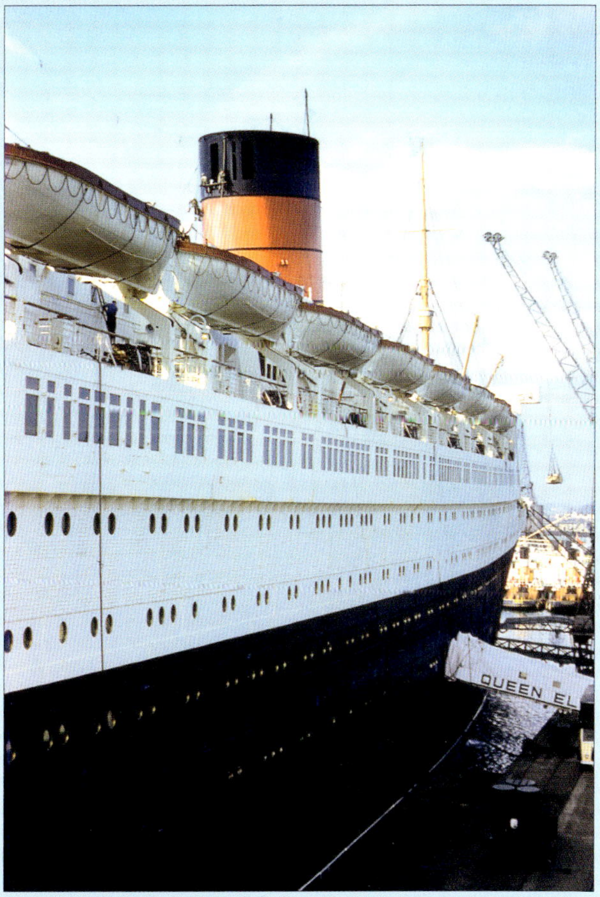
QUEEN EL

Above: The *Queen Elizabeth* became a victim of Brambles Bank on 14th April 1947, after failing to take a turn. Finally freed, after many attempts, she arrived in Southampton more than a day late, with most of her passengers already tendered ashore. An inexperienced pilot was navigating the *Queen Elizabeth* at the time of the grounding – Cunard's regular pilot having missed his flight to Cherbourg where he was to have joined the ship. (Philpot Collection)

Opposite top: Edgar Hodges used to drive down to Southampton in the 1950's, just to look at the *Queen Elizabeth*. The ship looks resplendent here, kissed by the early-afternoon sun. (Edgar Hodges)

Opposite bottom left: Twice a year, the *Queen Elizabeth* entered Southampton's King George V Graving Dock for service and reconditioning. The first was a short, mid-summer revamping lasting about a week, followed by a longer winter inspection and overhaul lasting up to six weeks which was carried out any time between December and March. (Michael Lindsay Collection)

Opposite bottom right: The big ship is being loaded, prior to the start of another North Atlantic crossing. (Michael Lindsay Collection)

Above: Large crowds line the dock as well as up on the observation decks of Ocean Terminal, bidding farewell to friends aboard the liner which has now distanced itself from her berth. The captain, with the aid of tugs, had to race against time in order to get the ship backed into the River Test before the arrival of a strong whirlpool which forms off her stern as the tidal movement changes. (Michael Lindsay Collection)

Left: 1968: Her full length now in the river, a tug starts to align the *Elizabeth* downstream. (J.K. Byass)

Bottom left: A late-1950's image showing the ship being turned just off her berth. (Michael Lindsay Collection)

Bottom right: 1967: The tug *Calshot* works alone for the last few moments of the turning – the ship just about ready to sail ahead under her own steam. (Edwin J. Webb)

August 17 1965: The direction of smoke emanating from the tugboat's stacks and the *Queen Elizabeth's* notable list to port indicate that as is often the case in Cherbourg, a stiff westerly breeze is blowing across the dock. Tugs will have their work cut out for them trying to keep the stern from swinging to port once her bow is protected by the lee offered by the large terminal building. (Tony Bullock)

On this occasion, the winds are absent and the ship, checked by just one tug, is safely inside the inner harbour, edging closer to her berth. The Inner and outer breakwater can be seen in the background. (Philpot Collection)

A tranquil scene from 1966, showing the 'Queen' docked in Cherbourg's Darse Transatlantique. On the right of picture is the *Ingenieur Minard*, formerly the *SS Nomadic*, the last remaining vessel of the White Star Line, used to tender 274 passengers to the ill-fated *Titanic* on the 10th of April 1912. The *Ingenieur Minard*, now restored as the *Nomadic* and on display in Belfast, was retired from tendering duties on the 4th of November 1968, the very same *day RMS Queen Elizabeth* made her final departure form Cherbourg. (Philpot Collection)

A 1950's aerial view showing the *Queen Elizabeth* docked in Cherbourg's Darse Transatlantique adjacent the historic Gare Maritime building. (Philpot Collection)

into their city, New Yorkers never tired of seeing the "Lizzie". Like a glamorous Broadway show, she entertained the masses whenever she was in town. Rarely was she overlooked. Her presence at Pier 90 often beguiled motorists as they drove past her along the raised West Side Highway – the drivers forgetting for a brief moment where they were, gaping just a little too long at the majesty before them, resulting in collisions with other vehicles or the guardrail. Often, the traffic slowed right down opposite the docked Cunarder, causing congestion and delays.

The phone lines to Cunard's New York Offices were also abuzz whenever the "Mary" or "Lizzie" was in town. People asked Cunard employees for facts and specifications that would help them settle bets made with friends, while some called to offer advice or make complaints: "You know your boat has a big scratch with paint missing on the left side – near the pointy end?" or even: "Excuse me, did you know there is mud and seaweed dangling from your boat's anchor?" Some people even called to complain that the crew shouldn't be allowed to fish from the ship's windows while she was docked; the well-to-do callers mistaking homemade radio aerials, permitting better reception to the city's radio station broadcasts, for fishing rods.

A "Queen's" turnaround time in the Big Apple was normally less than 24 hours, with the *Queen Elizabeth's* record being 16.5 hours, set in January 1961 – her crew were trying to make up for a delay in getting into New York due to uncooperative weather.

During a typical turnaround, the ship was loaded with stores which included 8,200 tons of oil fuel, 6,000 tons of fresh water, 58 tons of food and 20,000 pieces of clean linen. Pier gangs also loaded approximately 6,300 pieces of luggage, sometimes up to 15 automobiles, 150 tons of general cargo and 150 bags of mail. This load had the effect of increasing the ship's draught, which is the depth of the loaded hull under the surface of the water. This is a critical figure is used to calculate the minimum depth of water needed for the ship to enter and depart her various ports of call at their differing tidal states.

In New York Harbour there was always ample water in the main channel, thus imposing less of a restriction to docking and departing than in Southampton. The act of turning off her berth was always a tricky manoeuvre, but made less difficult during slack water periods – the brief time in between tides when the river was not flowing in either direction.

On a number of occasions, the *Queen Elizabeth*, was forced to tie up alongside her pier in New York minus tugboats, which in effect were her fore and aft thrusters. The adroit feat of manoeuvring the 1,031-foot giant, tug-less, into a space where the width between piers was less than half that of the ship itself, would always make the

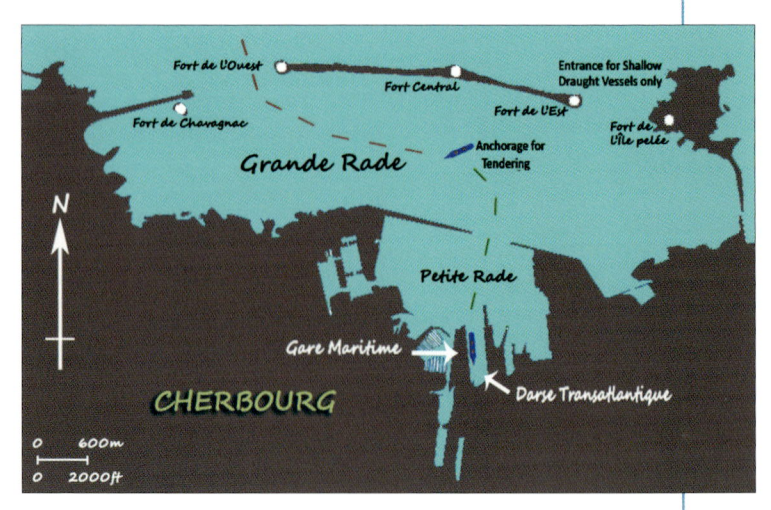

Map of Cherbourg Harbour

newspaper headlines whenever it was carried out. Commodore Geoffrey Marr explained:

"When berthing without tugs, on the south side of Pier 90, turning is absolutely vital. There are only two 20 minute periods each day when this is possible, so you must arrive off the dock steaming the last of the flood tide, meaning about 15 minutes before the period of slack water begins and when those ashore confirm that the surface flow has stopped. Start your turn, hoping to have your stern inside the dock with the lines ashore, before the first of the ebb catches it and carries it across towards the other pier. Even then there is a large amount of luck and calm weather is essential."

Casting Off

Several hours before departing New York, the Captain of the *Queen Elizabeth* would normally pay a brief visit to the Cunard Offices Downtown. Upon his return to the ship he would order his officers to check key equipment – the steering gear, the compasses, the telegraphs in the bridge as well as those in the engine rooms and the all-important steam whistle. As the ship was making ready to sail, the signal flag "Blue Peter" – a white rectangle on a blue background, was flown from the top of her foremast.

Thirty minutes prior to casting off and with all passengers boarded, staff rounded-up stragglers, the last dawdling visitors, and ushered them off.

One of the last persons to come aboard prior to sailing, apart from a vain Hollywood star wanting to make a last-minute grand entrance for the press, was the Undocking Pilot. His task was to get the ship backed into the river and turned downstream. Boarding about the same time as the Undocking Pilot was the Harbour Pilot. His responsibility

Top: With the *Queen Elizabeth* well clear of her berth, she will now be swung around to line up with the entrance into the Grande Rade of Cherbourg Harbour. (Philpot Collection)

Above: It has taken approximately 1 hour to steam the 12 miles from the Ambrose Light ship to the Verrazano Narrows Bridge. It will take her a further hour of slow steaming before she is alongside her berth at Pier 90 - ten miles further upstream. (Philpot collection)

Right: Map of New York Harbour

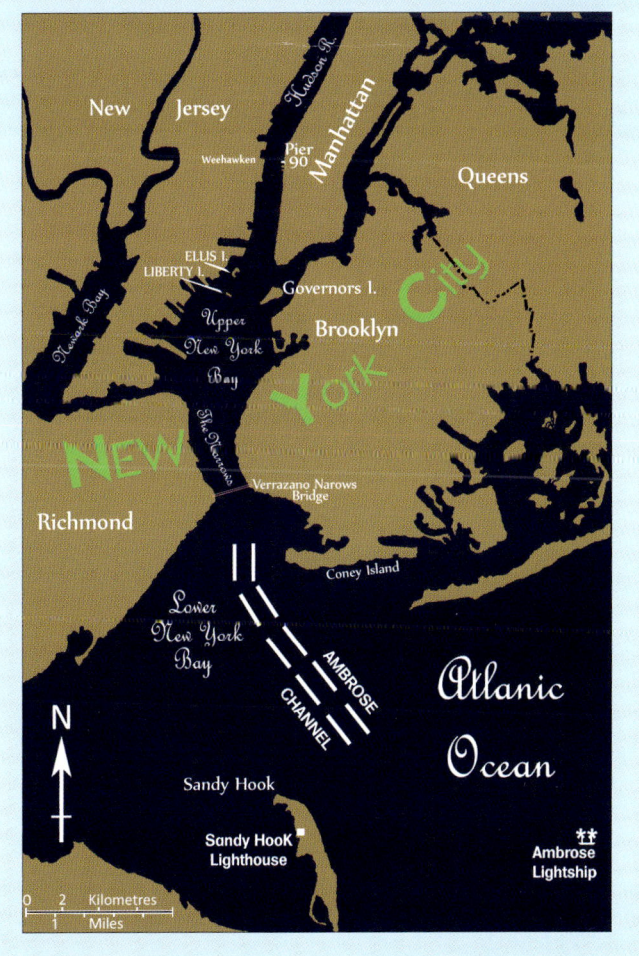

RMS Queen Elizabeth: the Unruffled Cunarder

was to guide the ship down the river to sea. Both pilots were technical advisors to the Captain, who put great trust in their local navigating knowledge.

The Undocking Pilot's work was of short duration but of great complexity, having just 2,500 feet of navigable river width behind him in which to manoeuvre the great bulk of the "Queen." With this task, help could not be expected

Above: For two days of each week, there would be one or the other 'Queen' berthed at Cunard's Pier 90. In this publicity image taken in the 1960's, the illuminated *Queen Elizabeth* looks like a dazzling jewel in the New York City night. (Philpot Collection)

Below: Battery Park, on Manhattan's most southerly point, has always been the favourite place from which to observe the big ships come and go. This is the *Queen Elizabeth's* May 13th 1958 arrival into New York. (Philpot collection)

Southampton – Cherbourg – New York: Earning Her Keep

Right: This view, from April 4th 1966, shows the dressed 'Lizzie' arriving into New York for the first time following her major 1965/66 cruising refit, sporting a new lido deck with swimming pool. (Philpot Collection)

Above: Manhattan's skyscrapers slowly appear from out of the early morning mist, as the *Elizabeth* nears the completion of a crossing in 1965. (Philpot Collection)

Above: A Moran Tugboat delivers the Docking Pilot to take over the *Queen Elizabeth's* pilotage from the Sandy Hook Pilot, who had guided the liner from the Ambrose Lightship to this point. Captain George Mason is seen boarding the ship through the R- Deck shell doors, a very precarious operation between two moving vessels. He will soon be on the bridge, for the complex job of docking the huge ship. (Capt. Parslow - Philpot Collection)

Below: August 1968 - lone visitor: By this point in time, New York's luxury liner row was becoming ever more desolate, exhibiting none of the life it once did just a few years earlier, when liners of all shapes and sizes occupied almost every pier. (Carl House photo – Philpot Collection)

Above: With a slight starboard list and her hull riding high in the flooding tide, the ship has less than two miles to before reaching her berth. It was not uncommon for the *Queen Elizabeth* to arrive into New York with a reduced stability, caused by the emptying of ballast water from her tanks, 100 miles from the US coastline. The water was pumped into her oil tanks in Southampton, allowing Cunard to take advantage of the cheaper price for bunker-C grade oil in New York. (Philpot Collection)

Summer 1955: With fleet mate *Scythia* occupying the south side of Pier 92, the *Queen Elizabeth*, with the aid of at least four tugs, slightly touches the corner of the pier while attempting to squeeze into her Pier 90 berth. On several occasions, whenever they were out on strike, the 'Queens' had to be berthed without the aid of tugs – or today's side thrusters. No mean feat. (Port Authority New York)

As the Author's entry into this world, so too, on July 5th 1961, The *Queen Elizabeth* makes a grand entrance - onto the stage that was luxury liner row. This was a time when the Hudson's finger piers were the maritime equivalent of New York's JFK Airport today. From bottom to top are the liners: *Independence*, SS *America*, SS *United States*, *Olympia*, aircraft carrier *Intrepid*, *Mauretania II*, and beyond the docking QE - *Sylvania*. (Philpot Collection)

During the momentary slack tide, the ship is moved to her berth on the south side of Pier 90. This is this brief period when the river's tidal movement stops and no pressure is exerted on the ship's sides. The *Cristoforo Colombo* is seen berthed at Pier 88. (Marc Piché)

69

A night view taken in November 1966: Beauty and elegance – any time of day. (Richard Weiss Collection)

Below: This wonderful image of her knife-edge bow was taken as the *Queen Elizabeth* was preparing to leave on her final cruise to Nassau, from April 12th to April 16th 1968. (Philpot Collection)

Above: July 30 1959: Crowds watch as *Queen Elizabeth* again leaves the slip which she only left the day before. She returned after colliding with the freighter American Hunter in dense fog in lower New York Harbour – one of the few times she was ever involved in a collision in her long career. (Philpot Collection)

from the rudder because it was of no use to a ship the size of the *Queen Elizabeth* when she was backing slowly. The Pilot instead steered the vessel, through the skilful use of assisting tugs and the four propellers.

Shortly before the *Queen Elizabeth* cast-off her lines, a Cunard employee, stationed at the end of the pier, looked carefully up and down the Hudson. Satisfied the river would be free of traffic for a considerable length, he switched the traffic lights atop the roof at the pier head from red to green.

Finally, the moment passengers and the well-wishers amassed at the end of the pier had waited for. Three blasts of the liner's whistle sounded, signalling "I am going astern".

The term "whistle" is somewhat of a misnomer, conjuring up the impression of a high-pitched sound. The *Queen Elizabeth's* powerful voice was a throbbing note, two octaves below middle "C", analogous to a ripe, resonant bass baritone. It was so thunderous, possessing such a depth and reverberation, that it must have assisted in dislodging any old flaking paint from the pier's sheds.

Up on the bridge, the Undocking Pilot began his work with the command: *"Begin to single up,"* which translates to: *take in all but four lines at the stern and four at the bow* (of the twenty-four lines that have held the *Queen Elizabeth* fast to the pier).

"Take gangways in. Let go aft," and the last four lines aft were reeled in. *"Let go forward!"* Another long booming blast from the whistles high up on the forward funnel and she was almost set to move.

Depending on wind conditions at the time of departure, there would either be two tugs in the slip at the bows or, if it was too windy, one tug stationed at the bow and another at the stern. When excessive westerly winds blew across the Hudson from Weehawken, on the Jersey Side, the Undocking Pilot would station one tug at the bow and another at the stern. His first manoeuvre would be to have the rear tug pull the stern away from the pier upstream about 100 feet, with the front tug holding her bow in place. Thus she would be partly turned downstream before she even started to back, and the difficulty of turning against the wind was that much less by the time the ship was in midstream.

Above right: Close-up of the damage shows it was confined to the area around her anchor well, which was repaired with tons of cement and the temporary welding of some slightly damaged plates. (Philpot Collection)

Right: High-wire act: Immediately prior to the ship's departure, a seaman climbs up the ratlines, to lash the topping lift tackles in readiness for the sea. His skills are being followed by Officers below on the fo'c'sle and a small crowd of onlookers at the bow of the ship. (Philpot Collection)

1965: *Barbara Moran* and *Moira Moran* hard at work, pressed against 'Lizzies' massive, raked bow. (Bill Cotter Photographer)

A fond, fifties farewell. (Philpot Collection)

RMS Queen Elizabeth: the Unruffled Cunarder

Left: For every arrival and sailing, the visitor's platform at the end of the Cunard White Star pier, would be overflowing with people. What's for certain is that they most definitely had the better view. Note that the traffic light on top of the pier to the right, shows green – the river is free of traffic and the 'Queen' may make her exit. (Philpot Collection)

Below: Mid-1960's: majesty backing up into the Hudson. (Titanic Historical Society, Inc., Indian Orchard MA/Louis O. Gorman Collection)

'Full ahead port, slow ahead starboard' and the *Queen Elizabeth's* backward movement is arrested, thus preventing her from hitting New York Central System's Pier 2 on the Weehawken side of the Hudson. This command simultaneously turns her bows to starboard. Passengers take in proceedings from the very spacious Raised Boat Deck, which is also the cabin-class games deck. June 1964. (Philpot Collection)

Undated view of the *Queen Elizabeth*, outward bound on a milky-looking Hudson. The bow anchor was always partially lowered whenever the ship was steaming in the river – a safety precaution, meant to save time in case she had to come to a rapid stop in an emergency – especially a collision. (Philpot Collection)

RMS Queen Elizabeth: the Unruffled Cunarder

The *Queen Elizabeth* begins to pick up speed as the New York skyline becomes ever-smaller. Manhattan and Governors Island are left behind in her wake and she will soon be passing under the Verrazano Bridge, then out to sea. (Philpot Collection)

"*Engines slow astern*" – three very short, but nonetheless ear-splitting blasts on her sirens signalled that her propellers were turning. Down came the Blue Peter and up went the Stars and Stripes, the traditional gesture of a vessel entering or leaving a foreign port.

"*Full astern all,*" and the *Queen Elizabeth* moved a little quicker in reverse. The tug at the stern now went to assist the other tug to push hard against the bow as she moved clear of the pier.

"*Full ahead port, slow astern starboard.*" This command set the two port propellers into a strong forward thrust while the two starboard props continued to pull slightly astern, having the effect of slowing the ship's reverse movement while helping her turn to face directly downstream.

"*Dead slow ahead all*" — the ship had turned enough to permit all engines to run forward. As her speed crept up to 7 knots, the rudder began to take hold. The undocking was now over and the Harbour Pilot took over from there.

It takes one hour to get from her Pier 90 berth to the Verrazano Narrows Bridge – a distance of 10 miles.

Steaming the Hudson River

Steaming at slow speed in such a busy harbour was crucial in case the massive bulk of the *Queen Elizabeth* needed to stop suddenly in an emergency and also to avoid her 'taking a run' or 'sheer'. New York Harbour's Ambrose Channel is as shallow as 44 feet in places, meaning that the *Queen Elizabeth* only had a clearance of only three to four feet between keel and river bed. Should she move too fast, water would accumulate under the front part of the hull causing the stern to squat or drag down even closer to the river bed which then affected her steering, causing her to veer off to one side. For a ship as large as the *Queen Elizabeth*, to lose control by sheering, in a confined body of water and in the presence of other shipping, would be a recipe for disaster.

Taking the *Queen Elizabeth* to sea from the Hudson River meant the Harbour Pilot calling off a series of compass courses – with zero referring to a North Heading.

From Pier 90 to about 23rd Street, the course was "210", "190" was then steered to reach The Battery at the southern tip of Manhattan – also identified as Castle Gardens. "Steer a course 195," took her to 31-buoy off the Statue of Liberty, "207" to Robbin's Reef abeam near Bayone, "185" was steered through to 69th Street in Brooklyn, "167" passing under the Verrazano Narrows Bridge and bearing "147" through The Narrows, swung the ship towards Ambrose Channel. Finally a course of "117" brought the liner to Ambrose Lightship which, since 1967, has been replaced by the Ambrose Light Tower.

Close to the Ambrose lightship, a pilot ship, which was home to the Sandy Hook Harbour Pilots between jobs, would cruise the area constantly. The Pilot, having safely guided the *Queen Elizabeth* to this point, was picked up by a smaller launch from the pilot ship, and with the liner now travelling at a brisk speed he climbed down the Jacobs Ladder from the shell doors into the bobbing launch fifteen feet below.

High up on the flying bridge of the *Queen Elizabeth*, the Captain waved the Pilot farewell. The liner now raced "full-ahead," starting another run across the North Atlantic.

Chapter 4

Adornment of the North Atlantic: A Nicer Shade of 'Grey'

George (Grey) and Miriam Wornum – RMS Queen Elizabeth's Interior Architects: From the collection of the Wornums's daughter, the late Brigit Fletcher. (Reproduced with the kind permission of the family of Brigit Fletcher)

CUNARD

Introducing their new flagship to the public for the first time, the Cunard brochure read: "Upon entering the *RMS Queen Elizabeth*, the liberated passenger takes a deep breath and starts to realise that he or she has just crossed the frontier into a new world. Crossed, moreover, into a world where space is everyone's heritage and time is of little account. The new passenger starts to explore the ship, feeling the same sort of emotions of wonder and excitement as he or she might experience when exploring the city of Venice."

When the *Queen Elizabeth* finally entered commercial service in 1946, she truly was like a "new world", where passengers joyfully settled into a hitherto unseen version of ocean-liner-grandness. From the outset, passengers were enveloped with a cosy sense of being "at home", in a very spacious and grand English country manor. The *Queen Elizabeth* was beyond question unlike any other passenger liner before her and quite definitely "no slavish copy of her sister," as Sir Percy Bates pointed out.

The *RMS Queen Elizabeth's* interiors are often mistakenly and too simplistically described as being Art Deco – even though she was conceived in the late 1930s when the streamlined Art-Moderne was the emerging style. The *Queen Elizabeth* was neither Art Deco nor Art Moderne, despite sporadic displays of both styles within. She did, to a far lesser extent, exhibit *some* of the ornate opulence of the *Queen Mary*, but in comparison to the *Mary*, the *Elizabeth* was architecturally more correct, showing effortless and logical symmetry through a simple and balanced flow of straight lines and repeating rectangular patterns, within larger, more ample interior spaces. The man responsible for the creation of this unique "new world" the Cunard brochure referred to was British architect George Grey Wornum.

Affectionately known as Grey, he was renowned for designing the Royal Institute of British Architects headquarters at 66 Portland Place, London. His entry for the 1934-completed building was judged the best of 3600 entrants in the competition and it stands to this day as a testament to his brilliance.

The following is a chapter from Grey Wornum's unpublished biography – written by his wife Miriam, who was part of Grey's design team on the *Queen Elizabeth*. The chapter is reproduced here, thanks to the generosity of Grey and Miriam Wornum's surviving family.

George Grey Wornum (17 April 1888 – 11 June 1957) Interior Architect of the *RMS Queen Elizabeth*

Winning the RIBA competition would certainly have appeared to be the most spectacular act of a lifetime, and probably it was, but no one can deny that even the possibility of working on the finest British passenger ship,

RMS Queen Elizabeth: the Unruffled Cunarder

August 1968 - looking forward and to starboard: The inner section of the First Class Main Lounge rose to three decks high. The lounge was veneered predominantly with Canadian Maple cluster finished with trimmings of elm burr. On the pillars are leather-covered squares in blue-grey, buff and a gold inner trim – a trademark of architect Grey Wornum used tastefully throughout the ship. (Philpot Collection)

was a very close second. Grey went time and time again to the Cunard offices to be scrutinised, to be questioned, more drawings of past work were asked for – more background of his personal life were gone into. I doubt if he had ever been so thoroughly investigated before, and certainly not since.

The only work he had done on the interior of a ship had been the yacht *Nyria*. It was a beautifully finished job, luxurious and sophisticated, small in scale and utterly suited to its purpose. The *Queen Elizabeth* was another problem, being on such a big scale in both size and luxury that it would quite dwarf anything Grey had done before. When the work on the ship was finally started it was even more exciting than imagined, and at that stage Grey had only one fear. This was the unlimited scope that Cunard were giving him. "Nothing can be too luxurious" he was told "Whatever has been done in decoration or comfort must be done better on our ship. You must surpass not only what is the latest thing, but design so that in two-years-time when the ship is finished, it will still be ahead of any other vessel."

Again it was a good thing that the future was hidden, and that no one knew that it would not be two years but nearly eight years before the splendid ship would be used for her real purpose, and that during these years she would build for herself one of the finest war records.

"You see", Grey said to me, "this sort of 'the sky's the limit' is almost too much of a responsibility. I wish there were far more restrictions. Every restriction an architect faces creates a shape, and brings with it its own solution; no restriction in material or cost is formless and remains formless. It means groping about and so often ends in vulgarity." I laughed, "You won't. You've had too much experience in using plywood and paint to get results on a shoestring to go berserk when you use marble and gold leaf" "I don't know," Grey continued, shaking his head, "they are giving me too free a hand."

However, this was before Grey had met the problem of air conditioning every room, or the engineers (naval and Scotch (sic)) who, with the utmost conscientiousness, thought of contingencies of storm and high seas that had never existed on our planet in the memory of man, and of fires started from pipe smokers to poltergeists. Later, when Grey had worked on a vista or a particularly happy ceiling, he would come home distraught with a complete change in height or proportion necessary because one of these engineers would have told him "Mr Wornum, we need anotherrr girrrderrr, herre."

Tom Timms - tenor saxophonist for Horace Bagaley's first class band - poses in front of an art-deco lighting fixture and beautifully-burred maple panelling in the first class lounge. (Cass Caswell)

Above: An aft-looking view of the First Class Main Lounge. Her Majesty Queen Elizabeth's portrait hangs in the space formerly occupied by a large, wood marquetry. (Philpot Collection)

Below: The inimitable comic team of Dean Martin and Jerry Lewis put on an impromptu show for lucky passengers in the First Class Lounge. They were aboard the *Queen Elizabeth* in June of 1953 on their way to their first-ever overseas engagement at the London Palladium. (Cunard)

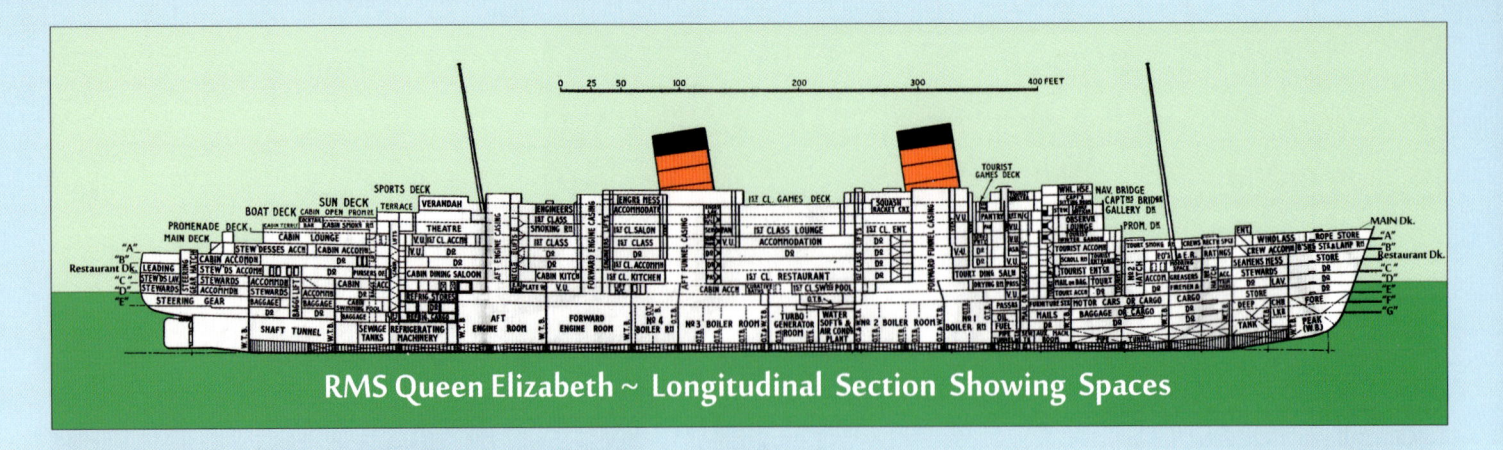

RMS Queen Elizabeth ~ Longitudinal Section Showing Spaces

Bingo! a popular pastime in the First Class Lounge. (Cunard)

The writing recesses in the Main Lounge were lined with grey-blue leather to match the leather decorations of the pillars in the room. The window curtains and carpets in the room were specially designed Grey and Miriam Wornum . (Robert Lenzer Collection)

A string sextet performs, in the Main Lounge in 1947, in front of the wood marquetry 'The Canterbury Pilgirm's Journey'. It was designed by George Ramon and executed by Mr. J. Dunn. The almost 20-foot tall marquetry was relocated to a landing in the Main First Class Stairway in 1948. (Philpot Collection)

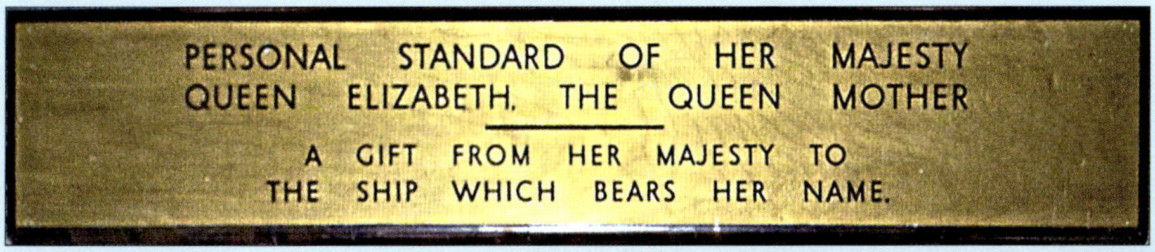

PERSONAL STANDARD OF HER MAJESTY QUEEN ELIZABETH, THE QUEEN MOTHER

A GIFT FROM HER MAJESTY TO THE SHIP WHICH BEARS HER NAME.

Above: A close-up of the original signage to Her Majesty's Royal Standard, seen in the photo below. The sign and pennant were removed from the ship when she was de-commissioned in 1968. The Royal Banner, minus the wooden sign, has been on display aboard the *M/v Queen Elizabeth*, but thanks to the benevolent work of ship-buff and collector Mitchell Mart, the original sign and the Royal Standard have been reunited once more aboard the latest 'Lizzie'. (Mitchell Mart)

Right: The Entrance to the First Class Restaurant on 'R' or Restaurant Deck. Above the doors, is Her Majesty Queen Elizabeth Bowes-Lyon's Royal Standard and Banner of Arms which can be seen in colour on page 182. A Royal Standard was always flown whenever Her Majesty travelled on the ship. The two rows of wood carvings depicting birds and fish were executed by Bainbridge Copnall. This is a replacement set, re-carved by Copnall in 1946, after the original ones, covered in silver-leaf, went a.w.o.l during WW2. (Philpot Collection)

Below: Agnes Moorehead, best remembered for playing the role of 'Endora' in the 1960's TV series Bewitched, is photographed exiting the First Class Restaurant. (Cunard)

Bottom right: Four rectangular columns gave grandeur and importance to the 111 feet by 111 feet First Class Dining Room. (Philpot Collection)

RMS Queen Elizabeth: the Unruffled Cunarder

There was no argument; in went another girder, and Grey went back to the drawing board to create another scheme – no need to worry any longer about a condition of formless licence!

Before Grey actually started any drawings he thought about and discussed the principles on which his work would rest; he never went off in a blaze of enthusiasm and half-baked ideas. When he got down to it, he really knew what he was doing in the widest and deepest sense. A central idea established, meant to him that the details would arrange themselves and slowly the body would, in its material form, convey the atmosphere and feeling, which was all-important. This was the reason for the great quality in his work; the fire of an idea never went out.

"We do not want a floating nightclub" Grey said very firmly, "we are not going to stunt, so that the first time a passenger sees a room he says, 'How amusing', and the second time he begins to be bored, and later irritated.

The eye-catching columns of the First Class Restaurant, were sheathed with a polished ornamental metal-work framed in teal-green leather and adorned with bronze, seven-point stars and woodwork. (photographer Ernest Arroyo - David Boone collection

A rare close-up of the huge tapestry that was specially commissioned for the *Queen Elizabeth* in 1938. The idea for the tapestry's design came from the painting titled 'Venus in the Waves with Her Attendant Sea Horses and Mer-Children', produced by by Miss E Esmonde-White and Mr. Leroux S Leroux. The tapestry was 5 metres (16 foot) wide and 4 metre (13 foot) high and was woven in three parts by a small team of persons and then sewn together. The tapestry hung on the aft bulkhead in the First Class Restaurant, just behind the Captain's Table. Does it still exist somewhere today, or was it left on board during the ship's conversion in Hong Kong in 1972 and thus destroyed, like everything else aboard, by the all-consuming fire? (Photographer Ernest Arroyo – Scott Becker Collection)

Adornment of the North Atlantic: A Nicer Shade of 'Grey'

The Hargreaves family celebrating in the Main Dining Room in 1959. Who said the most fun was to be had in third class!! (John Hargreaves)

—Decorative glass panels like this, realised by Jan Juta, were fitted inside three private dining rooms which adjoined the First Class Restaurant. (Philpot Collection)

This intimate cocktail bar was found next to the First Class Restaurant Foyer. The walls were panelled with champagne-coloured leather and white-bleached London Plane tree, with the bar itself veneered with beautiful Sycamore curl (Philpot Collection)

Above: The First Class Smoking Room was also adorned with rows of repeating leather squares - a design in keeping with Grey Wornum's distinctive recto-linear style. Wood carvings by Dennis Dunlop - 'Hunting', 'Fishing' and 'Shooting' – are also to be seen on the aft bulkhead. (Photographer Ernest Arroyo – David Boone Collection)

Left: Auctioning of the ship's 'pools' in the First Class Smoking Room. This game worked on the basis of miles the *Queen Elizabeth* would cover each day - usually between 700 and 780. The Captain would send down 22 numbers and celebrity passengers would auction them. The following day, the exact number of miles was posted outside the Purser's Office with the person holding the number closest to the correct distance winning the monetary prize. (Cunard Archive)

RMS Queen Elizabeth: the Unruffled Cunarder

Left: First Class Smoking Room: Macdonald Gill was the creator of this glass-engraved map of the North Atlantic which contained two moving models of the 'Queens' showing their current position. Above the map casing is an ornamental clock face with carvings of two fish and a sailing ship, by Dennis Dunlop. (Richard L. Weiss – William Brennan photo)

Above: The Dance Salon was essentially the ship's cabaret nightclub. The bandstand is on the aft bulkhead. (Philpot Collection)

Above right: The First Class Dance Salon or Ballroom, on Promenade Deck, had its bulkheads covered in glistening, natural satin, buttoned quilting and high quality draping. It was one of the most exquisitely-decorated rooms aboard. The tables and chairs were constructed of bleached wood, giving them an almost pure white colour and were upholstered in red and green. (Philpot Collection)

Right: Peruvian soprano Yma Sumac (centre) and her party in the First Class Dance Salon. Seen in the background – on the forward bulkhead - is Jan Juta's painted glass mural, an exotic animal frieze in gold, bronze, yellows and browns. (CUNARD Archive)

83

Chapter Title

Because a large part of the passenger list consists of people who cross constantly, we don't want the ship to look like a cinema either. No sinking into plush carpets, and windows with great velvet curtains with swags of gold cord, and tassels that swing when the weather is rough. The ship is to be English and its decoration must never dwarf the passengers, or make the women's pretty dresses fade into insignificance. People must feel assured as they move about the rooms, which should be a background. "So," Grey concluded, "we will model these rooms in proportion and in decoration on the stately homes of England; the great houses in which the English gentleman has lived and felt at home for hundreds of years. Like him we will go to the artist and sculptor studios and buy his best work to hang on our walls. We will have works of art, not frivolous decoration. When the ship is broken up, they will still be works of art. If, at the end, all these things melt into a unity that is hardly noticed, that is exactly what I wish."

On this idea there was no disagreement, and everything possible was done to produce a gentle background that held the essence of a drawing room; of informality allied to elegance. Some rooms had to be more formal than others, and some were brighter and gayer, but this only added variety and made the work that much more fascinating.

Except for the slope of every surface, wall, ceiling and deck, which in a ship never makes a right angle, there was very little difference in the actual planning that would have arisen in rebuilding the interior of an already existing palace or large hotel. The real divergences lay in the fact that it would be a violently moving palace, subject to continuous earthquakes and hurricanes, and that the people subject to this agitation should be helped to be as little aware of this as possible. Anyone who has experienced a rough crossing can sympathise with Grey's efforts. To forgive and forget a nasty sea during the process of being its victim is almost beyond human charity.

He realised that he had to avoid designing any object that was loose enough to swing, or of a colour scheme that might be bilious. Also to be shunned was a feeling of being trapped in an enclosed space. This he had felt on a foreign liner

Often, the *Queen Elizabeth's* captain, browsing through the passenger list, would take full advantage of the wide selection of celebrity passengers aboard his ship and prevail upon some of them to demonstrate their skills, be it singing, magical acts, playing an instrument, comedy or even swinging a golf club! Here, members of the Walker Cup Golf Team were persuaded to demonstrate a 'swing' of a different kind in the first class dance salon. (Cunard Archive)

Whenever Commodore Marr entered the ballroom, the band would stop whatever song they were playing and strike up the 1921 hit tune 'MA! – He's Making Eyes at Me'. The tradition followed him throughout his career. (CUNARD Archive)

Jan Juta completed many works for the *Queen Elizabeth*, but none as large or spectacular as this work - a 23-foot-long by 7-foot-tall, hand-painted decorative glass mural showing a jungle scene with wildlife. It is made up of seven vertical panels. The work was landed during the room's complete refitting in 1964 and today it can be seen in a hallway leading to the Lord Mayor's Office in the Southampton Civic Centre. (Philpot/QEHS Collection)

During the ship's January 1964 winter lay-up, the Ballroom was transformed into the Midships Bar – the new, First Class Cocktail Bar. The space was an honest (failed in the eyes of some critics and purists) attempt by Cunard at reorganising and modernising the ship's interiors in an attempt to keep up with the changing tastes of many of its passengers. The kidney-shaped bar is where the bandstand used to be. (Philpot Collection)

Above top: The ceiling has been dropped several feet from the Dance Salon's original two-deck height and fake shutters replace Jan Juta's mural. Those who criticized the Midships Bar rightfully argued that it was built in an uncomplimentary and too contrasting style to the rest of the ship's older and more striking interiors. The look was a preview, of sorts, to what the replacement ship QE2's interiors, would look like. (Photographer Ernest Arroyo – David Boone Collection)

Above: The Verandah Grill was an elegant and stylish room extending the entire width of the Raised Sun Deck. Grey Wornum's style is evident throughout. (Philpot Collection)

Left centre: For those not wishing to dine in the first class restaurant, the Verandah Grill provided an à la carte menu between the hours of 12 noon to 3 p.m. and 7 p.m. to 10 p.m. daily. The Verandah Grill was the most exclusive eating place on the entire ship with gourmet meals served, excellent sea views and the chance to dine amongst the elite of the passenger list. Each patron was required to pay a 10-shilling cover charge for the privilege, about $2.50 at the time. (Philpot Collection)

Left: Dancing in the highly desirable Verandah Grill - a combined first-class restaurant and night club. (Philpot Collection)

RMS Queen Elizabeth: the Unruffled Cunarder

where the dining saloon had been deep in the bowels of the ship and completely cased in, with no windows but great panels of highly decorated Lalique glass instead. Added to this was a series of steps and doors to be negotiated before entering the room, and this obviously offered no hope of being able to make a quick and inconspicuous exit, should a rough sea and a sudden loss of appetite, makes this desirable.

The Cunard Company asks the Patersons, Grey's young partner Tony Tripe, and Grey and me to travel on, wherever possible, every great liner of every nationality afloat, and when in port, to stay or dine at the best hotels and restaurants, and to go every night to as many nightclubs as could be managed -this was an invitation not likely to be made again. All that was asked in return was to sample the cuisine and wines as fully as possible, and to make a note of decor, gadgets, service and comfort. Needless to say, each in his own way saw and did his duty. It was a wise move on the part of Cunard, as between us, the French, Dutch, Italian and Swedish ships were all inspected, as were the German and the few American passenger liners then existing. Sample menus were designed to test and compare the difference in restaurants and the specialities were tried. Waiters, beauty parlour and barber shop attendants were questioned about their ideas as to how their work could be helped by better planning; secrecy was promised and kept, and they disclosed some of the shocking conditions under which they lived and worked behind the facade of the greatest luxury. Much was learnt and many mistakes avoided in consequence; not to do something is often as great a contribution towards excellence as the positive inclusion of a desirable feature.

Although our grand tour was over, the blank white paper of the drawing board awaited, and heavy breathing was heard throughout the office as every-one sweated out the complications of this most complicated job. It never became dull or routine; in fact it is quite realistic to state there was not a dull moment! Again, the artists and craftsmen had to be selected, instructed and inspired, and materials of every

Top right: The First Class Observation Lounge and Cocktail Bar. At evenings, intimately lit by spotlights, the room took on a more sophisticated look. On the negative side, the room was unpopular during heavy seas due to its forward location in the ship, where pitching of the bows is more pronounced making it an uncomfortable place to be. (Robert Lenzer Collection)

Centre right: The walls in the Observation Lounge were panelled in sycamore, stained a distinctive shade of light, 'lobster-shell' red. Eighteen large square windows wrapped around the room providing very good illumination during the day. This space was assigned to tourist class from 1964 onwards. (Philpot Collection)

Bottom right: The lofty, First Class Main Hall, at Promenade Deck level was two decks high. The main woods used were burred English Olive Ash and myrtle burr. Within the hall was a series of shops, a travel bureau and a radio office for booking telegrams (Philpot Collection)

Adornment of the North Atlantic: A Nicer Shade of 'Grey'

A crew member cleans the bronze sculpture by Mr. Maurice Lambert, above the starboard entrance to the Promenade Deck main hall. This piece, together with a similar sculpture above the port-side entrance, across the hallway, was of a female figure entangled with a sea-serpent, anchor and chains. (Philpot Collection)

The Main Hall, looking forward in the ship towards the First Class Grand Stairway. The marquetry, 'The Pilgrims Journey', can be seen on the staircase's bulkhead and protruding from a flower bed at the head of the stairway, is the bronze statue titled 'Oceanides'. (Philpot Collection)

The magnificent First Class Main Stairway, seen from the landing between Main and Promenade Decks. The walls lining the stairway were covered in Arbele burr, with the burl pattern on each panel almost identical the next. Because of this, most passengers imagined that the panels were in fact replicas of one another, rather than continuous shavings from the same log. The balustrade was done in dark-green leather with hand rails a highly-polished silver-bronze. (Philpot Collection)

'Oceanides': The bronze sculpture took its name from a musical work by Finnish composer Jean Sibelius and it shows male and female figures in harmonious and pleasing animation. The work was not originally commissioned for the ship - its creator Maurice Lambert had the finished piece sitting in his studio when it was spotted by chance, in the early 1940's, by Cunard chairman Sir Percy Bates. (Philpot Collection)

Fixed above the entrance foyer to the First Class Restaurant, was Her Majesty's Royal Coat of Arms, intricately carved in lime wood by British sculptor Edward Bainbridge Copnall. Before being installed on the ship it first had to be vetted by The College of Heralds. It survives to this day aboard QE2 and a colour close-up can be seen on page 184 (Philpot Collection)

The First Class Main Staircase terminated here, at the R-Deck lobby, directly in front of the entrance to the First Class Restaurant Lobby. In the distance are the starboard shell doors. (Philpot/QEHS Collection)

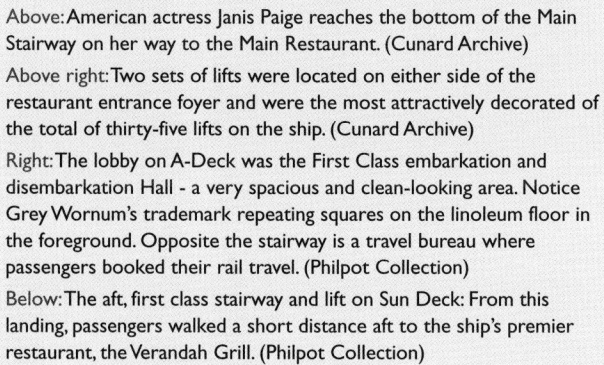

Adornment of the North Atlantic: A Nicer Shade of 'Grey'

Above: American actress Janis Paige reaches the bottom of the Main Stairway on her way to the Main Restaurant. (Cunard Archive)

Above right: Two sets of lifts were located on either side of the restaurant entrance foyer and were the most attractively decorated of the total of thirty-five lifts on the ship. (Cunard Archive)

Right: The lobby on A-Deck was the First Class embarkation and disembarkation Hall - a very spacious and clean-looking area. Notice Grey Wornum's trademark repeating squares on the linoleum floor in the foreground. Opposite the stairway is a travel bureau where passengers booked their rail travel. (Philpot Collection)

Below: The aft, first class stairway and lift on Sun Deck: From this landing, passengers walked a short distance aft to the ship's premier restaurant, the Verandah Grill. (Philpot Collection)

known shape and form started pouring into the office.

In the kind of designing in which Grey excelled, there was always one special problem. If every moulding, doorknob and lighting fixture is created specially, not to mention rugs and textiles, furniture and decorated glass, every one of these has to be made. This takes time, and for anyone who has had the experience of having had even one thing made to order, the prodigious amount of time it takes can be appreciated. When you multiply this by the score it is easy to understand how long ahead of the moment of completion these orders, with their full working drawings, must be given. Not only were these designs original, but often the very principle on which they were based was a revolutionary one.

"Won't work, sir." "Can't be done, old man." These were all familiar phrases heard round the office, uttered by workmen and managers, until Grey proved they were wrong. However, the greatest feat of all, aside from being creative enough to design new shapes, was his amazing ability to visualise every detail, as it would fit in a future whole. Many a time Grey would discuss the fringe on a pelmet in a room that had crude brick for walls and holes for windows, and here on the ship there would be even less than that. Practically no artist or craftsman would set foot on the ship until his completed work would be put on board, and it was Grey alone who was capable of the vision necessary to give the orders that set the machines clanking and the looms turning. His was the final responsibility, literally years beforehand.

So although Grey was the only one who saw the ship as she was to be, all the artists working to adorn her had to see in some measure why they were doing what Grey wanted. Grey explained, and I became a form of liaison officer to keep on explaining and to soothe the artistic ruffled temperament, so as to keep the various works of art in some proportion to each other. Artists are apt to get illusions of grandeur and suddenly produce much larger canvasses or carvings than will fit, as well as changing the subject matter entirely.

"No," they will state calmly to one's surprised face, "I am not painting swans – that idea seemed wrong when I worked on it. This big face with the one eye, I like placing it in the

Top right: Looking forward in the ship, along a first class corridor on M-Deck. Staterooms M.118 and 120 are to the left and M.123 to the right. The bulkheads are lined with golden maple, with Australian Walnut dados. (Philpot Collection)

Centre right: Two garden lounges were located on the promenade deck, on either side of the ship. They were situated on a raised terracing which meant that the windows were much lower to the floor than on the rest of the Promenade deck thus giving passengers sitting at the tables a far better view of the sea below. (Philpot Collection)

Bottom right: Amidships, on the port-side of Promenade Deck, was the lovely first class writing room. The room was lined with both sycamore and betula veneer, with etched glass panels cut to ornamental shapes surrounding the stairwell. (Philpot Collection)

Adornment of the North Atlantic: A Nicer Shade of 'Grey'

Right: A view of the First Class Swimming Pool taken in December 1967: Mosaic coloured a delicate shade of sea-green surrounded the pool area, interlaced with wavy, inlaid metal strips of silver-bronze. The familiar Wornum theme of square shapes, works well with the linear design of the pool area. (Philpot Collection)

American actress, dancer and singer, Ginger Rogers, in the Writing Room, Ca 1948. (Cunard Archive)

The first class pool on C-Deck: The whole area was totally re-tiled in the refit following WW2, with the destruction of an original Grey Wornum mosaic mural. The pool was open from 7 a.m. to 7 p.m. daily, seas permitting. (©SCOTLANDIMAGES.COM - The National Archives of Scotland)

The First Class Library as envisioned by Grey Wornum, in this 1939 sketching. The term 'Cabin' was, for a while in the 1930s, used as the top class aboard a ship. By the time the *Queen Elizabeth* commenced commercial service in 1946, Cabin Class reverted back to its original designation for the middle or second class, with 'Tourist' referring to Third Class (Cunard Archive)

This 1946 photograph of the First Class Library, shows that the space was eventually fitted-out as originally penned by Wornum seven years earlier. (Philpot Collection)

There were eighteen extra-large and luxurious, First Class Staterooms on Main Deck and forty on A-Deck - each was individual in style and configuration. Betula, Burr Ash, bleached Queensland Maple, Indian White Mahogany, maple burr and many more varieties of delicately contrasting woods, gave each room warmth and individual character. (Philpot Collection)

The same stateroom seen in the previous two black and white images, this time in colour - 23 years later in 1971, while the ship was laid up in Port Everglades Florida. The patina of the wood veneer has substantially darkened over the years. The Roanoid plastic, Pukah louvers remain untouched. (Robert Lenzer Collection)

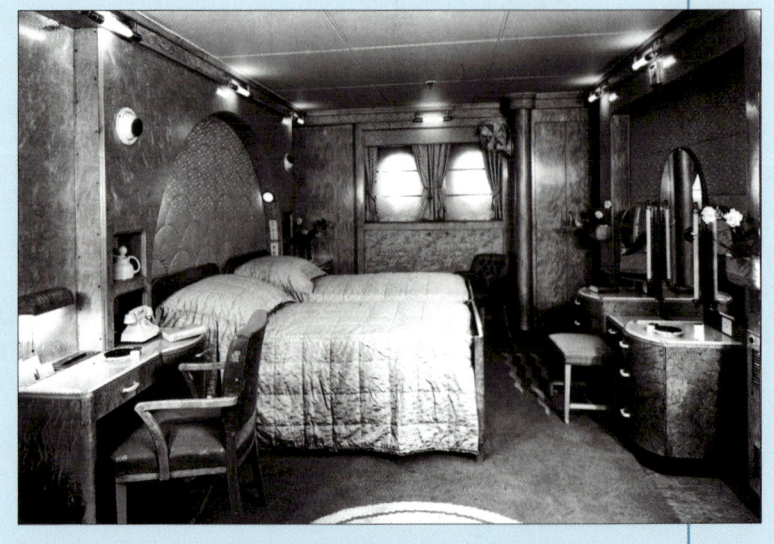

An outboard view of the same cabin: The forward and aft recesses are covered in quilted, natural silk fabric. (Philpot Collection)

Adornment of the North Atlantic: A Nicer Shade of 'Grey'

The stateroom used by the Queen Mother during her 1954 trip to America. The wall recess behind the dressing table is bordered with a screening designed by Miss Margot Gilbert. (Cunard Archive)

Early 1971, Port Everglades, Florida: The carpet, bedspreads and the furniture coverings are not original to this former First Class Bedroom, however the green damask fabric on the walls certainly is. (Robert Lenzer Collection)

A Cunard publicity photograph, released in 1963, showing the recently-refurbished First Class Stateroom A.101 (Philpot Collection)

First Class Cabin A.109, after the major, 1962 winter upgrading of the *Queen Elizabeth's* cabins. (Philpot Collection)

Child star Margaret O'Brien, seen here in her First Class Stateroom, is travelling to Europe with what appears to be a replica of herself in the form of a porcelain doll. (Cunard Archive)

chin, don't you? Was so right – I knew at once this was what you really wanted. Being six feet instead of two is much more significant although I am not really convinced, ten feet wouldn't be better."

To know a two-foot recess was where this decoration was to go and that the swan motif was echoed in the room meant a very firm hand to guide the painter back into a possible path. Cries and screams and bitter accusations of being a Philistine were part and parcel of the routine. The great thing was to get him back complete with painting. Sometimes his indignation was such, and his refusal to work on an established size and subject was so violent, he left, refusing to work at all in this horrible atmosphere where an artist was just not understood!

Grey was very patient with these moods, but it was trying and often discouraging. The artist would become more and more bewildered and produce new sketches, each more wide of the mark than the one before, until he would be given a cheque and at the last minute someone else would be called in to save the day. Very often this turned out to be my job, but being the wife of the architect created a delicate situation, so this was never officially mentioned, an arrangement Grey and I agreed was preferable. Yet if Grey felt the artist was really trying, he would sweat it out with hire, until the block was broken and the right idea came through. Usually, the men chosen were full of ideas and capable of grasping a problem, though they were told specifically only about their small part in it. Working with most of them was a pleasure, though there were enough of the others to create a steady dull headache as a background. Grey and I knew exactly what we were letting ourselves in for, but the *Queen Elizabeth* was one job that had to use artists in abundance. A ship was no longer supposed to look like a ship -when it reached this size it became something else. No longer were the rivets exposed so that lying on one's bunk (now replaced with beds of course) did one see rows of what appeared to be fat white marshmallows marching across the ceiling, and could gaze upon a brass porthole set in a painted steel wall. The purists have a right to scoff; Grey in a great measure would have agreed with them, but his job was to provide the background of five days of gracious living, regardless of where this took place. The "nasty great snarling Atlantic" as Jan Juta calls it, must be made as unimportant as possible: to this end the artist was indispensable.

Despite Grey's firm policy of going to the studio and selecting work from paintings or sculpture already there, it was still necessary at specific points on the ship to have special works of art made for them. A good example of how both these measures worked is shown in the sculpture of Maurice Lambert R.A. In his studio was one of his finest works, "Oceanides". Grey chose this group for the central piece of the main hall, at the top of the grand stairway. There was no difficulty in convincing the Cunard directors that this was a work of art they needed.

When it came to casting in bronze, Maurice knew he

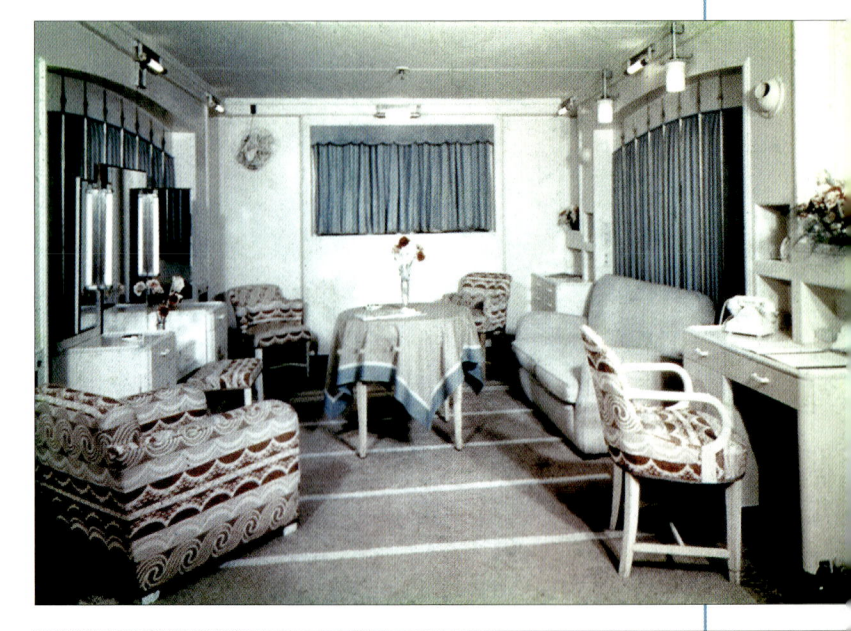

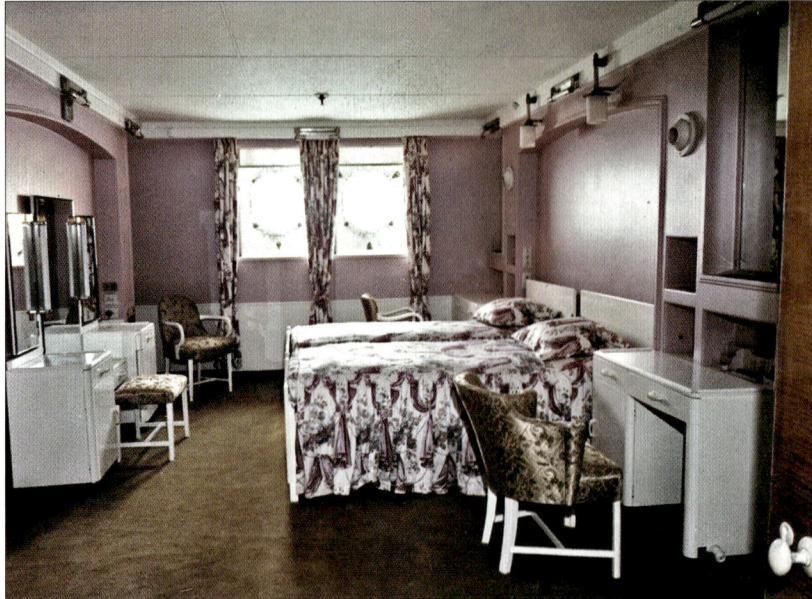

Top: In the mid-1950's, approximately ten years after the *Queen Elizabeth* had been in service, most of her staterooms underwent their first reconditioning. The First Class Cabin seen here, originally a bedroom, has had its furniture reupholstered and has been reconfigured as the sitting room to a suite. The striped mat has remained original from 1946. (QEHS Collection)

Above: The same cabin seen in the above photo following the winter 1962 refit: The bubble-gum-pink walls were to the liking of Hollywood actress Elizabeth Taylor, who booked this particular stateroom on more than one crossing. (Robert Lenzer Collection)

had to bear in mind that his group would be subject to constant vibration as well as, at times, violent motion. He strengthened it accordingly, but although Grey was convinced this was more than adequate, not so the engineers. They not only insisted upon a thicker core of

Adornment of the North Atlantic: A Nicer Shade of 'Grey'

Above: First Class Stateroom M.72 as originally configured in 1946: This space was used as the dining room to a suite of three adjoining cabins, with the wood panelling a beautiful Indian White Mahogany and Maple burr. The recess on the aft bulkhead was covered with padded blue hide. (Philpot Collection)

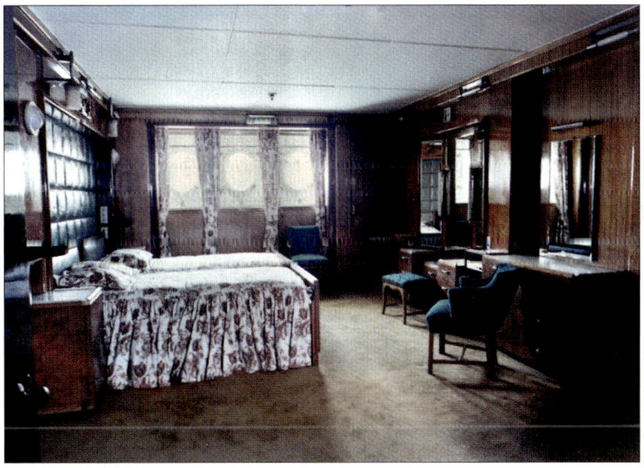

Right: Stateroom M.72 was reconfigured to a bedroom once the *Queen Elizabeth* commenced part-time cruising in the early 1960's. This Image of the Stateroom was taken in 1970, during the ship's time in Port Everglades, Florida. (Robert Lenzer Collection)

metal; they actually demanded a change of design. Whether they visualised a moment when the great ship would rise and be shaken by a monster wave as yet unheard of; which would hurl a rain of bronze bodies and fish upon the innocent passengers, no one could guess, but the sculptor was told more fish, bigger fish, and nearer the mermaid to hold her firmly in place.

Maurice grimly set to work, and not only did he do all they demanded, but managed to achieve it in a way that did not destroy the beauty of his design. The statue stood on a pedestal with a low rim of green plants out of which it rose, but alas, the taste of that strange group of salt water gardeners, has gradually raised these plants to a height that leaves the bronze barely visible, and have added cumbersome yellow and red and pink blooms, so that the cool green colour is lost.

The answer in high places to the outraged complaint made by me over this was so astounding as to leave me practically breathless. "Mrs. Wornum" was the reply, "we have to plant this way. We don't dare leave any space at the base of the statue, because if we do, it gets filled up with

RMS Queen Elizabeth: the Unruffled Cunarder

cigarette stubs, burnt matches, and candy-bar wrappings!"

Besides "Oceanides" there were two niches and places over each door leading to the outside deck that Maurice had to fill. So his work came under the two categories; finished work brought from the studio and specially commissioned for specific places.

Dennis Dunlop and Edward Copnal carved in wood and modelled in plaster, in the smoking room and dining room, and framed various clocks scattered throughout the ship. There were several sand-blasted and etched glass panels and walls by Jan Juta in the Ballroom and Veranda Grill, and above all, the use of marquetry that Grey felt was the ideal decoration for a ship. "It is smooth and an integral part of the wall, and people can get as close as they wish and feel it, and no matter how near they go, it still looks beautiful."

Grey assumed that the public who would travel on the *Queen Elizabeth* would be both sophisticated and capable of appreciating the work of the best artists available, but the turning of "Oceanides" into a litter receptacle makes one wonder. Every time I cross on the *Elizabeth* I wonder even more.

At that time the favourite colours in both ships and restaurants were hot, especially a red-rust tone. This shade came originally from Germany where the new school of decoration had used it to great effect. It admirably filled spaces and created a sense of warmth and gaiety. Grey, however, came to the conclusion that perhaps the passenger did not want the dining room to be done in these hot tones, when the mere thought of food might put him off; "Let's try a cool colour" Grey suggested, "it might actually help."

To be certain that this was a good move we redecorated our own dining morn in Hamilton Terrace in pale blue and white, and carefully watched the effect on the appetite of our guests. As this seemed excellent, it was decided to use this same ice blue with deeper tones, throughout the ship. This was a good foil to the natural and warm coloured wood veneers, which formed most of the walls.

The floor of any dining room, big or little, is always a

Below left: A stylish First Class Stateroom on Main Deck: commodious, uncluttered discreet and unique. (Philpot Collection)

Below right: A First Class Stateroom seen in 1968 - the ship's final year of service for Cunard. (Photographer Ernest Arroyo – David Boone Collection)

Bottom left: 1959: First Class passengers enjoy pre-dinner drinks in the sitting room of their Stateroom. First Class cabins would always be decorated with fresh flowers at the beginning of each voyage. (John Hargreaves)

Bottom right: The Richards (couple on the far right) enjoying drinks and hors d'œuvres with a group of shipboard friends, in their First Class Stateroom in 1948. A cabin get-together for pre-dinner cocktails was the fashionable thing to do when travelling by ocean liner. (Warren Kendrick)

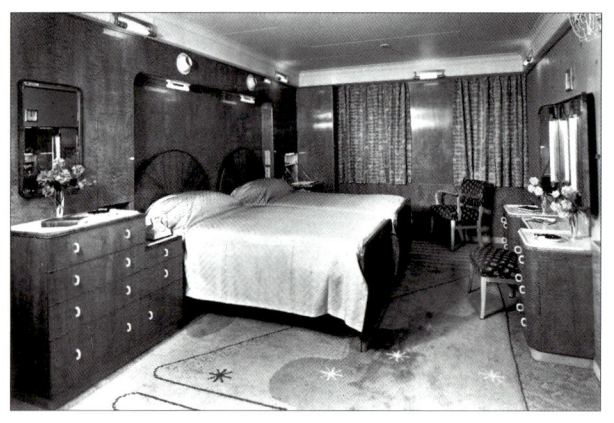

Adornment of the North Atlantic: A Nicer Shade of 'Grey'

Mother and daughter travel to Europe in a big way – in a luxurious cabin aboard the world's largest ship. (Cunard Archive)

difficulty; one spilled tray and the finest carpet is ruined. So Cunard wisely insisted upon linoleum; a most useful material but very difficult to marry to fine wood, gold leaf, etched glass and leather. Grey had his designers turn out drawing after drawing until the pattern, colour and scale satisfied him. Unfortunately the war years that were to follow gave this linoleum such hard wear that it had to be replaced before the ship was in commercial service, and this was done by a totally different designer and was completely at variance with the colour and feeling of the room.

The most amusing episode in the working out of this dining room came from the tapestry which formed the main decoration on the far wall. The designers were two young people, then in partnership, Miss E Esmond-White and Le Roux Smith Le Roux. Its background was the sea, in the same shades of blue that flowed through the ship, and showed Venus being towed upon a shell by rearing, white sea horses. In front the shell were three small mer-babies; frolicsome and without clothes. When the tapestry was hung for the first time, one of the directors who was inspecting the ship, was perfectly horrified by the little boy in the middle, a child possibly two or three years old. Pointing with a shaking finger at what he imagined to be the little masculine appendage, which he claimed should not be there at all, he demanded its removal. It is hard to say how many passengers travelling on the ship would have noticed, and if noticing would have cared, but the tapestry was sent back to the factory and painstakingly by hand, the offending 2 inches were unpicked, and then blandly featureless, woven back. Now the tapestry hangs pure and blameless, endangering none of the passengers by its bold announcement of the facts of life. It never ceased provoking

RMS Queen Elizabeth: the Unruffled Cunarder

The Cabin Class Lounge had artificial, floor to ceiling windows made of spun glass panels which were silvered on the reverse side. The reflected light given out helped to give the appearance of natural daylight entering the room. (Philpot Collection)

An attractive, curved bar was set into the forward bulkhead of the Cabin Class Lounge. (Robert Lenzer Collection)

Vaudeville singer, Sophie Tucker affectionately known as 'The last of the Red-Hot Mamas', made several crossings on the *Queen Elizabeth*. She performs here in the Cabin Class Lounge, where the carpeting has been rolled up and used as front-row seating. (Cunard Archive)

The Cabin Class Lounge was remodelled into the 'Caribbean Room' during the 1964 winter layup, a change that came about as the result of the decision to introduce the *Queen Elizabeth* to part-time cruising. The room was designed with the younger traveller in mind and was given a tropical island look (Philpot Collection)

Because the Cabin Class Restaurant did not run the full width of the ship, the entry of natural light was not permitted. Nevertheless, the room was not lacking in illumination thanks to a clever method of lining the curved side-bays with a silver-coloured material which reflected the indirect light into the centre of the room. (Philpot Collection)

Adornment of the North Atlantic: A Nicer Shade of 'Grey'

The curved side bays had the effect of removing the walls relieving the room from having a closed-in feeling, a well-thought manipulation to create the feeling of space. The Cabin Class Restaurant could seat 377 passengers at one sitting and was rechristened the 'Windsor Restaurant' during the 1966 cruise-refit. (Photographer Ernest Arroyo – David Boone Collection)

a chuckle from Grey when he saw it, and the incident was a cause of great pleasure to his entire staff.

On the deck below the dining room were the Turkish bath and swimming pool. The Turkish bath is deliberately without decoration; white, clean and soothing. Many "witty" designs were considered but all were discarded in favour of hygiene and peace. The swimming pool was another involvement altogether, and so sore a point to all those who worked on the ship, that it is questionable if it should be mentioned at all. Inasmuch as the public had been continuously puzzled about the bleakness of the first class pool as compared to the highly embellished pools of other classes on board, and the luxury shown in this feature in other ships, perhaps the story of what happened on board the *Elizabeth* had better be told.

The original scheme was restrained, it is true, but it was bright both in colour and subject, and was very, very expensive. The pool was to be done entirely in mosaic and tile; the mosaic was to be of the finest Venetian glass. At first the idea was to do an elaborate decoration on the floor of the swimming pool, and let it be seen through the water. It was typical of Grey, to say that the water itself was the most important feature in the room and that it should dominate. Also typical of him was his way of finding out if this were as practical as he thought. So he and I chose the moment when the *Queen Mary* was doing a 'turn around' in Southampton, and fighting our way through the loading and cleaning process going on around us, made our way to the *Queen Mary's* swimming pool. Lying flat on the floor we dropped one by one the bright coloured pieces of mosaic with which we were armed. We watched the little squares of brilliant emerald green, turquoise, curve to the bottom, but as the water deepened it did horrid things to the brightness, so that when they finally landed, each looked like mud and made the idea of the decorated floor impossible. The one thing that came from this was that the gold and silver pieces of mosaic that were also dropped retained their glitter and although they turned green they were still alive.

Rising from the floor and dusting himself off, Grey then and there decided on his scheme. It would be expensive but he became quite enthusiastic about it. "Whatever we do," he said, "we will not mark the line running round the edge of the pool, as this is subject to distortion as the water is thrown about by the kind of sea there is outside. The level of the pool is rarely steady, and nothing is less happy than a design that should be static, moving about because of the water line." So Grey ordered the entire pool to be lined with silver mosaics. When the water is tilted they would form their own water line, bright silver above the deepening silver green below. He was very cunning and gave orders that the individual mosaics were to be set in the walls and floor slightly unevenly, not achieving a completely smooth

RMS Queen Elizabeth: the Unruffled Cunarder

The Cabin Class Smoking Room was often mistakenly considered to belong to the first class due to its luxurious, expensive appearance. More than any other public room aboard, it had an Art-Deco look. (Cunard Archive)

A cheerful group of passengers gather for farewell party in a side bay of the Cabin Class Smoking Room. The smoking room was renamed the 'Club Room' in the major, 1966 cruise refit. (Philpot Collection)

The Cabin Smoking Room's main decoration was a group of nine bas reliefs that were located above a marble-framed radiator. Designed by Norman Forest, the motifs were made of the principle materials used in the construction of the ship. Starting from the top left of each row downwards, are 'White-Metal', 'Glass', 'Aluminium', 'Lead', 'Wood', 'Rubber', 'Bronze', 'Steel', and 'Copper'. (Photographer Ernest Arroyo – David Boone Collection)

The streamlined arrangement of the Cabin Class Cocktail Bar was Grey Wornum's adaptation of the then contemporary Arte Moderne style - a request by Sir Percy Bates, who wanted, as much as possible, a style which would especially please American passengers. (Robert Lenzer Collection)

Not only did the title of each relief correspond to the medium it was created from, each design introduced symbolism suggesting its origin, use and quality. This relief is 'Aluminium' - Light and strong. A copy of this relief was made using the original mould and it currently hangs on a wall in the retired QE2's Crystal Bar. (Philpot Collection)

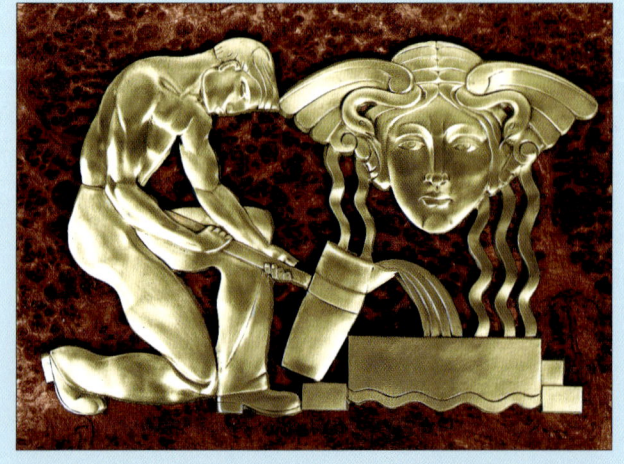

'White-Metal': is an alloy of various metals and often used as a base for gold and silver plated ornaments (Philpot Collection)

101

Adornment of the North Atlantic: A Nicer Shade of 'Grey'

American tourists took a special liking to the overall design of the Cabin Class Cocktail Bar, no doubt reminding them of the diner-like ambience found back home. (Robert Edmiston)

The Cabin Class Drawing Room: This space also served as a Chapel for the celebration of Mass and other small religious services. Behind the central curtain stood an altar and a glass panel with an etching of the Madonna and Child. (Philpot Collection)

The Cabin Class Library: Although not very large, the library was especially attractive due to the handsome graining of the horizontally laid veneers of Australian Walnut. Also interesting was the room's shape - two sections with a semi-circular apse at the forward end (Robert Lenzer)

RMS Queen Elizabeth: the Unruffled Cunarder

A parapet wall surrounded the Cabin Class Swimming Pool, keeping the surrounds dry. The pool itself was tiled with golden quartzite, giving the impression of a sandy bottom. Marine-themed designs by the artist Hector Whistler decorated the walls. This space has always been considered prettier than the first class pool area. (Philpot Collection)

The main, Cabin Class Stairway was the longest stairway on the *Queen Elizabeth*, serving eight decks in total and ending here, at the Promenade Deck Hall. In the background is an Austin Reed men's shop – one two aboard. The door, at top right, gave crew access to the baggage-lift well. (Philpot Collection)

The walls of the split, cabin stairwell were panelled with a bleached, Silky Oak wood from Queensland, Australia. The starboard entrance to the Cabin Class Smoking Room can be seen at the top of the stairs. (Philpot Collection)

Replacing a large photographic mural that was originally displayed here, on the raised Prom. Deck landing of the stairwell, is this superb painting of *Aquitania* - the 'ship beautiful' - under tow to the breakers yard in Faslane Scotland. (Photographer Ernest Arroyo – David Boone Collection)

The R-Deck lobby of the main, Cabin Class Staircase: On the left is the Cabin Class Purser's Office and in the distance, a travel bureau and a branch of The Midlands Bank - one of three aboard where telegraphic transfer of funds to passengers, via the ship's radio, could be sent from the UK and where passengers could make payments to recipients on either side of the North Atlantic. (Philpot Collection)

Adornment of the North Atlantic: A Nicer Shade of 'Grey'

Above: One of the most luxurious Cabin Class Staterooms aboard the *Queen Elizabeth* (Philpot Collection)

Below: Cabin Class Cabin R.62, for three persons: Features for this cabin are: adjustable ventilation vents, separate wardrobes for each occupant, a combined writing desk and dressing table with cheval wing mirrors, night tables, stools, a wash basin and large tub arm chairs. (Philpot Collection)

Below right: A three-bed Cabin Class Stateroom – quite simple but nonetheless a roomy and elegant design. Most 'cabin' staterooms came with a telephone, and a large number were outboard rooms possessing skylights (portholes). (Philpot Collection)

surface. This way the light filtering through the water struck little sparks from the different angles, and all through the pool these glittered and shone. Grey claimed that this was quite enough decoration for this part of the chamber. He added pillars of intense lapis blue and green from floor-to-ceiling, and at one end of the pool he put a wall about two feet high on which was to be an ornate mural. Here was to be centred all the colour and richness of the entire scheme.

A young painter was chosen to make this design, but though he tried yen-hard, working in an unknown medium baffled him, and he could not produce an acceptable design. He was paid for his time, but by then with no drawing and a short span only before a drawing had actually to be in the

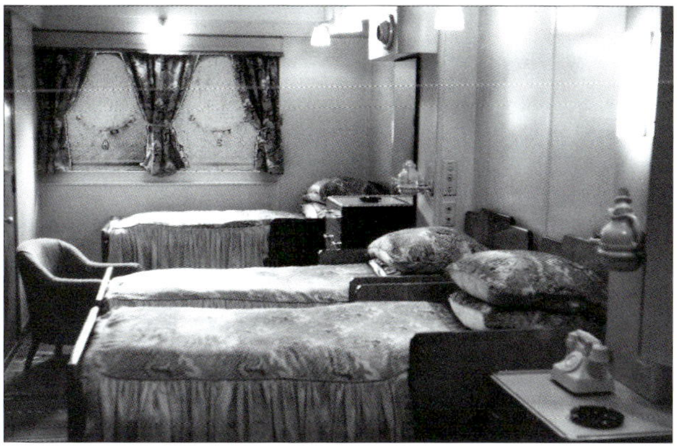

RMS Queen Elizabeth: the Unruffled Cunarder

hands of the firm who were to do the job, things were desperate. There was neither the time nor the hope of finding another painter to do the work, so Grey and I dropped everything and did one of our dashes to the continent, this time to Italy. There we went to all the towns, churches, and buildings where the finest mosaic decorations were to be seen, the older the better. We had long talks at the factory near Venice where the actual mosaics had been manufactured for several hundred years, and where to our astonishment, the floor of the factory, over which many carts holding great loads of sand and other heavy material had rumbled, was paved in the vitreous mosaic itself "Hardest wearing material there is," we were told. But, Grey added, far too expensive to be used anywhere except in its own factory. So, finally I finished the design for the swimming pool and sent it off to Italy to be made. The mural was simple; huge shells and seaweed filling the wall in as big a scale as possible. Unfortunately the engineers had been particularly unkind and had gradually, by inserting their beastly 'girders' lowered the ceiling, so that it was all out of proportion.

As soon as possible after the war Grey and I visited "our" ship; a strange way to see Grey's work after all those years, clad in her war uniform of grey, and filled inside with all the trappings of war. The pool had been used for a sewing room, boarded over, and covered with dustsheets, but the mosaic mural glowed through the spaces left clear, and one presumed the silver shone within the pool although it was not possible to see it. A great sigh of relief went up, that this was indeed a hardy material, but it was a most unwise sigh to have breathed for when the pool was uncovered it was found that due to some fault in the wartime cement that had been used to fix the mosaic, individual pieces were falling out leaving great patches where they had been apparently impossible to mend. The cost of new silver was too great so the order went out, "Knock them in out, and replace them with white." To this day I do not know the true story of what actually happened; only that somewhere an order went wrong, for the workmen who broke up the swimming pool, also knocked out the entire mural. Grey did not allow one an official protest, for once he was tight lipped and cold towards the storm of grief and indignation, which assailed him. Eventually he said that it had not been an accident at all; the directors had never really liked the design.

Whatever the cause, something that had had its own beauty was destroyed and never replaced. Now the pool could not have been more dull; dreary is really the proper word, all tones or rather dirty white with no decoration of any kind. It is a sad story, and one that must raise wrath in the heart of any artist to whom the wanton destruction of any work of art is a little murder.

The main salon was subject to the most intense care in every feature. It was used by the passengers for restful

Top right: The Tourist Class Lounge: On the far bulkhead is a painted decorative panel by Margot Gilbert. Side-bays, resembling those in the cabin class areas, line the starboard side, into which are small settees. (Philpot Collection)

Above: The artist at work: Margot Gilbert was commissioned to create works for all three classes aboard the *Queen Elizabeth* – both in Staterooms and Public rooms. Her speciality was the creation of graceful figures in oil colours, in a definitive style which often depicted movement. She's seen here adding finishing touches to 'Venetian Carnival' - on the forward bulkhead of the Tourist Class Lounge. (Cunard Archive.)

Adornment of the North Atlantic: A Nicer Shade of 'Grey'

—Seen here in 1967, performing in the Queen Elizabeth's 'Tourist' Lounge is the tourist-class trio. They are, from left to right, Cass Caswell – Bandleader and double bass, Jeff Kingscott – drums and John Asher – piano. In addition to evening dances and functions, the trios on board would play for numerous daytime events such as children's parties, morning coffee music, afternoon tea music, dancing classes, sing-songs and - when the sea was too rough for dancing - passenger talent shows. (Cass Caswell)

The Tourist Class Dining Room was located towards the forward end of R-Deck, spanning its entire width. It sat 400-plus passengers arranged at tables of between two and ten people. The prominent décor was a large glass panel on the central forward bulkhead, with etched animal and plant motifs and clock dial. (Philpot Collection)

The wood used in the Tourist Class Restaurant was contrasting veneers of golden Canadian Birch and dark-brown Australian Walnut. These two lands supplied the majority of the wood varieties used to decorate the *Queen Elizabeth*. Beverley Philpot is about to give her lunch order to the waiter as her husband Harold snaps this picture during their crossing in June 1964. (Philpot Collection)

In a mid-1950's overhaul, the Tourist Class Smoking Room was given a noticeable face-lift. Furniture was re-upholstered using bright coloured materials and an equally-colourful linoleum floor was laid. From the late 1960's this space became known as 'The Ambrose Room' - used daily for recorded concerts, talent shows, news broadcasts, musical matinees, tea time music and evening dancing with the ship's resident, musical trio. (Philpot Collection)

Above: The Tourist Class Smoking Room was a large, airy room, occupying the entire width of A-Deck. Three, large wood-marquetry inlays, depicting bird life by W. Borthwick, decorated the room - one of which is visible in the background, to the left of the photo. (Philpot Collection)

Left: The 'Ambrose Room' - the former 'tourist' smoking room, is here the scene of a rousing display of Scottish dancing accompanied by a lone bagpiper. (Philpot Collection)

Adornment of the North Atlantic: A Nicer Shade of 'Grey'

Although not evident in this photo, the Tourist Class Winter Garden was semi-circular in shape - the ship's curved, front superstructure being the forward bulkhead. The room's décor boasted a long glass panel onto which was etched 'The Birds of Life', by Ralph Cowan. Towards the end of the ship's commercial life, the Winter Garden was renamed The Fastnet Room - a groovy, late-night spot for the younger or young-at-heart 'tourist' passenger. (©SCOTLANDIMAGES.COM - The National Archives of Scotland)

When it's too cold up on deck: A group of female passengers huddle-up close to receive singing tuition inside the Tourist Class Winter Garden during a 1964 crossing. (Philpot Collection)

The A-Deck hall of the Tourist Class Main Stairway: This foyer served the smoking room, the ladies and gentlemen's hairdressing salons and the souvenir shop, pictured here. Tourist class stairways and halls on the *Queen Elizabeth* were, thanks to the ship's enormous size, far more spacious than their equivalent on other passenger liners at the time. (Philpot Collection)

RMS Queen Elizabeth: the Unruffled Cunarder

reading and a pleasant spot in which to relax with friends. It was also unfortunately used for the "organised gaiety" which now seems a prerequisite of travel. No longer are the passengers deemed capable, within a veritable Arabian Nights Palace of Delights, to manage to be amused by their own efforts. Games and "get-together" parties crowd the rooms, and have to be ploughed through by the fastidious traveller attempting to find sanctuary in the smoking room, where the soothing quiet and perfect service of the Cunard staff was at its best.

The carpet in the original scheme was a great challenge, inasmuch as it covered area of acres of floor and Grey wanted it to be on a big scale, yet to keep the design flat. To add to this difficulty, it had been decided to use a motif throughout the ship, which we termed 'acordage' that is, rope; made with its special texture, its coils and knots. Right at the beginning a note of high moral import was struck, and what is more, was kept. This was that of never losing an end of rope, no matter how intricate it's interweaving, nor how complicated the knot; every piece had to be brought to its logical end, and must never be abandoned. This led to

Above: An inside, single-berth Tourist Class Stateroom: This was one of the smallest cabins aboard the *Queen Elizabeth*. (Philpot Collection)

Below: Size isn't everything: The small confines of their Tourist Cabin, doesn't seem to bother these passengers. (Philpot Collection)

Adornment of the North Atlantic: A Nicer Shade of 'Grey'

A passenger confuses her twin-berth Tourist Cabin's chamber pot for a champagne glass - easily done. (Robert Edmiston)

many groans of "Oh, Hell I've lost an end, where is it?" There was always some severe critic to point out exactly where his 'faux pas' had occurred, and no feeble excuse of "Well it's just got to stay lost, it will ruin the design if I try to pick it up again" was allowed.

The final full-sized drawing of the repeat of this carpet actually covered the entire floor of the dining room in the office at Devonshire Close. It is sad to think that the only piece of this carpet extant is the original sample sent by the manufacturers, now in the country house of our daughter, standing up to the children, animals and the English climate tracked over it in winter.

However the great decorative feature of the room, the "pointe riche", was the large marquetry panel designed by George Ramon, based on the story of the Canterbury Pilgrims. It dominated the wall at the far end: natural

A typical, twin-berth Tourist Class Stateroom, photographed during a 1962 crossing. In 1965, due to the ever-increasing demand for berths in the most economical class, a number of the smaller First Class Cabins were allocated to tourist class. (Robert Edmiston)

coloured wood, shading from cream to a brown that was almost black, with gold leaf and here and there an insertion of mother of-pearl. Its mood was enchanting, the people were done with the lightest and gayest touch, the horses and dogs and little rabbity creatures had the charm of those shown in old tapestries, and the composition was superb.

There was never any doubt about the design; the difficulty that confronted Grey and George was who was going to make the actual marquetry itself. This was most delicate work requiring the greatest skill. There were two candidates, one a quiet man and dependable, but that summed him up. The other had a touch of genius, but was unreliable as he had been known to leave a job for his own personal interests.

Grey decided to take a chance, and he appealed to the artist in the more talented craftsmen, promising him, that if he would stick to the job, the biggest binge of all time afterwards, if he wanted it. The finished result, which could not be bettered technically, proved Grey's trust in him amply justified. The decoration drew one to it, and it was a joy to peer as closely as one wished and to stroke its polished surface.

Later this decoration was moved to the stairway and in its place was hung a portrait of the Queen Mother. The size of this portrait was insignificant and left a great empty space around it that had no reason to be there.

As well as the large carpet, there were any number of scatter rugs to be designed, some quite as large as good-sized carpets. Everything was on such a vast scale on the ship that the greatest care had to be taken to keep this in mind, at the same time not allowing the human frame to be dwarfed. With anyone but Grey in charge, this paradox might have been too difficult to achieve, but he was like a symphony conductor, keeping control and not allowing a single false note.

One thing, however, did escape him and amused him mightily. In the small library there was a specially woven rug. The design was colourful but simple and it had a border going its full length. This line went along sedately until suddenly it had a most unhappy wiggle. Grey would chuckle whenever he saw it, knowing that a handful of unfinished drawings had been taken before they could be finalized, and this one had been copied far too faithfully for all time.

There was always a quandary when it came to showing a decorative scheme to the committee for their approval. The accepted method is to do this by making a careful watercolour of the room, but it is not a very good way as the scale is too small and really can convey very little idea of what a room is going to be to the layman. Beside Grey's office was not one that took kindly to pretty little watercolour perspectives. Grey and I never use anything but the roughest of quick sketches and worked in the actual materials themselves. Sometimes when magazines asked to publish the drawing for some work of Grey's, there just weren't any. At one point Grey was very keen to get the

committee to agree to a vivid Chinese vermilion for the seats of the ship's theatre, and was very afraid that this colour would not be passed by them. "It's hopeless to try to put this in a drawing" he said, "They'd have to see how the entire theatre would brighten before they could possibly realise what this colour could do for it." Just before he left, looking rather gloomy, I put a little package in his hand. "I think, Grey, this will do the job", I said. "What on earth is it?" Grey asked. It was a quarter of a yard of chiffon velvet of exactly this shade Grey wished, although obviously in the most unsuitable of materials for upholstering seats. Nevertheless, it's gorgeous tone and even the feel of it as it was passed from hand to hand by the committee, won the day, and thereafter whenever there was a special colour desired, a length of any fabric having the exact shade was used to demonstrate. There was a 100% acceptance by this method, and there is no doubt that the sense of touch allied to visual pleasure is a factor that is very important in capturing the interest, and even the enthusiasm of people.

The end of the war released the *Queen Elizabeth* from her wartime service, and made it possible for Cunard to put her into a kind of passenger carrying role very different from the transportation of troops. She had done this on a tremendous scale; thousands upon thousands of men had been taken across both the Atlantic and Pacific Oceans, including our own son in the RAF on his way to train in Canada. Now she would have to prepare herself to carry thousands more but under very different circumstances.

To do this was not an easy task, as her fitments had been deliberately scattered about the world, so that heavy bombing of any single seaport would not destroy the entire lot. Many cities had guarded her treasures and now was the time for their return, but from some of these places there was no return: Singapore for instance.

Some of her most costly dining room fitments had been jettisoned into the sea near Australia because they took up too much space. Costing over $1,000 each they lie at the bottom of the ocean, while their replacements shine and glitter in the luxurious dining room of the ship today.

Piece by piece everything was collected and gradually' put in its proper place. As had been said, very unfortunately when there was a question of replacement Grey was rarely consulted, and furniture and carpets were chosen that did not harmonise with the existing scheme, but there was nothing Grey could do about it.

Finally came the day when everything was aboard, and the ship was ready for her official maiden voyage. The word had gone out that before this, on her voyage from the Clyde to Southampton, she would carry a selected few by invitation. Rumour added that the ship would be theirs and every luxury it held would, for this one night voyage, be at their command. Only those people connected with her creation or whose name would add to the glitter of the

At first, only public toilet facilities were available to such small 'tourist' staterooms, but in later times, most were renovated to include private or semi-private conveniences. Public baths with showers were provided in near proximity to the staterooms on each deck level. (Philpot Collection)

occasion were to be invited, and this list would be secret to the last moment. The Grey Wornums started to panic, both suddenly fearing that for some reason they would not find themselves on this list. We got like this sometimes and would go around in despair for no logical reason. However the invitation arrived and it was a party!

From the time we left London on the special train to our return, there was not a minute that we were not the guests of Cunard, and no Renaissance Prince nor Roman Emperor could have been more lavish.

As we travelled up to Scotland, little by little we were able to forget the grim ran behind us, and the tremendous task it had been, in the face of danger and destruction, to bring this great ship to this day and hour. It was a friendly, easy group that left the train to embark on the tender that was to take us the short distance from shore to ship. Grey held my hand as we stood very close together, both of us deeply moved as across the quiet dark water we approached "our ship" blazing with light, huge beyond belief; waiting and ready. After all the dark years of the blackout, here she floated in shining beauty: peace could have no finer shape than this.

As our small crowd wandered through the enormous rooms, we really began to believe that luxury and peace would once more enter our lives. Morning came too soon but we all left the ship with a new look in our eyes. In the years that followed we travelled many times on "our" ship. It was always "ours" in a special way from the moment we stepped from this gangplank and were greeted with, "Nice to have you aboard again", to the, "Well, we'll see you again soon," answered by, "Of course!"

Although we were not to travel again as the guests of Cunard, we always felt, no matter how expensive the passage was, that we were dropping it in to the piggy-bank of a very large and beloved child.

Chapter 5

The Sixties and Beyond: A Difficult Time for an Ageing 'Queen'

The portrait of HM Queen Elizabeth by Sir Oswald Birley: Her Majesty unveiled the oil during her visit to the ship on July 28th 1948. The painting was prominently displayed aboard the QE2 for her entire career. (Philpot Collection)

From the late 1950s and into the 1960s, the degree to which transatlantic aeroplanes were taking passengers away from the liners had not only increased, but increased exponentially. Competition between the passenger ship lines for the ever-dwindling numbers of passengers who still preferred to cross the North Atlantic by steamer was fiercer than ever, as each tried to keep their fleet full and their companies afloat.

Cunard started a campaign of well-researched and psychologically motivating adverts, running them in virtually every single major newspaper and magazine in Europe and North America. Some even appealed the wives of executives into coaxing their husbands to go by ship: "*Something went out of travel when speed became a fetish. Tensions increase. Health and efficiency suffer. Why not try a little gentle persuasion and get him back to the sea? Three days to catch up on work, a weekend off and he's in Europe, fighting fit -and you'll probably sleep easier yourself.*" (*Fortune* Magazine, May 1963).

Some ads even resorted to using reverse-psychology: "Well, if you're so mean, or in so much of a hurry as to think we are out-of-date, then you're not for us. Otherwise welcome aboard and let's live a little." (*Time Magazine*, June 1966).

It was proven however, that no amount of media slogans – regardless of the angle – would arrest the flow of passengers that were turning their backs on the transatlantic liner once they got the taste for air-speed. Times had changed – losing time meant losing money and with this, fewer people wanted to procrastinate on a luxury liner for five days.

Cunard, from very early on, were mindful of the significant future role that air travel would have in transporting passengers across the North Atlantic, even if – like most – they underestimated the speed and the degree of the turnaround. It soon became apparent that ocean liners could never hope to successfully compete against the new age of the jet aeroplane, which had now cut the crossing time to just seven hours. The only hope left of deriving any meaningful profit from the two "Queens", was to introduce them to part-time cruising during the quieter winter months, which was far more profitable than sending them back and forth across The Pond half full.

Cruising Their Liners

Cunard was no stranger to the cruise trade with the *Laconia* making the first world cruise in 1922, the second *Mauretania* and the *Britannic* cruising to the West Indies and Europe in the 1950s, and in 1949, introducing an extremely popular, permanent world-cruising-liner, the *Caronia*.

Cunard first cruised the *Queen Elizabeth*, ahead of the *Queen Mary*, in 1963, beginning with a five-day trip departing

RMS Queen Elizabeth: the Unruffled Cunarder

New York on the 21st February, heading for Nassau in the Bahamas and back. Two more consecutive trips to Nassau immediately followed before the ship returned to her transatlantic commitments.

As a one-class cruise ship, the *Queen Elizabeth's* passenger carrying capacity was reduced from just over 2,000 to approximately 1,500 and for most of her total of 30 cruises she sailed at full or near-full capacity. All but one cruise – her last – began in New York.

Cruise passengers were mostly Americans who were treated to a well-organised "house party", led by three social directresses and a dozen or so cruise staff. An impressive list of activities was performed daily throughout the ship and conducted in a casual country-club atmosphere. The typical British style of service, attentiveness and courtesy, a legacy of the transatlantic crossings, remained unchanged during cruising, bolstering the American passenger's egos.

The musical entertainment during the cruises didn't change much from her transatlantic crossings. Apart from the introduction of reggae and calypso numbers during Caribbean cruises, the biggest difference was seen in the stamina of the musicians themselves. To cater to a younger, more revved-up group of passengers than those travelling on the crossings, the musicians found themselves playing much longer in the evenings, well into the tiny hours of the mornings in the various bars aboard. The *Queen Elizabeth* was described as being alive with music from stem to stern during her cruising days.

Old Girl, New Age

A totally new atmosphere prevailed on the *Queen Elizabeth* during cruises. Large signs located everywhere made it seem as if London's Savoy Hotel had been turned into a holiday camp. But the signs were necessary, for they

April 1966: The *Queen Elizabeth*, heading back to Southampton following her cruising refit, meets the *MS Kungsholm*, performing her sea-trials. Also built at the John Brown Yard at Clydebank, the Swedish America liner, however, represented the most up-to date breed of passenger liner, designed specifically to spend several months of the year cruising. The ageing 'Queens' were facing a difficult time against such modern competition. (Philpot Collection)

The Sixties and Beyond: A Difficult Time for an Ageing 'Queen'

Above: The *Queen Elizabeth* races a Boeing 377 Stratocruiser prop-plane, to New York on May 7th 1951. The image is a symbolic preview of how aeroplanes would inevitably overtake the ocean liner as the quickest, most-preferred means of crossing the oceans. In just six years, planes and ships would, for the first time, be carrying equal numbers across the North Atlantic. Like the dinosaur, the days of the transatlantic ferry was numbered. (Philpot Collection)

Below: A collection of Cruise brochures for the *Queen Elizabeth's* cruises. The one on the far left is for her first cruise ever, departing New York on February 21st 1963. (Philpot Collection)

helped direct visitors off the ship as well as helping bewildered and lost passengers during the cruise – for the majority of them were Americans who had never been on a ship before, let alone the biggest in the world. The crew too had seen nothing like it and needed to adjust slightly to the new breed of passengers aboard – much less self-restrained and more adventurous than the sedate transatlantic ones.

Departures were also a different affair. Four bands aboard played the ship away from the Pier in New York and the ship would always be dressed in colourful bunting. Thousands of streamers hurtled downwards from the railing of the ship, in scenes reminiscent of sailings from tropical ports like Honolulu or Port Vila. Mobile bars and buffet tables were positioned along the covered promenade daily, to cope with the larger consumption of food and drink. Midnight suppers and buffets were held every night in the main lounge and Cunard even began hiring professional entertainers from various parts of the world, in an effort to attract more clientele from rival shipping companies. On shorter cruises, the *Queen Elizabeth* was at sea for only 72 hours meaning that some passengers would get very little sleep and could, should they wish, dance from noon until dawn.

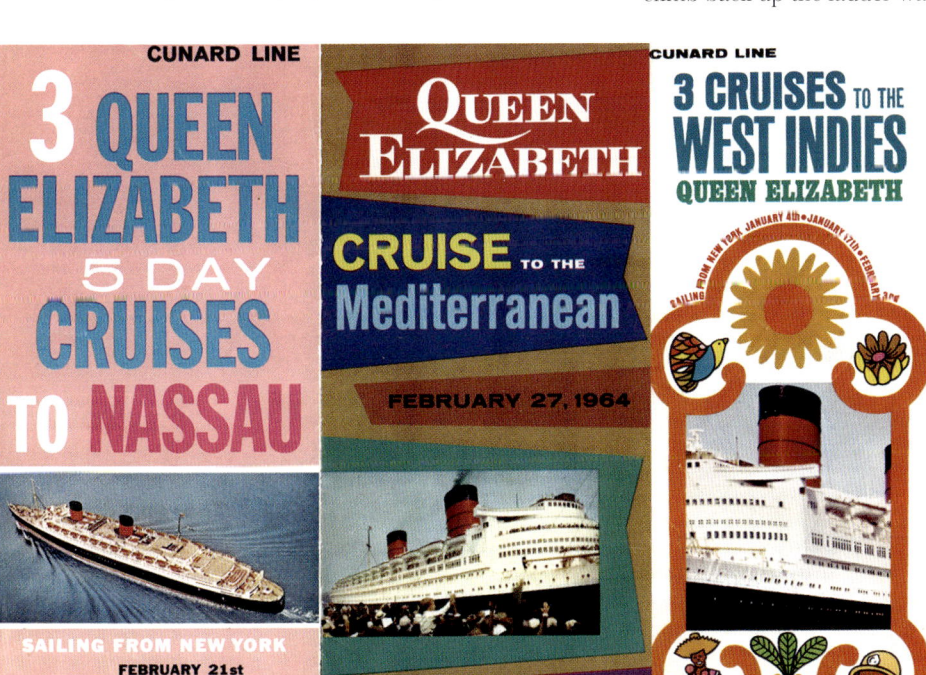

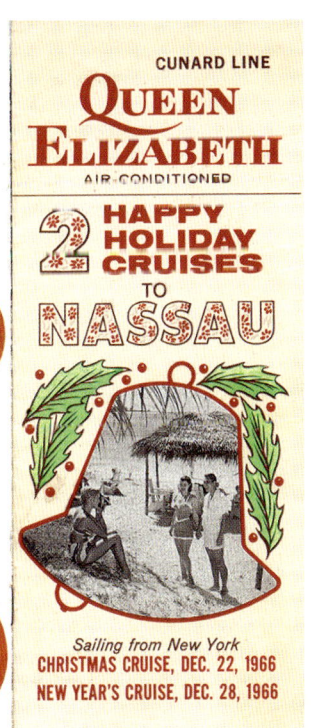

For cruises prior to 1966, passengers had to disembark the anchored ship via the Promenade Deck shell doors, and then face a long walk down an accommodation ladder to the waiting launches. Returning to the ship, the steep climb back up the ladder was a major feat for elderly

passengers and for some, the risk of having a coronary before reaching the top was quite high. Therefore, during the ship's cruising refit in the winter of 1965/66, to accelerate and make safer the embarkation and disembarkation of passengers, two off-landing platforms, resembling cages, were added. Each was the length of a life boat, replacing Boat 9 on the starboard side and Boat 10 on the port side. The "cages" were lowered on the davits to the waterline, providing a platform where tenders from both shore and the ship's own covered launches could berth alongside.

Passenger numbers for the 1963 and 1964 off-season cruises were heartening, not only for the *Queen Elizabeth*, but for all of the 23 transatlantic luxury liners engaged in special cruises during that period – each sailing either fully-booked, or close to it. By the end of the 1965 cruise-season, Cunard realised a 55% jump from the 1963 figures, with 14,622 passengers taking cruises on their ships. The signs looked good for the future, and Cunard's policy of increasing the number of winter cruises each year had, according to them, "been having its full effect."

Hard Times for Cunard

More sobering however, were transatlantic passenger numbers. In 1963 the entire Cunard fleet of eight ships carried a total of 178,296 passengers collectively across the North Atlantic, with the two "Queens" responsible for 60% of this figure – split approximately 30% each. The following year that number fell by 10% to 160,293. With each passing year, both "Queens" were exponentially losing passengers. Ten years earlier, between 1953 and 1955, the *Queen Elizabeth* alone, managed to carry 142,362 passengers, or just below 9% of the total sea-born transatlantic travel – more than any other ship in that service.

Cunard could at least take small solace in the fact that they were not alone, with all 20 of the shipping lines operating passenger service in the North Atlantic suffering similar losses in trade – a phenomenon directly attributed to the introduction of regular transatlantic jet flights. Although the results of both "Queens" initial cruise efforts were positive, even netting them a profit, the progress made was negated by the huge financial losses made from 1960 to 1962. Furthermore, as the 1960s progressed, both liners were showing their age. They weren't as efficient to operate as the smaller, newer vessels, as running and maintenance costs ate ever-larger chunks from their dwindling profits. Drastic reorganisation of Cunard's fleet was necessary. It was obvious that cruising would not be the "miracle" that could or would save them or the company.

The very graceful 'Green Goddess', was Cunard's full-time, world-cruise ship. *RMS Caronia*, was launched in 1947, and was very popular with American cruise passengers. (Philpot Collection)

Retirement: The Unavoidable Destination

Cunard continued its commitment to cruising in 1964 and 1965, and to prove their seriousness, they dedicated money and effort into giving their fleet a fresher look that reflected the many design changes that were emerging in the mid 1960s. The transformation began with both structural and decorative modifications applied to sisters the *Saxonia* and the *Ivernia* – refitting, restyling and even renaming them as the *Carmania* and the *Franconia* respectively.

Despite the company's precarious financial situation, cautious optimism was the feeling at Cunard when it was announced publically, early in 1965, that £1.5 million would be invested, so that later that same year the *RMS Queen Elizabeth* could be extensively refitted and upgraded for her cruising role. It was envisioned that she would emerge as the North Atlantic's showpiece for Cunard's new-found, spirited style of decoration. It was a brave decision, stemming from the fact that the "Lizzie's" total carryings were up slightly compared to the previous season, and on one voyage, in June 1964, she sailed from New York with 2,138 passengers – the highest any North Atlantic passenger liner had carried since 1960. The Cunard fleet carried just under a quarter of the total North Atlantic passenger traffic in 1964 and on more than one occasion, the *Queen Elizabeth* sailed virtually full.

Cunard had not given up hope of the ship making them money on both her North Atlantic runs and as a cruise ship, feeling she fully deserved this refit. They planned to keep her sailing for another eight to ten years, as a worthy running mate for the "Q4" project – the replacement "Queen" for the soon-to-be-retired *Queen Mary*. "Q4" would emerge as the *Queen Elizabeth 2* in 1969.

The Sixties and Beyond: A Difficult Time for an Ageing 'Queen'

Dressed overall, the *Queen Elizabeth* backs out into a still-thawing Hudson River on the 6th of March 1963, heading for the warmth of the Bahamas, on her third cruise voyage. (Philpot Collection)

The ship's First Class, 7-piece band, with Bandleader Horace Bagaley (standing), played stirring songs like *'A life on the Ocean Wave'* on the covered Promenade Deck as the ship started off on her cruise. (Bob Malinowski)

Record breakers: Passengers on deck are rugged up as the world's largest liner heads off, on the 21st of December 1967, for a 5-day, 'Happy Holiday Cruise' cruise to sunny Nassau. Down-river is the world's longest liner - *SS France* and to her right, the world's fastest - the *SS United States*. The *France* followed the *Queen Elizabeth* down to Nassau. (Philpot Collection)

The only times in the past that the *Queen Elizabeth* was dressed overall with bunting, was during special occasions including her maiden peacetime voyage, the Queen's Coronation in 1953 and the ship's final voyage from New York - to name a few. Now, for every cruise, she was always adorned with an array of colourful signal flags. (Bob Malinowski)

A roped-off buffet table in the First Class Restaurant awaits the hungry masses to arrive. The cruises almost always saw to a larger consumption of both food and drink compared to the transatlantic crossings. (Philpot Collection)

Below: Anchored off Nassau in December 1966. The line coming from the stern of the ship is attached to the local Nassau Harbour tug, which was always on hand during blustery conditions like this. The tug towed the ship's stern to windward, so as to hold a good lee on the port side and make it easier for the tenders to load passengers going to shore. (Philpot Collection)

117

The Sixties and Beyond: A Difficult Time for an Ageing 'Queen'

The wondrous sight of the world's largest liner - lit by the tropical sun and at anchor in the transparent, turquoise waters off Nassau. (Southampton City Council)

The best islands in the Caribbean have propellers: The *Queen Elizabeth's* beginning and end-of-year cruises to Nassau - the palm fringed capital of the Bahamas, were an important part of the Cunard Line's operations and in most respects, very successful trips. For the five-day experience, fares started at $185 per person for a D-Deck inside room (two beds and two upper berths and toilet), all the way up to $1,300 for a suite for two on Main Deck. Optional shore excursions cost just $5.00. (Richard Weiss collection- Jack Goodrich photographer)

West Indies Cruise, February 1968: A crew member tenders passengers to shore in one of the ship's covered launches (Robert Lenzer)

Above: December 22 1967: When the *Queen Elizabeth* anchored off Nassau, large shore tenders arrived from the harbour and pulled alongside the R-Deck shell doors and passengers were ferried ashore. Nassau was one of the few harbours with such large tender boats, making it unnecessary for the ship's off-landing, gantry-cages to be used. (Philpot Collection)

A lovely stern-view taken from a launch as the ship rides at anchor off Bermuda in 1966. (Philpot Collection)

RMS Queen Elizabeth: the Unruffled Cunarder

The beautiful mountainside city of Funchal - capital of the Island of Madeira – forms the backdrop to the *RMS Queen Elizabeth*, in November of 1966, during the Indian Summer Cruise. (Luis M. Correia Collection)

The SS France had also now reached Nassau, giving passengers from both liners quite a spectacle. France, with 1,292 passengers on board, was on a two-week, 1967 Christmas-Cruise. The *Queen Elizabeth* was also close to fully-booked. (Philpot Collection)

Final call at Nassau, April 13 1968. The port, off-landing gantry or 'cage' is visible amidships at Promenade Deck level. They greatly sped up the time required for getting passengers ashore and back. (Richard Weiss collection Herb Frank photographer)

Refitting For Cruising

The *Queen Elizabeth* entered the 1964-built Inchgreen dry dock in Greenock, on 11th December 1965. Two thousand men from John Brown's yard and a further 500 from the Firth of Clyde Dry Dock Company and subcontractors were given four months to get the work finished. It was hoped that the external and internal modifications made on the 25 year old liner would not only make her more suited to cruising, but would also serve at making her interiors more attractive to the ever-diminishing number of North Atlantic passengers.

A Lido Deck was added, as too an outdoor heated swimming pool and a large sea-water distillation plant, which had the effect of lengthening her steaming range thus permitting for longer cruises without having to stop to take on fresh water. In addition, a new and more efficient ventilation system was installed so that the entire ship, including all passenger and crew accommodation, was air-conditioned.

Three hundred First, Cabin and Tourist Class cabins were upgraded, which included new décor and furnishings in Tourist staterooms, and the addition of private showers and toilets in all Cabin and Tourist accommodations.

Previously unnamed Tourist Class public rooms were given individual names in an attempt to rid them of any "Third Class" stigma and thus make them more appealing.

A teenagers room was created aft and starboard of the Caribbean Club on Main deck, on what was previously open deck space, but which was covered-over by the new Lido Deck. This spot was later renamed the Cavern, a popular name given to live-music venues throughout England in the 1960s. Next to the Cavern on the port side of the ship was a small bowling alley which was also a rendezvous-point for teenagers.

Two landing gantries or platforms were hung from davits amidships, on the port and starboard side, simplifying the disembarking of passengers when the ship was anchored.

The Sixties and Beyond: A Difficult Time for an Ageing 'Queen'

Top left: The *Queen Elizabeth* is ready to leave the Inchgreen Drydock, on the on the 9th of March 1966, following a three month cruise refit. The Lido Deck and outdoor swimming pool have been added but internally, not one of the 300 cabins being upgraded was finished. (Mike Triplett)

Top right: Before…

Bottom: And after: The new Lido Deck was an extension of the Promenade deck up to the aft docking bridge. The pool was originally designed to be kidney-shaped like the one on the *Carmania*. The rows of glazed-glass screens, added to protect sunning passengers on the open decks, were precursors to the ones added on the after decks of the *QE2*. (Philpot Collection)

The cruising refit was far more costly than planned, and due to a shortage of skilled workers it could not be completed on schedule. Whether the effort would pay for itself remained to be seen.

A new Cunard management took over at this time, headed by Sir Basil Smallpeice. Their snap decision to scrap 26-year-old the *Mauretania* in December 1965 – a ship just one year older than the "Lizzie" – because she wasn't making it as a cruise ship, showed what the determined, younger breed at Cunard, were prepared to do in order to get themselves back into profit.

Strike and New Regulations: The Beginning of the End

Sporting a new aft profile, the *Queen Elizabeth* began her sixteenth cruise on 7th April 1966 – another successful New York to Bermuda trip. Then, after just two return voyages across the North Atlantic, one of the most infamous and consequential strikes in the history of the country brought every port in England to a dead stop. For a total of 47 days, from 16th May until 2nd July, the *Queen Elizabeth*, losing tens of thousands of Pounds every day, remained laid-up in Southampton, kept company by a congregation of other out-of-action liners and cargo vessels that were blocking every single berth of the docks.

The disputing members of the National Union of Seamen dealt a crippling financial blow to Cunard at a time when it was already on its knees. The repercussions were many for the line, beginning with a plot that would ultimately dethrone both "Queens".

On 26th April 1967, an urgent board meeting was held at the Cunard Building at pier Head, Liverpool. A letter was read out: "It is felt that release of our forward plan, which includes the intention to withdraw the *Queen Mary* in the autumn of this year and the *Queen Elizabeth* in the autumn of 1968, will be made probably on the 15th of May."

Also revealed at the meeting, was that every one of Cunard's passenger ships was experiencing a revenue shortfall. Moreover, the planned 1967 budgeted-loss of £721,000 was already, in the first three months of the year, £1,059,000 worse off. The poor cruise sales of the *Queen Elizabeth*, the *Caronia* and the *Carmania* were blamed – particularly the longer-duration cruises. Moreover, North Atlantic sailings were expected to bring further losses of £1 million, boosting the total expected deficit to budget for the initial nine months of the year 1967 to around £2.5 million. This was in addition to £4 million in lost revenue caused by the 1966 seamen's strike.

The short and long term future of Cunard was not yet sealed, but it was in grave doubt. Whichever way they turned, they were faced with obstacles to raising revenue. The company could no longer rely on the "Queens" to bail them out.

It was proving extremely difficult to fill both ships with 1,200-plus passengers on either short or long-duration cruises, especially since neither ship was suited to cruising in the first place. Their length and deep draught prevented them from tying-up in most of the major cruise ports around the world. Rival companies on the other hand, could carry almost the same amount of passengers in their newer, 20-25,000 ton ships at lower average prices, with better accommodation and benefit from lower running costs. And importantly, these ships did not have to anchor in a roadstead and tender their passengers to shore like the

Sporting her new cruise-profile, the Queen Elizabeth *departs Scotland for the last time on the 12th of March 1966. Strong gales delayed the boarding of her refurbished lifeboats which now included eight covered launches, built by adapting the existing 36-foot boats. The ship performed sea trials in the Firth of Clyde that day. (Mike Triplett)*

"Queens" were forced to do during cruises – always a tricky manoeuvre, even in the best weather conditions.

The other major player in this turbulent time for Cunard was the IMCO – the Intergovernmental Maritime Consultative Organisation (now the IMO – International Maritime Organisation). In 1966, amendments to fire safety regulations for passenger ships required expensive alterations be made to both the *Caronia* and the *Queen Elizabeth*. Without these alterations, the ships would not be allowed to sail.

In the end, with their passenger ships "sailing in a sea of red ink", having lost £25 million from 1961 to 1967, this latest dilemma was the straw that broke the camel's back – forcing Cunard to announce the early retirement of their

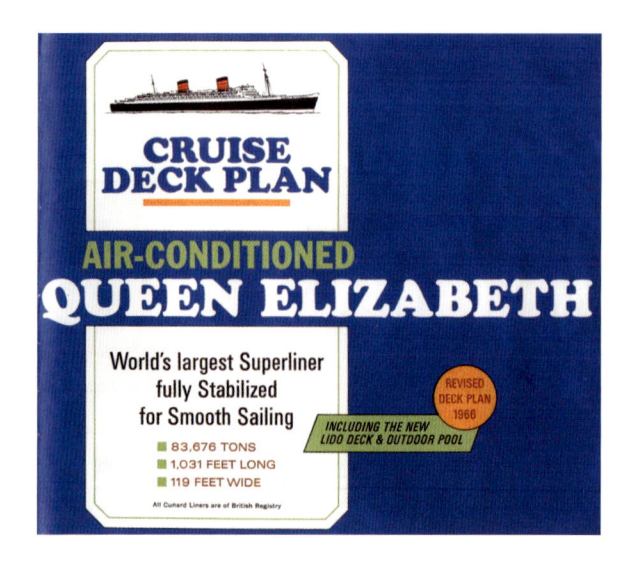

The Sixties and Beyond: A Difficult Time for an Ageing 'Queen'

Just three days prior to announcing that the *Queen Elizabeth* would be retired, Cobh was added as a port of call on the North Atlantic run, with the first visit taking place on May 5th 1967. This was a last, desperate attempt to attract more passengers for the crossings, by spicing-up the Itinerary and bringing some Irish on board. 14th of July 1968. (Philpot Collection)

"Queens". The *Queen Mary* would be retired in December 1967 – a year earlier than originally planned. Then, on the on the 29th October 1968, the last day before the IMCO fire-improvement legislation became operative, the *Queen Elizabeth* would also be retired – at least five years earlier than originally planned.

Cunard management prepared a question and answer sheet with scripted responses to the most likely questions the press would be throwing at them regarding their decision to retire the most famous ships in the world.

When was this decision made?
At Cunard Steam-Ship Board 26th April 1967.

Was the decision influenced by the new IMCO safety regulations?

Not directly. The decision to withdraw the "Queens" was made on the commercial considerations, but over and above these the new regulations would have involved at least half-a-million Pounds expenditure on the 27 year-old Queen Elizabeth and this naturally added weight to the decision.

Has the decision been influenced by the Shareholders Committee?
No.

Why was 1½ Million Pounds spent on converting the Queen Elizabeth?
This decision was taken in February 1965. The expenditure was not by any means related solely to cruising. The air conditioning and modernisation of passenger cabins which represented the major part of the cost were needed to bring the ship up to modern standards for the

RMS Queen Elizabeth: the Unruffled Cunarder

Above: 25th of May 1966 - Going nowhere: The image shows the *SS United States* astern the *Queen Elizabeth*, which is tied up alongside 106 Berth at the Western Docks, during the National Seamen's Strike. She is devoid of crew except for her officers. The image was taken from Holland America's *Maasdam*. (Yvonne Thompson)

Right: During 1967, a diorama display featuring a waterline model of the forthcoming *Queen Elizabeth 2*, was placed aboard both the *Queen Mary* and the *Queen Elizabeth*. The QE2's designated Master, Bil Warwick was at hand to talk about his new command (David Golby)

123

The Sixties and Beyond: A Difficult Time for an Ageing 'Queen'

Atlantic, quite apart from cruising.

What savings do you anticipate from the withdrawal of the "Queens?"
The whole purpose of this decision is to eliminate losses. The "Queens" are trading currently at losses of about 750,000 Pounds a year.

Why do you expect the Q4 to pay if the two "Queens" do not?
The "Queens" were brilliantly specialised vehicles in their conception, designed for the express run to New York and back. They are deep-draughted, wide in the beam and with bunkering and fresh water supplies needed for their capacity, are far from ideally suited for cruising. For a start they will pass through neither canal and there are a limited number of ports where they can go alongside. Q4 on the other hand passes through both canals and draws far less water, and is far more flexible to operate – besides, as the newest passenger ship she is of more modern design than any other ship and will attract a lot of passengers for that reason.

Do you anticipate scrappings of other Cunard ships?
Not immediately, but ships get older and markets change so inevitably, ships have to go or be replaced.

Was this decision made as a result of the seaman's strike?
Not directly, of course, but no one should think that a strike like that can take place without having a catastrophic effect. A 4 million Pound cash loss has left us with no margin in hand and we have undoubtedly had to take this decision earlier than we might have otherwise done.

Farewell Announcement

At 13:00 aboard the *Queen Elizabeth*, on the 8th May 1967, one day from arriving into New York, acting Captain Joseph Woolfenden was given radio word to open the sealed envelope that was given to him in Southampton before departure. He was filling in for regular Master Commodore Geoffrey Marr, who was ill. "It was like the sealed orders of wartime," Captain Woolfenden said to reporters after arriving in New York. As soon as word was radioed through, he opened the safe in his stateroom and first read the letter to himself. Feeling somewhat stunned, he then called several of his "crowned heads", the name he gave the various department heads aboard and read the news to them. Chief Purser Fergus Pritchard, who was also later interviewed in New York, said: "There was a moment of shocked silence. We all knew the *Mary* was due for scrapping, but we didn't believe the *Elizabeth* was going too."

Every department head aboard the ship was eventually notified, and that same afternoon a notice was placed on public bulletin boards for the passengers. Captain Woolfenden added: "The crew took it the only way they could. It was inevitable. It is a sad moment, but if it will keep Cunard going, it will benefit everyone in the end."

On that historic voyage, the ship was carrying a mere 632 passengers, with just 171 in First Class. 502 passengers boarded in Southampton, 85 in Cherbourg and making her first Irish call – 45 embarked at Cobh. Such low numbers of passengers, only served to confirm the real reason why the "Queens" had to go: "They rattled around in accommodation that could take 2,000 easily," pointed out a restaurant steward, commenting on the small number of passengers aboard. More than 120 sailors from the *Queen Elizabeth's* crew had remained with the ship since her secret maiden voyage on 3rd March 1940: "We are sort of stunned", said one quietly, while another expressed: "As far as I am concerned, it was shattering. From now on it will be like a wake."

The news reached the convalescing Commodore Marr at his home, but to him it came as no surprise:

"It was what I predicted at the beginning of the seamen's strike. It was obvious that if the strike continued, as it did, then it was the end of the "Queen" liners. It is a terrible pity. I have been associated with them one way or another since I started with Cunard in 1934. But it had to be."

Joe Woolfenden, on the bridge of the *Queen Elizabeth*, just eight hours from reaching New York, said it best when speaking by telephone to a media representative: "We all realised it was the end of an era. It was the end of two of the greatest things Britain has ever produced." Then the ship's siren sounded: "Did you hear that?" asked the Captain, "We are running through some heavy mist at the moment. But just like the Cunard troubles, we hope there is some fine weather ahead."

Goodbyes – The Final Crossings

The start of the *Queen Elizabeth's* last scheduled transatlantic return crossing began in Southampton on the 23rd October 1968, with the ship arriving at New York for the last time on the 28th. For two full days the ship was host and venue to private and official parties and events, all leading up to her New York farewell on the 30th.

A heartfelt speech was read out by the Mayor of New York, John Lindsay, in front of invited guests in the ship's Verandah Grill: "We New Yorkers Love thoroughbreds, we love champions, we love beauty, we love style. And this great liner is indeed every inch a "Queen" who commands our admiration".

In the hours before the ship sailed from New York, between four and five thousand visitors made their way aboard for a last look and to farewell friends making the trip to Southampton. In her lifetime, she had crossed The Pond

RMS Queen Elizabeth: the Unruffled Cunarder

close to a thousand times, in both war and peace, and in those 28 years, she had steamed 3,472,672 miles.

"Larry" was just one of the 1,600 passengers on the *Queen Elizabeth*'s final crossing of the North Atlantic. He still remembers something of the event, despite his self-confessed indulgences during the trip:

"The last crossing was truly a gala experience, from the grand send-off out of New York Harbour, with fireboats and their salutary sprays, the thousands of balloons and streamers, the toots from a flotilla of tugs and other floating well-wishers as we sailed down to The Narrows. It was an unforgettable experience.

"We spent all our waking hours – and there were more of those than sleeping ones – partying, reminiscing and looting, all at the tacit encouragement of the crew who were, by the end, hard to distinguish from the passengers.

"The First Class 'rabble' was something out of an Agatha Christie mystery. Nobility, theatre and rock & roll impresarios, women of dubious morals, all mixed it up with 'Cunard-o-maniancs' and assorted hangers-on. Having crossed on her before, I knew my way below to the Pig and Whistle crew's pub and I would lead the bejewelled and tuxedoed down greasy companionways to the artificial heart of a great ship to show them how real people lived.

"Our last night, we lay at anchor off Southampton so as to arrive at prime time in mid-morning for the hoop-la that was planned at that end. That night, our part of the ship literally rocked with music and conspicuous over-indulging. My fellow-traveller and I had a late party in our small

Once the *Queen Elizabeth*'s fate officially became known, cartoons like these began appearing in the newspapers. (Philpot Collection)

The Sixties and Beyond: A Difficult Time for an Ageing 'Queen'

A tired-looking *Queen Elizabeth* arrives into New York for the final time on the 28th of October 1968 - 28 years since her first call into the Big Apple. (Philpot Collection)

stateroom for fifty or sixty assorted Dukes, tycoons, Madams and busboys! I distinctly remember forcing loose the winged securing nuts from the portholes to get fresh air and to see better the large number of boats lying in wait for our ceremonious entrance the next day. It was then that I decided that Cunard would no longer need two of the porthole "dogs", and threw them into my luggage.

"She was a majestic jewel on the Atlantic. She had a remarkable history helping win the war and then paving a glamorous highway between post war worlds. The *Queen Elizabeth* was formidable, and I believe that if she hit an iceberg the iceberg would have not had a chance."

The Final Passenger Voyage

The *Queen Elizabeth* called into Cherbourg one last time on 4th November, and boarded 280 passengers for her final cross-channel trip. She arrived at Southampton the following morning, signalling her entrance to the docks with three blasts of her whistle, but neither crowds nor fanfare greeted her at the end of her long transatlantic career. In the end, American interest in the *Queen Elizabeth's* last days at sea was shown to be keener than in her own land. In compensation, one of the ship's keenest admirers, Elizabeth Angela Marguerite Bowes-Lyon – Queen Elizabeth, The Queen Mother, was not going to let the ship bearing her name leave British waters without first bidding a personal goodbye of her own. She made her final tour of the liner on the 6th November.

An eight-day final cruise to Las Palmas and Gibraltar, from the 8th until the 15th November, would be the *Queen Elizabeth's* final, paying passenger-carrying voyage. The ship sailed with a full passenger list, including eight members of Commodore Marr's family. It was the final boatload of passengers out of a total of more than 2,300,000 souls the ship had carried throughout her commercial lifetime.

As the ship was departing Gibraltar, in what Commodore Marr described as, the Farewell Cruise's "only incident of note," both the Royal Navy and jet-fighters of the Royal Air Force joined forces to give the still-British liner, the spectacular send-off she deserved. The air-show greatly impressed all on board, none more so than her master Commodore Marr who later wrote in his autobiography: "It was a wonderful farewell. The dreadful thought behind it was that it was farewell."

The final ceremonious gathering of people to be held aboard the *Queen Elizabeth* was a very lively officer's farewell dance, on the evening of the 18th November in Southampton. Nearly one thousand of the ship's present and past officers attended in what must have truly been a night to remember.

Of her nearly 1,200 crew, only 193, mostly engineers, would stay on with the ship on the trip to her new home on the East Coast of the USA.

The newest "Queen" – the *QE2*, would absorb some of the "Lizzie's" younger crew, including some officers and catering staff, but the greater majority would be forced to "swallow the anchor" for good.

RMS Queen Elizabeth: the Unruffled Cunarder

On the morning of the final departure, a reception was held on board in the Verandah Grill, where New York's Mayor Lindsay, read a speech that began with: 'Today, a great 'Queen' sails to glory - we shall see her here no more. We shall miss her….' From left: Commodore Marr, Mrs. Lindsay, Mayor John Lindsay and Nicholas Anderson from New York's Cunard Office. (Philpot Collection)

Final NYC departure: Amassed at the stern were cooks, stewards and deck hands, many of whom would be out of work in a month's time. Above them, on the Lido Deck, were many of 1,600 passengers aboard for the final westbound crossing, listening to the emotional and lamenting sounds of bagpipes playing the great ship off. (Philpot Collection)

127

The Sixties and Beyond: A Difficult Time for an Ageing 'Queen'

At 12.32 p.m. came three long blasts from the 'Lizzie's' sirens signalling, 'I'm moving astern'. This was followed by the ceremonial unfurling of a 280-foot-long paying-off or 'homeward-bound' pennant - ten feet of length equalling one year of year of service. The Blue Duster or Ensign, on the stern post, was then taken down and raised on the mainmast. (Philpot Collection)

Above: Saying their last goodbyes were Oswald Brett (left) and Walter Clarke - shipmates on the *Queen Elizabeth* from December 1942 until October 1945. Both men were Able Seamen on the 'Lizzie' during the war years and had remained close friends ever since. They are aboard the tugboat *Doris Moran* and the man on the left, with his back to the camera, is Walter Lord, ship historian and author of the famous Titanic book, *'A Night to Remember.'* (Oswald Brett)

Right: At the head of Pier 92, the Gleneagle Highland Pipe Band skirls an emotional farewell to the 'Lizzie' as she starts to move away. A huge crowd has amassed on the viewing area and more than one person managed to find their way up onto the roof of the pier for a better view. (Bob Malinowski)

128

RMS Queen Elizabeth: the Unruffled Cunarder

An Understated Departure

Shortly before 08:00 on 29th November 1969, the *Queen Elizabeth*, carrying a skeleton crew, slowly started to distance herself from Berth 107 at the New Docks in Southampton. Cold and cloudy with fog patches – not even the weather provided a minimum of cheer on that sad, final departure from home shores. No significant crowds gathered for the last couple of arrivals and departures from her home port, and at this inconvenient time of day with the weather so frigid and bleak, not many well-wishers bothered to show-up either – final departure or not.

This was probably the biggest disappointment of the *Queen Elizabeth's* long, illustrious career. The *Elizabeth* had come through an entire world war unscathed, so this snub certainly wasn't going to ruffle her. However, for the more sensitive souls aboard, especially her proud Master Commodore Marr, this rebuff was a very bitter pill to swallow.

Dr. Allan Ryszka-Onions of the Solent Maritime Society was one of a small group of early-risers which did gather at the Hythe Pier to pay homage to the departing liner. This is his recollection of that cold, foggy Saturday morning, nearly 50 years ago:

"On November 27th, I noticed that the *Queen Elizabeth* was scheduled to leave for the last time at 7.30 a.m. I reckoned that a quick visit to the end of Hythe Pier to catch her and take a few photographs would still give me time to get to work for nine o'clock.

"November 28th dawned cold, grey and misty, a typical November morning in England, but I managed to get myself

The huge ship is being turned mid-stream. As with all final departures, strong and mixed emotions were felt by all on board that day. (David Boone)

The Sixties and Beyond: A Difficult Time for an Ageing 'Queen'

Completing her final eastbound crossing from New York, the *Queen Elizabeth*, still flying her Paying-Off Pennant arrives into Southampton on the 5th of November 1968. Cunard's North Atlantic ferry service is no more. (Mick Lindsay Collection)

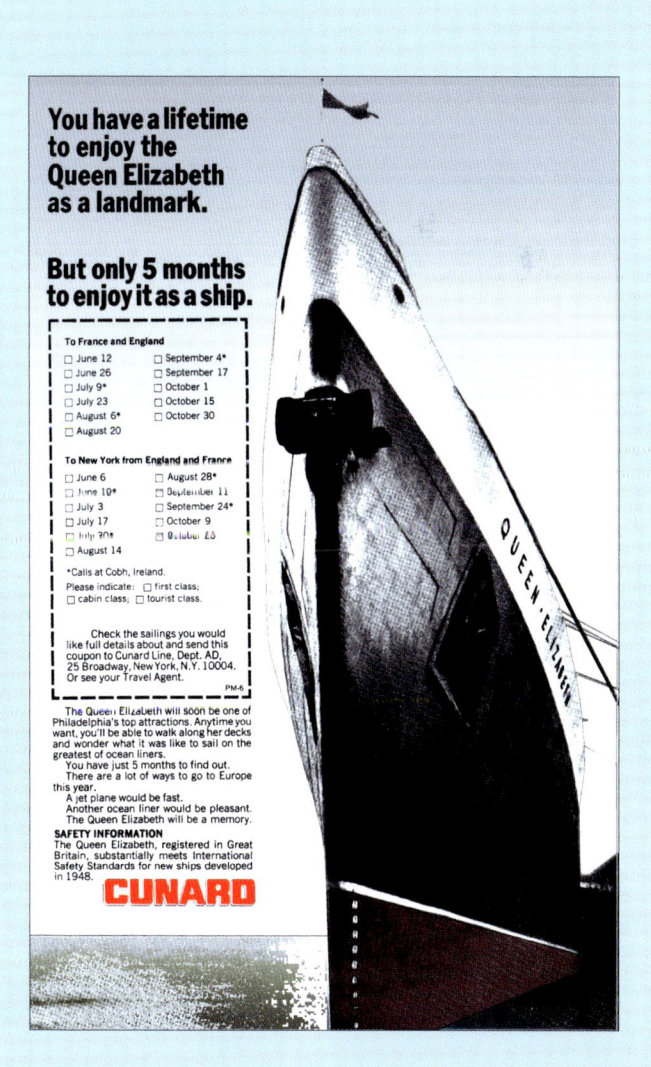

Top left: The Doris Moran, carrying spectators on her stern deck, accompanies the departing liner down to New York's Upper Bay. (Richard Weiss Collection)

Above: Right on cue the wind caught the enormous Paying-off Pennant and at the same time, a Statue of Liberty ferry, with bag-pipers aboard, raced out to meet the 'Queen', breaking into the very touching Scottish tune, *Will Ye No Come Back Again?* (David Boone)

Right: In June 1968, Cunard released this ad stating that the *Queen Elizabeth's* future home, once she had finished her transatlantic and cruising commitments, would in Philadelphia. But had anyone even checked if she would fit in the Delaware River? (Philpot Collection)

RMS Queen Elizabeth: the Unruffled Cunarder

down to the end of the Hythe Pier in good time. After a short while, the huge grey form of the *Queen Elizabeth* appeared out of the mist, passing Southampton's Royal Pier, moving serenely down river from her berth at Western Docks. No ceremonial send-off, no helicopter fly-pasts and tugs spraying their water cannons that had been afforded the *Queen Mary* when she left. No! The poor old "Elizabeth" was making her own solitary way out of her home port for the last time, alone but for a small harbour tour boat along her side with a few ardent fans aboard and as far as I can recollect, just a couple of people besides myself at the end of Hythe Pier.

"When she reached the Eastern Docks, passing Berth 41 and moving towards Dock Head, I was amazed to see all the dockside cranes slowly bowing in salute as she passed, a truly moving moment that brought tears to my eyes. At least the Southampton Dockers were wishing her "bon voyage" on her last departure. The *Nevasa*, on 38/39 Berth offered her own farewell with blasts from her horn, graciously acknowledged by the "Queen". As she passed Hythe Pier, she gave one last long lingering blast on her powerful horns that seemed to echo around the empty river forever. Putting on the power, she added to the mist and gloom-laden atmosphere, with her own pal of black smoke, before disappearing down Southampton Water for the last time, on her way to Port Everglades and an uncertain future."

Philadelphia And Florida

A purchase agreement was finally accepted by Cunard in London on 5th April 1968, almost a year after they placed the *Queen Elizabeth* up for sale. The successful buyer was a team of three entrepreneurs from Philadelphia that had made an unsuccessful bid for the *Queen Mary* the year before, namely Charles Williard and the brothers Robert and Stanton Miller (hereafter referred to as C.B.S.).

The Queen Mother arrived at Southampton on the 6th of November to say a personal goodbye to the ship bearing her name. She is seen greeting ship's officers with Cunard's Chairman Sir Basil Smallpiece, standing behind her and Commodore Geoffrey Marr to her right. (Philpot Collection)

The Sixties and Beyond: A Difficult Time for an Ageing 'Queen'

Above: The ship was made resplendent for the Royal visit, leading Commodore Marr to make the comment: 'She really did look like a ship everybody could be proud of that day.' He is seen here pointing something out to the Queen Mum on the port flying bridge. (Robert Lenzer)

Below left: The Queen Elizabeth departs on her first-ever cruise from Southampton - 'The Farewell Cruise' - leaving on the 8th of November 1968 and returning on the 15th. (Mick Lindsay Collection)

Below right: Her last night at home: In a few hours the Queen Elizabeth would sail out of Southampton for the very last time. (Mick Lindsay Collection)

RMS Queen Elizabeth: the Unruffled Cunarder

A thin crowd gathered at the end of Southampton's Royal Pier to watch as the *Queen Elizabeth* left English shores for good. *'Compared to the send-off received in New York and Gibraltar it was as though the British world of ships and ship-lovers, looked the other way until she was gone'*, wrote Commodore Marr years later. (Philpot Collection)

Devoid of any celebration, the *Queen Elizabeth* literally steals away from Southampton for good on that foggy morning of 28th of November 1968. The *Nevasa* at right acknowledges the significance of the occasion and blows her whistles in salute to the once-proud Cunarder. (Mick Lindsay Collection)

Above: Ship-enthusiast Allan Ryszka-Onions captures the *Queen Elizabeth* from his vantage point on the Hythe Pier. Like many, he was saddened by the lonely departure the ship had to endure in her own home port. As the ship passed the Eastern Docks, the cranes, one by one, bowed in salute - a poignant moment which brought tears to the eyes of the photographer. (Dr. Allan Ryszka-Onions)

133

The Sixties and Beyond: A Difficult Time for an Ageing 'Queen'

Dubious Beginnings

In its June 1968 edition, the analytical journal *Philadelphia Magazine*, published a very frank exposé on the sale of the *Queen Elizabeth* to C.B.S. "Jack", was a jolly barman aboard the *Queen Elizabeth* who came from Liverpool. He was asked by the *Philadelphia Magazine* what he thought of the ship going to Philadelphia:

"Well, it's a nice enough place I suppose – never been there myself. I suppose you yanks might as well have her now that you've got the 'Mary'. And now I hear that one of you blokes bought the London Bridge. I suppose it won't be very long before you buy the bloody Palace too. Great people the Americans."

In a much more serious tone, the article went on to reveal that the slick, fast-talking and super-confident C.B.S. were in fact not the "great people" Cunard had thought them to be. While the *Philadelphia Magazine* was very much in favour of having the *Queen Elizabeth* as a convention centre and tourist attraction in their city, they wished to bring to light the dubious integrity of C.B.S., stating that: "Owners Stanton and Robert Miller are closely associated with people to whom this publication is anathema" and that: "third owner, Charles F. Williard was attacked directly by us last year for playing 'funny games' with a freewheeling labour boss." There was strong suspicion that C.B.S. was mafia-funded and even long after the purchase agreement was signed, there were still conflicting claims as to who had put up the initial deposit for the ship and exactly where the rest of the money would come from.

The exposé pointed out that "notorious hoods" were known to meet frequently with the Millers and that C.B.S. resented anyone questioning them as to where the money was coming from to buy the world's biggest ocean liner. When part-owner Charlie Willard was directly asked about the forthcoming funds for *The Elizabeth*, as the ship was to be renamed, he did not hold back his displeasure to the question: *"Where the financing will come from is nobody's damn business."* Willard exclaimed. He made it perfectly clear that it would also be nobody's business what exactly would become of The Elizabeth once she was moored in Philadelphia. That was their "business."

In selecting a buyer, Cunard had always said that the prospective new owner of their "Queen" must first prove that they would provide the ship a suitable home. Having accepted the promised $7.7 million from C.B.S. for the ship, but without first sending a representative to see if indeed the chosen site was suitable, Cunard were embarrassed to find that the "Lizzie" was too big to even navigate the Delaware River in order to get to the proposed site. Added to this were other major problems: a nearby airport presented a possible hazard with low-flying aircraft both on approach and departure, there were still no roads or even tracks leading to the ship and in one final astonishing oversight, the presence of substantial environmental pollution made the site unattractive, both from incessant aeroplane noise and the strong chemical stench coming from a nearby oil-refinery. These crucial factors, along with their inability to meet both the first and second deadline for paying Cunard the balance of the purchase price, meant that C.B.S. had to urgently find a new site to moor the ship and beg Cunard for time.

Amazingly, Cunard decided to continue negotiating new terms with C.B.S. What transpired was the formation of The Elizabeth Corporation where Cunard, with 85% of shares in the company, would retain outright ownership of the vessel and C.B.S., holding the remaining 15% of shares, could lease the liner from Cunard for $2 million per year – only gaining outright ownership after ten years of regular payments.

A previously considered 100 acre site at Port Everglades in Florida was the new goal, and plans to permanently moor the *Queen Elizabeth* there were quickly underway. With a bit of luck, she would have a flourishing life as a tourist attraction on the US East Coast, just as her former running mate and ex-pat, the *Queen Mary* was hoping to do on the West Coast, but even this plan seemed to be getting off on the wrong foot.

C.B.S. had run into potentially serious delays after local Governmental Commissioners became concerned about the integrity of a 50 year land-lease for 135-acres of prime public land – incredibly, with the first four years rent-free. As well as this, nobody quite understood where the money for the infrastructure, enabling a ship the size and complexity of *The Elizabeth* to permanently berth alongside, would come from and this led to the suspicion of more dirty deals. It seemed that The Elizabeth Corporation would be facing a long battle in obtaining both the land-lease and official permission to moor the ship at the Port Everglades site.

The Philadelphians, who in reality were holding onto nothing, warned the Floridian politicians that they would refuse to 'play' any further should the land lease be withheld. They threatened to pack-up and take 'their' ship somewhere else. Cunard, finally losing patience by the delay in securing a home for the ship, in turn warned C.B.S. that if an immediate solution was not forthcoming, they would abolish all deals and instead scrap the *Queen Elizabeth* once they were finished with her on the North Atlantic in November that same year, only a few months away.

Sitting Pretty

On the 16th August 1968, after behind-the-scenes wheeling and dealing, C.B.S. was given the all-clear to bring the liner to Port Everglades. Despite ongoing doubts

and speculation surrounding the whole deal, her long-awaited new home in the Florida backwater was settled and all that was left was for Commodore Geoffrey Marr to bring the ship in. This finally happened on the 8th December 1968, after the "Lizzie" completed her last ever crossing of the North Atlantic.

By 11:30 that Sunday morning, the *Queen Elizabeth* was docked. By noon, she was fast and "finished with engines". Commodore Marr spoke the following words to waiting journalists: "It's a very sad moment when the end of a ship has to come. She seems to have a heart that is beating when she is out there battling the elements – she almost becomes a living thing in a way. It was more like a ghost-ship voyage with miles and miles of empty staterooms. I'm a little sad and a little nostalgic."

The ship was spruced up before she could be opened to the public for guided tours, in what would be the first phase of the *Elizabeth's* eventual transformation into a hotel and convention centre which was expected to attract three million visitors annually and make a profit of $50 million each year.

The *Elizabeth* was open to the public for the first time on 14th February 1969. From that moment, there was tremendous pressure on The Elizabeth Corp. to generate sufficient money to keep the project afloat. Despite the docking fees being waivered by the port authorities, which raised more than a few eyebrows, the ship still had to earn considerably more than the conservative figure of $3,000 per-day it would cost to keep her docked there. This included the crew's wages and the 40 tons of oil needed daily to keep the ship self-sufficient.

Commodore Marr and 152 of the last crew to sail with the *Queen Elizabeth* lived on board the ship: "We are manned on the basis of a laid-up ship" said the Commodore who strode around in his crisp white uniform and talked to as many visitors as possible. "Technically we are here on what is known as a 'prolonged delay', in an 'extended voyage' and if you want to further complicate that, I'm retired from active sea duty. The company decided younger and better-looking captains would be more appropriate on its new ships."

Commodore Marr thought it was a damned shame that his ship should be sitting next to a parking lot, with himself reduced to having to look out his porthole and count the number of cars in order to estimate how business would be that particular day. He described such conditions as "a little silly," but he could not change them. He went on to reveal:

"The ship looks magnificent I think. We're painting her completely. It breaks my bloody heart; I think she should be still running. Properly promoted, she could be... and at a profit."

"It's all so complicated. First the Miller Brothers in Philadelphia made a down payment of $650,000 on an asking price of $7.7 million and didn't get it up – so we

The Philadelphia Magazine, in its June 1968 issue, ran an exposé on the ship's three 'gentlemen' buyers from that city. In the end the author was proven right - it *was* no place for a 'Queen'. (David Hutchings Collection)

Front page news: Commodore Marr saved this clipping from the Fort Lauderdale's daily newspaper dated December 8th, 1968. (Philpot Collection)

The Sixties and Beyond: A Difficult Time for an Ageing 'Queen'

—The *Queen Elizabeth* enters the breakwater at Port Everglades on Florida's Gold Coast – her new home. She is about to pass the Point of Americas high-rise apartments in the background, whose height she matches. (Christophe Walter Collection)

came here. Look at this scrapbook, it's full of the wheeling and dealing of the Miller Brothers, and Florida's Governor Kirk and Jimmy Hoffa – yes, Hoffa! Oh it's a cast of assorted thousands."

"We settled on $2.50 because that seemed the basic charge for what they call the tourist traps around here, but this isn't developing the ship's potential at all. If she can't get back to sea, I'd like to see her opened up as a restaurant and hotel because obviously she'll never make a fortune on tourists just walking through. Who knows, in a few months the snowbirds will have departed to their homes in the north and we may go down to just a couple of hundred visitors a day."

After just three months of running at a loss, Cunard had had enough of both paying her upkeep and the ongoing negative publicity the ship – still wearing Cunard livery – was receiving. The latest controversy, made public by a Port Everglades Commission Investigation, revealed that the land-lease contracts made by the C.B.S. reeked of illegal behaviour. This prompted Cunard in early May 1969, to put her up for sale yet again. Unless they received a satisfactory offer for the luckless ship before the 11th July that year, they would fire up the remaining boilers and sail her to the scrappers. Whichever way it turned out, Cunard would very soon once and for all disencumber themselves from their former Flagship.

Queen Ltd

On the morning of 19th July 1969, the *Queen Elizabeth* was finally sold to new owners for $8.6 million. The sad moment had come for the Commodore and the remaining loyal British crew to finally be sent home.

The successful bid came from the Utilities Leasing Corp. backed by two investment companies and an insurance firm. The *Elizabeth's* new owner was called Queen Ltd. The principal executives of Queen Ltd. were Robert B. Cosden: President, and Edward M. Moldt: Vice President, Treasurer and Design Superintendent. Financing for the purchase would come from a major life insurance company and although C.B.S. would still be involved, their interests supposedly would be limited to just 15% of the project.

The plans for the ship were impressive to say the least. Apart from having 1,000 hotel rooms, seven restaurants, even more in the way of bars, a disco, maritime museum and shops, she would be land-locked at the bow and the stern, forming part of a multi-million Dollar resort complex spreading around her. This would feature a convention hall, concert arena, cinema, a bazaar, more shops and restaurants. Further to this, on private land south of the port, a 3,800-apartment complex would be built which, according to the hype, would "stimulate The Elizabeth's tourist-attracting potential."

RMS Queen Elizabeth: the Unruffled Cunarder

Early in 1970, in an effort to raise the desperately needed money for the grandiose scheme, it was decided to make Queen Ltd into a public company by floating stock worth almost $14 million. The millions in dividends flowing back in would, in theory, pay back creditor loans as well as the balance of sale still owing to Cunard. Not long after it was announced however, the sale of stock was suddenly cancelled. A poor share market environment and the threat of a full investigation into Queen Ltd. by the Security Exchange Commission in Washington – just one of a series of inquiries directed toward the dubious agreements entered into between Queen Ltd. and the Port Everglades Port Commission – had caused the wheelers and dealers in charge to "jump ship" on the whole project. It was revealed that Queen Ltd. owed debts of over $12 million – a sum rising daily – while their assets totalled only $11.5 million. In May of 1970, Queen Ltd. filed for voluntary bankruptcy proceedings.

It seemed that the ship was jinxed. The liner was, in effect, all the time a hostage in Port Everglades – the sacrificial lamb which in reality wasn't as important to C.B.S. and Co., as the 135-acres of prime land surrounding her. Her heavy shell doors were closed to the public for good. Her boilers were shut down and the lights went out.

New Owner, New Name

The ship was now on sale for a third time, to be auctioned off free and clear of liens and encumbrances and complete with her contents including gear, fittings, quality objects of art, fine furniture, furnishings and ship, hotel and restaurant equipment. The sale was planned for the 9th and 10th of September 1970, in the Continental Ballroom of the Galt Ocean Mile Hotel, Ft. Lauderdale. Inspection of the ship, located at Eller and Sliphead Road, Port Everglades, Hollywood/Ft. Lauderdale, was from 2nd September through to the 8th, and by appointment only.

Of the more than 200 creditors holding liens or a security interest against the debtor's asset, Cunard was at the front of the line, having only received, until then, $3.1 million of the $8.6 million sale price from Queen Ltd. This amount was nevertheless more than the total sale price of the *Queen Mary* to the city of Long Beach, California.

Prior to the auction, rationalists predicted that the ship would be more interesting to ship-breakers for scrap metal. This was almost confirmed, after a submission of a tempting pre-auction offer of $2.4 million by India Trading and Transport Corp., representing Italian ship breakers from La Spezia.

On the morning of day one of the sale, lawyer Isidore Ostroff, retained by Thor Eckert and Co. of New York and representing his client "C.Y." (Chau-Yung) Tung, put in a bid of $3.2 million. An effort was made to better Mr. Tung's offer by auctioning the vessel piecemeal in 800 separate lots. This failed miserably, with many highly-valued oil paintings and inlaid murals on board attracting offers of just $50 to $100, with the entire contents and hull only managing to raise about $2.3 million. Following court approval a few days later, the world's largest passenger ship was handed over to C.Y. Tung, the charismatic Chinese shipping magnate and founder of the Orient Overseas Line (today the Orient Overseas Container Line). Judge Emil F. Goldhaber, of the U.S. District Court Philadelphia, approved the sale on the 17th September 1970. The first thing Mr. Tung did was rename the RMS *Queen Elizabeth*, the *Seawise University*.

The Maiden Voyage Of The SS *Seawise* University

The *Seawise University* was barely afloat, listing and partially scuttled at her berth. Commodore Geoffrey Marr and Chief Engineer Robert "Ted" Phillip, along with sixteen of the *Queen Elizabeth's* former engineers, were effortlessly coaxed out of retirement by the ship's new owner Mr. Tung, to assist the new Chinese crew sail the ship the nearly 13,000 nautical miles to Hong Kong, her new home port, for a major reconversion. Commodore Marr, acting as Technical Advisor for the voyage, arrived back in Port Everglades from his home in The New Forest, Hampshire, on the 17th November 1970.

Not one for mincing his words, Marr was to-the-point when he spoke to a journalist of *The Fort Lauderdale News* and *Sun Sentenial* on the 22nd November:

"My, that ship is a bloody mess, it's heart-breaking to see her in that shape. I guess you can't really lay any blame on anyone, but that ship certainly has been allowed to deteriorate into an indescribable condition since we gave her up. Her boilers, bearings and machinery, almost everything on board has been ruined to the point of uselessness. They (Queen Limited) obviously didn't maintain anything except to set up a set of plush executive offices – including one for the Governor's father! Everything else just went to hell!"

The implications of this neglect meant anxious times for the ship's new owner and her crew. The Commodore's bluntness led to a few uneasy moments between himself and the ship's new owner, as he explained later:

"Mr Tung told me not to be making comments to the newspapers because after he employed me to sail the 'Queen' to the Far East, I created quite a stir in London by telling newsmen she could become the biggest damned cork in the world if things went wrong going out of Port Everglades.

"Mr Tung called right away and said, 'Commodore, don't talk like that please. After your comments the insurance people rushed right over and said if he feels it's

that much of a risk we've got to increase your insurance premiums! Please use caution,' he asked me."

Getting There… Without the Fun

In her present deteriorated state, getting the ship in working order again, ready for a voyage half way around the world, was going to be time consuming, costly and tricky. Commodore Marr had a difficult time predicting exactly when the neglected liner would be seaworthy once more: "They tell me soon, but from what I saw touring her yesterday and today, I wouldn't want to guess… about the middle of January (1971) at the earliest. But do not make that sound official," the Commodore added immediately, not wishing to worry Tung or his insurers any further. Regarding the upcoming voyage, Marr stated: "This morning we were carefully discussing the course we may take once we get her to sea, but I have no idea the time that may be involved. There's an unbelievable amount of imponderables to be weighed."

The state of decay of the ship's boilers and the presence of thousands of tons of oil-contaminated water in the ship's flooded fuel tanks and Nos. 1 and 2 cargo holds, initially convinced those responsible that the easiest way to get the *Seawise University* to Hong Kong would be under tow. But after careful consideration, it was felt that even with the aid of six tugs, the required energy needed to move her 83,000 tons ahead and astern in the confined space she found herself in, could only come from her own propellers. Work thus began at trying to restore a pulse to the lifeless ship.

After replacing hundreds of corroded boiler tubes, half of her twelve boilers were to be made operational. On the last day of 1970, a faint heartbeat was heard when the first two boilers were fired up. Two of the main generators could now be restarted, creating sufficient power to restore essential services, including lighting a ship that had been in total darkness since May. The huge red and black funnels were floodlit and once more a welcome feature of the Port Everglades night sky.

Nobody aboard was more determined to see the ship brought back to life than Commodore Marr himself. "There's a feeling one gets when one walks this ship these days, that she's trying to get born again," Commodore Marr said. "She'll sail again! It will take more than a swab of paint here and a bit of shine – her guts have to be torn apart, polished and fixed, then put back together again – but she'll sail. That is, if Mr Tung doesn't run out of money first!" – "Don't worry, he won't," interrupted Commodore Hsuan, who was standing beside him.

Commodore Hsuan, of C.Y. Tung's Orient Overseas Line was given the honour of captaining the famous ex-Cunarder on her maiden voyage as the SS *Seawise University*, with Commodore Marr supporting him. Hsuan was initially accompanied to Florida by a crew of 200 Chinese and Taiwanese crew, but because the overhaul was more involved than first thought, a further 100 men were sent over to support him with preparations.

Prior to sailing, the ship's navigational and radio equipment was overhauled, watertight doors tested to the approval of Lloyds surveyors, two years of marine growth scraped from the under-water parts of the hull, and the landed lifeboats as well as the anchors and cables returned to the ship. Engine trials were held on the 3rd February 1971, and for the first time in more than two years, steam was spinning the huge turbines in the after engine room. In a few days these engines would rotate the two inboard propellers, giving the ship just enough thrust to escape from that narrow, intra-coastal waterway which had held her prisoner.

During the night, on the eve of departure, a boiler developed leaks and had to be shut down. The ship would have to depart with just five boilers operating. The leaking boiler wouldn't be missed at the start of operations, since the six tugs were mainly responsible for guiding the ship into the turning basin. It was on the final run through the 300-foot wide entrance channel, on the way out to open sea, where the extra power would be needed most.

Once the *Seawise University* was properly aligned in the entrance channel, "full-ahead" was rung on the liner's long-silent telegraphs. Commodore Marr immediately called down to his old friend Ted Philips in the after engine room: "We are committed to the channel now. See that they give her everything they can!" The engineers, in numbers 3 and 4 boiler rooms brought up the fires, whereupon a huge black cloud of smoke rose up from the aft funnel.

The "*Seawise*" was approaching a speed of 5 knots, the minimum that would allow her rudder to have effect and sufficient speed to get her out of the channel to sea, when misfortune struck. Yet again, a water tube suddenly burst in another boiler, causing water to leak into the furnace and creating a spectacular display of contrasting white steam and black smoke exiting the funnel. The boiler had to be shut down as quickly as possible.

The four remaining boilers along with the six tugs would now have to get her through the breakwater entrance and prevent the ship from becoming the world's "biggest damn cork" that Commodore Marr had predicted. Fortunately she had picked up enough momentum to carry her clear of the dredged channel and stay on course out to sea.

Crowds of onlookers waved and honked their car horns from the south jetty and the beaches along the channel just as they had done when she arrived. This time however, some of the onlookers had tears in their eyes. Commodore Hsuan wanted so badly to give three long blasts of the sirens to signal "goodbye" to Port Everglades, but steam pressure was way down and the first blast

RMS Queen Elizabeth: the Unruffled Cunarder

merely fizzled away to a miserable and inadequate moan.

Working up to a speed of almost 10 knots, the ship made it safely out of Port Everglades and was now steaming out into the Atlantic headed for her first stop, Curacao in the West Indies, where she would take on fuel and water supplies. The *Seawise University* was classified as cargo ship for this single voyage to Hong Kong and was carrying just over 300 souls on board.

It wouldn't take very long for the next piece of disturbing news to make its way up from below. The ship had barely sailed for 48 hours when, approaching the Caribbean, number 4 boiler room had to be shut down completely. The evaporators weren't working properly, unable to produce enough distilled water for boiler feed. The ship still managed to sail a further three days on three boilers doing between 7 and 9 knots. Then, the most serious problem yet developed.

On the 13th February, with the western end of Cuba in sight, a fire ignited in the only boiler room still operating – boiler room number 3. The fire was extinguished after thirty minutes, but the damage caused to the boiler was sufficient to render it incapable of further use. With all boilers inoperative, the ship was now drifting off Haiti and she had to be urgently towed to a port of refuge for major repairs. Commodore Hsuan immediately called for towing assistance, but the ship would have to endure three days of drifting, at the mercy of wind and currents, before motive power arrived in the form of a tugboat.

Adrift in the Caribbean

At midnight, on the first night of drifting without power, the NCL cruise ship the *Starward*, spotted the two red "not under command" signal lights on the *Seawise University's* foremast. The brightly illuminated the *Starward* closed in and shone searchlights all along the desolate-looking liner, providing a spectacular view for the hundreds of passengers lining the rails of the all-white cruise ship. Through her loud-speakers, the *Starward*, called out: "Is there anything we can do for you?" "No thank you," was the brief reply from a megaphone on the Bridge of the *Seawise University*.

On the morning of the 16th February, the first of two tugs arrived to tow the dead-in-the-water liner to the Island of Aruba where anchorages were safer than either of the first two choices, Jamaica or Curacao. The second of the two tugboats arrived on the following day and between them, were only capable of pulling the ship at an average of 3 knots. The *Seawise University* arrived off Aruba on the 24th February, two weeks after departing Port Everglades – a leg that was estimated to take just four days.

As if the voyage had not struck enough bad luck, the

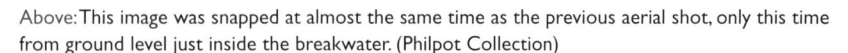

Above: This image was snapped at almost the same time as the previous aerial shot, only this time from ground level just inside the breakwater. (Philpot Collection)

Above right: The 'Lizzies' body guard: With the armed officer, turning his back on proceedings, the *Queen Elizabeth* sneaks past on her way to the Port Everglades turning basin, prior to her docking. (Philpot Collection)

Right: Port Everglades has a new landmark. The land surrounding the ship is yet to be fully developed however unfinished cruise terminals in the background are an indication of what is yet to come on this prime piece of real estate. (Philpot Collection)

COME ABOARD the ELIZABETH
QUEEN OF THE SEAS

The largest ocean liner the world has ever seen

Welcome to the ELIZABETH

You have just entered where all First Class passengers began their Trans-Atlantic ocean cruise. This is STATION #1 on your tour. The sounds you hear are those typically heard by departing passengers. Follow the markers which will direct you to one of the four elevators. This elevator will ascend six decks and you will exit on the Sun Deck STATION #2. Passing through the Port Corridor, walk up one flight to the Sports Deck. Then follow the markers to The Bridge STATION #3. Here pause for a recorded message. Next, move to the starboard side and descend two decks to the Boat Deck STATION #4. Pause for a recorded message. Following marked route, take stairway down to the Promenade Deck. This is STATION #5. Pause for a recorded message and gallery of murals. Again follow markers turning left and you will enter the Observation Bar STATION #6. Then enter stairway on the port side and down to the Main Deck. See the Fastnet Room, also known as the Winter Garden STATION #7. Again pause for a recorded message and gallery of murals showing ship's war history. Move next with the markers to the Fore Deck STATION #8, and pause for another taped message. Go along the port side of the Promenade Deck, STATION #9 and hear another recorded message and gallery of murals. Then enter the Main Lounge at Prom Square, STATION #10. Pause for recorded message. Move to the First Class Lounge STATION #11 and enjoy a recorded taped message. Then to the Mid-Ship Bar STATION 12. Pause for taped message. Next you will arrive at STATION #13, the First Class Smoking Room, where you may select newsreels of nostalgic flavor. Then enter the Cinema Theatre STATION #14 to relax and enjoy the film. Upon completion of the film, follow markers to the Lido Deck STATION #15. You are invited to continue your tour by moving down the Main Deck to the Caribbean Room STATION #16 (where ''Port of Call'' movies will be shown). STATION #17 Nursery. Then you will visit a selected group of first class suites, STATION #18. Down to the main stairway descending to B Deck Foyer, STATION #19 proceeding on Port Corridor to rear stairwell, you will enter the first class dining room STATION #20. Pause for recorded message, ship's model and visual display. Move with the markers to the opposite rear door into the kitchen area STATION #21. STATION #22 Cabin Class Restaurant (shopping). Then to the R. Deck Square to the Purser's Office STATION #23. Pause for closing recorded message and visual display.

We thank you and hope you will visit The Elizabeth often. Each time you come, you will see and enjoy NEW and EXCITING INNOVATIONS.

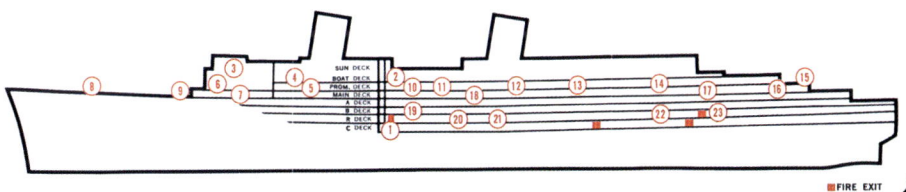

■ FIRE EXIT

Left: Mrs Cotton (pictured) agreed to take her son Charles to Port Everglades so he could see his idol the *Queen Elizabeth*. 'I will never forget my first impression of the ship, she was so huge! The ship just dominated the whole area as there was nothing built nearby, just that gigantic hull and beautiful streamlined profile.' (Charles Cotton)

Below left: Elated seventeen-year-old, Charles Cotton, poses with his mother at 'Station 15' of their tour of *The Elizabeth*. This was the rest spot, where the former 'Queen' had to suffer the indignity of red and white striped awnings, with visitors munching frankfurters and popping soda cans – not far from where, passengers used to dine on pigeons grilled to order and drank champagne. (Charles Cotton)

Bottom: Charles proudly stands to attention on the foredeck – 'Station 8' of the tour. The Teak decking still looks in fine condition. Behind Charles are the motorised capstans and the 9-inch, manila-fibre mooring rope used for docking. (Charles Cotton)

RMS Queen Elizabeth: the Unruffled Cunarder

Officially retired from active sea duty by his former employer, Commodore Geoffrey Marr was asked by Cunard if he would like to remain with his former command for nine months following her arrival into Port Everglades, to which he graciously agreed. Marr's new role was as P.R. Man, giving talks to visitors about his beloved ship and, as he put it, doing what he could to "improve Anglo-American relations". (Philpot Collection)

The Sixties and Beyond: A Difficult Time for an Ageing 'Queen'

anchor was then mistakenly dropped right on the edge of a steep underwater shelf. After a few days, wind and waves picked up causing the ship to drag her anchor off the edge of the shelf and into deeper water, thus rendering it useless.

The ship was once again adrift and being blown away from Aruba, but this time luckily over an offshore sandbank where she was able to re-anchor herself four miles from her original position. At this new anchorage, she was fully exposed to the force of the trade winds and made boarding the launch for shore a very dangerous procedure.

A tugboat by the name of the *Schelde* was sent out to help and quite incredulously its captain somehow imagined he could claim salvage rights to the powerless ship. Commodore Marr had a tough time explaining to him that they were not in any danger, but simply needed a tow to the sheltered anchorage off Oranjestad for repairs to be carried out.

To assure the ship's safe arrival into Hong Kong, it was seen as necessary to carry out a meticulous job of repair on all six boilers. More than 600 water tubes were flown to the ship from New York, with other spares air-freighted from England. The work took 74 days to complete, but in the end, all six boilers and engine rooms were restored to full working order. According to the former Cunard crew on board, the ship was now beginning to look like her former self again, and once the ship went back on main power, enabling all essential services to be restored, there was a distinct feeling she was given a new lease of life.

The voyage to Hong Kong resumed on the 10th May, exactly three months to the day since leaving Port Everglades. As the ship slowly steamed past the town of Oranjestad, all hands were on deck as the *Seawise University* saluted the town with three blasts of the powerful whistles. This time, much to Commodore Hsuan's delight, they worked just fine.

The trip to the neighbouring Island of Curacao was a short one, with the ship arriving in Caracas Bay the following morning. In just 48 hours the ship was loaded with fuel oil and fresh water and then she was off once more, this time headed for Trinidad, arriving in the Port of Spain on the 15th May. As a matter of precaution, fuel and water tanks were again topped-off and an overheating turbine bearing was opened up for examination.

After weighing anchor and getting underway again on the 17th May, the ship passed through the spectacular island passage of Boca Navios, beginning the first long sea voyage of the journey thus far – down the South American Coast to Rio de Janeiro. The ship was propelled at just over 11 knots for much of this leg of the journey, causing a definite pulse that could be felt throughout the entire ship – something that had been missing for over two years and which greatly raised the spirits of everyone on board.

The *SS Seawise University* reached Rio de Janeiro on Sunday morning, the 30th May. She made a magnificent sight next to the famous Sugar Loaf peak. With fuel tanks

Top: The former Cabin Class Restaurant on R-Deck, was used as a souvenir shop during the ship's time in Florida. Posters, 35mm slides, postcards, pennants, souvenir spoons and plates, tea towels - even used Cunard china was on sale. Each item had a small, 'The Elizabeth Queen of the Seas' sticker attached to it. (Charles Cotton)

Above: The view from the starboard bridge wing looking southwards along the intra-coastal backwater, where the *Queen Elizabeth* spent a total of two years in exile. (Charles Cotton)

RMS Queen Elizabeth: the Unruffled Cunarder

Left: May 6th 1969: After five months, the ship still looked amazing, thanks to the T.L.C. of her contingent original British crew, who kept up regular washing and painting of her hull, superstructure and funnels. (Rich Weiss Collection)

Centre left: A storm is seen brewing on the 25th of May 1970. The hurricane caused some of the lines holding the ship to snap and bollards to be ripped from the dock edge. The 70-mile-per-hour winds blew the ship some 100 feet into the middle of the waterway, just shy of the opposite bank. Passing vessels helped to get lines back on board. Thereafter, as a precaution, empty fuel tanks aft and the forward holds, were partially flooded so that the ship rested on the waterway's sandy bottom. (Philpot Collection)

Below: From November 1969, dining on *The Elizabeth* was no longer possible due to a ban on large gatherings and parties on board. The restriction was put in place by Port Everglade's Fire Chief who considered the ship's fire safety standards not up to par. This decision ended an important source of revenue for The Elizabeth Corp. (Philpot Collection)

Edward Moldt was Vice President and Treasurer of both the parent company, Utilities Leasing Corp. and The Queen Ltd. He was also Project Superintendent - responsible for inventing innovative ideas and new concepts that would keep The Elizabeth Ltd. from sinking. (John Patrick Moldt)

DINE ON THE ELIZABETH

Amid the splendor of the Ultra Grand Ballroom

Mere words are inadequate to portray the splendor of this shipboard setting as you sweep through the massive portals to the immense Royal Dining Room, where the unmistakable atmosphere of regal elegance and superb table service suddenly surrounds you in breathtaking enchantment . . . truly a dining experience fit for a Queen!

**CLASS AA
Captain's Table Service**

Serving from
4:30 P.M. 'til 10 P.M.
Complete Dinners from 5.95 to 7.95
For Reservation — 525-2076
The Grand Ballroom—The Elizabeth—
Port Everglades
Hollywood/Fort Lauderdale, Fla.
Use Eller Drive
Liquor is not sold aboard ship, you may bring your own favorite bottle.
Banquet Facilities Available

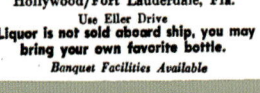

143

The Sixties and Beyond: A Difficult Time for an Ageing 'Queen'

Right: A Costa cruise ship prepares to dock alongside at berth number 21. Since her arrival, a very small cruise terminal has been completed and the car park adjacent *The Elizabeth* has been asphalted over. (Rich Weiss Collection)

Below: 1970 - in good company: From top-right, moving anticlockwise around the basin are the cruise liners *Europa*, *Carmania*, *Santa Maria*, *Fedrico C.*, *Ariadne* and *Franconia*. Port Everglades has continued to grow, with hundreds of acres of prime, port land having been developed for both cargo and passenger activity and a huge petroleum storage facility. (Philpot Collection)

RMS Queen Elizabeth: the Unruffled Cunarder

Above: September 9th 1970: Just days before the bankruptcy auction, the liner, by now closed to the general public, rests calmly and awaits her fate. Scrap merchants from Italy had placed a solid bid for her, which in the end wouldn't be enough. Inside the ship it was dark, quiet and virtually void of life. (Philpot Collection)

Left: Crude, hand-painted black lettering gives the initial impression of a name-change made for a vessel going to the ship breakers - with the ship's former identity still clearly evident. 'Seawise' was actually, a witty play on words derived from the phonetically similar 'C.Y.' - the initials of her new owner, shipping magnate, Mr Tung. (Philpot Collection)

145

Left: Albeit now on the Merchant Flag of the British Crown Colony of Hong Kong, the Union Jack is a reminder of the ship's provenance. (Philpot Collection)

Below: December 31 1970: After many months completely blacked-out and lifeless, the first sign of resurrection was in the form of smoke exiting the aft funnel following the lighting of two boilers. This allowed the re-starting of two main generators restoring power to run essential services aboard. (Rich Weiss Collection)

With her forward fuel tanks and two forward holds partially flooded as a precaution against breaking her moorings in a hurricane, the forward part of the ship rests on the soft, sandy bottom, giving the liner a starboard list - clearly evident in this photo taken in late 1971, just before her epic voyage to Hong Kong. (Philpot Collection)

On the 3rd of January 1971, the *SS France* made her maiden call into Port Everglades. She saluted the former *Queen Elizabeth* with a long blast of her own, deep-sounding Tyfon sirens. *Seawise University*, with insufficient steam, could sadly offer no reply. (©JP Basile)

full, she left the city the following day, providing a thrill to mesmerised passengers on passing ferry boats, as well as to those sunning on the Copacabana – the ship passing just a mile out from the world-renowned beach.

The ship crossed the South Atlantic, a 3,300 nautical mile run to Cape Town, in perfect weather. During the lonely crossing, in which not a single ship was sighted, the *Seawise University* managed her best average speed thus far: 11.26 knots. The speed – only a third of what she was capable of in her transatlantic days – would not be bettered for the rest of the trip.

The ship arrived at Cape Town on the 13th June. A press conference was organised by the owner's representative and was used to publicise the transformation of the ship into her new role as a floating university and cruise. The following day she left her anchorage in Duncan Harbour, the largest passenger vessel ever to call there, and headed for open sea once more.

University of the Sea

In his autobiography, *The Queens and I*, Commodore Marr recalls the next part of the voyage:

"After we rounded the Cape of Good Hope and were heading east, we found even larger, longer versions of the Cape Rollers waiting for us, with strong cold winds bringing up wintry showers from the south Polar Regions. So, standing on our vast, empty promenade deck watching the ship roll easily in the big quarter swell, it did not require a lot of imagination to picture the old lady as being back in her old stamping ground, the North Atlantic, where so much of her life had been spent in weather like this. With all of her tanks full of oil and water, she rode the 'greybeards' very well, and it was only when we passed the big tankers going the other way and shipping huge seas that we realised just how comfortable we were. We did sound very much like a ghost ship as, with every roll, dozens of cupboard and locker doors which had been left open in unoccupied cabins banged monotonously."

The rest of the voyage to Hong Kong was made in uncomfortable humidity and sweltering heat. The *Seawise University* entered Eastern waters on the 4th July. In the Straits of Malacca she was slowed to 8 knots, to arrive in Singapore on the 7th July. Two Shackleton aircraft of the RAF joined the ship close to Singapore, providing escort for about an hour and flying low around the ship. As she was proceeding to her berth, six RAF fighter aircraft flew over in tight formation, followed immediately by six Royal Navy helicopters – one final salute to the former pride of the British Merchant Marine.

Commodore Marr, devoid of energy in the overpowering equatorial heat, decided to remain on board the whole two days the ship remained in Singapore. During

10th February 1971: A fuming *Seawise University* leaves the Florida coastline behind in disgust, after plans to turn her into an East coast version of the *Queen Mary* went horribly awry from the start. (Philpot Collection)

that time, he was once more overcome by nostalgia and mixed feelings. He asked himself: "What is she doing here? Why couldn't she have stayed in Britain?"

Her new Master Commodore Hsuan, on the other hand, had gone ashore. When a reporter asked him of the future plans for the ship, he proudly replied on behalf of Mr Tung:

"Right now our plans call for the First Class compartments to be refurbished but remain basically the same. The Tourist section will be redesigned to carry 1,000 students with separate quarters for the teachers.

"Classrooms won't be much of a problem because they won't be formal as such and can easily be adapted from the many public rooms already on the ship.

"Her official language will be English although she'll be outfitted with an Oriental crew of no less than 800."

Local interest in the history of the ship that was once the *RMS Queen Elizabeth* was great, and a party of press, radio and TV personnel managed to get on board. Commodore Marr was asked to reflect on his former command:

"I realize that the sterile laws of economics leave no room for sentiment. With planes, we shall see the likes of her no more and it is now the end of a gracious era.

"The people who came on board her were a special breed, born to money and position, famous on the screen, or in some way made their mark on a world that's passed us by. She made life a little bit easier in a world where problems got harder.

"I am grateful from the bottom of my heart that she gets a second chance to sail again, no matter how she gets to do it. I would be thrilled and happy to see her sailing up Southampton Water with a vast crowd of students on board in her new role as a university of the sea."

The ship was bringing to Hong Kong with her the hopes and dreams of her new owner, and the best wishes from her admirers world-wide, for many years of life ahead. The former *RMS Queen Elizabeth* bravely steamed the remaining miles towards her fate.

The *Queen Elizabeth's* last Chief Engineer, Ted Phillip, took this photograph from the top of the forward funnel during the voyage to Hong Kong. Apart from a slight list to port, the picture reveals heavy rusting and weathering on the Fo'c'sle and top decks - the result of many months neglect in Port Everglades. (Philpot Collection)

Rio de Janeiro, Sunday 30th May 1971: Rio's two famed peaks - Sugar Loaf on the left and Corcovado on the right, form the backdrop to the departing *Seawise University*. (Robert Lenzer)

Seawise University spent a day and a night in Cape Town, the last chance for her European crew to enjoy cool temperatures before entering the stagnating heat and humidity of the Far East. Five months at sea have taken their toll on the ship, now rust-stained along the entire length of her hull above the boot topping. (Philpot Collection)

The *Seawise University* became the largest passenger vessel ever to enter Duncan Harbour in Cape Town, when she was there from the 13th to the 14th of June 1971. (Gerd Laschzok)

One final piece of ephemera: A colourful 1970's – style brochure for the floating university that never was. (Philpot Collection)

S.S. seawise university
(formerly R.M.S. Queen Elizabeth)

The Largest Passenger Liner
83,676 gross tons / Operated by
ORIENT OVERSEAS LINE

Chapter 6

Hong Kong: A 'Queen' Dies

Taken late in 1972 from aboard an aeroplane about to land at Hong Kong's former International Airport, Kai Tak, west of Kowloon Bay, the half-submerged wreck continues to release oil from her tanks into the already foul waters of the bay. An oil storage depot, to the left, on Tsing Yi Island, has been built on reclaimed land. Continual land reclamation on the island would see that by 2004, the edge of Tsing Yi would encroach out to, and cover-over, more than half of the submerged wreck's remains. (Michael Cairns)

CUNARD

Having survived the snail-paced trek halfway around the world, the former Cunard Flagship and world-famous ocean liner, the *RMS Queen Elizabeth* limped into her final port-of-call and new home, Hong Kong. It was a perilous 155 day journey that defied many odds.

She was still the biggest passenger ship in the world, still among the most beautiful, and now with a new name, owner and future, she was clinging to life.

As the *Seawise University*, she was set to embark on her fourth career, a meaningful role that seemed to suit her. Most importantly, she would continue steaming the vastness of the world's oceans which, considering her age, was cause for celebration among ship lovers, former passengers, crew members and the number of men who built her over thirty years earlier. The "Lizzie" would be around for years to come – or so it seemed.

What nobody could have guessed was indeed how "final" this Hong Kong homecoming would turn out to be.

The *Seawise University's* arrival into Hong Kong Harbour came in the small hours of Thursday the 15th July 1971. She had steamed north-west up the East Lamma Channel from the South China Sea at barely 4 knots. A flotilla of

onlooker craft comprised of assorted fishing boats, wooden sampans and Junks – all tiny in comparison to the huge liner. The curious, grinning occupants of this welcoming-party looked bewildered, bordering on nervous, as they moved in close and peered upwards at the mountain of steel from their frighteningly out-sized boats.

The emotions of Commodore Geoffrey Thrippleton Marr, the liner's last British master who was acting as technical advisor to Commodore William Hsuan, were torn as he silently watched the homecoming scene unfold before him. He was extremely happy that his former ship should be given the chance to sail-on into the future, but being a patriot, he resented that he was handing over a British icon, representing the very essence of Britain herself, to the Chinese, despite Hong Kong being a British Colony at the time. The Commodore thought to himself, "What is she doing here? Why couldn't she have stayed in Britain?" Such were the final, painful moments for Marr aboard his former home and command of many years; understandable sentiments from the man who knew her best and cared more for her well-being than anybody else alive.

Triumphant Entry

Not only was the "Lizzie" a conspicuously British-looking liner, she was undeniably Scottish, an unmistakable creation of Messrs. John Brown and Co. Clydebank – builder of the most recognisable ocean liners in the world for the most successful passenger ship line of them all. British ex-pats and non-Chinese tourists who came to say "hello" or "goodbye" to the old girl on her well-publicised arrival into Hong Kong, (including the RAF pilot who daringly landed his large helicopter on the Sports Deck between her two stacks) still regarded her, first and foremost, as Britain and Cunard's the *Queen Elizabeth*, regardless of her new name.

The former pride of the British Merchant Marine inched ever so slowly up the East Lama Channel bearing for Kau Yi Chau Island. She seemed to be gliding on a mirror-like sea, surrounded in all directions by a myriad of picturesque islands. The old liner was entering one of the most scenic harbours in the world, a harbour made all the more beautiful by her gracious presence.

As the ship approached the city, the welcoming flotilla grew steadily, giving the ship an exciting and triumphal welcome. Army helicopters buzzed overhead and vessels of the marine and fire services huddled in close, with the largest Hong Kong fire boat, the *Alexander Grantham*, putting on a world class display of water sprays, impressing everyone, especially Commodore Marr. Upon passing Green Island, she was met by four powerful tugs that would escort her to her anchorage. In the end their services were not required as the ship was still able to manoeuvre sufficiently despite her minimal speed.

The *SS Seawise University* dropped anchor at 09:30, just to the north of Kau Yi Chau Island. This was the first of two locations where she would ride at anchor within the harbour. Being the height of the typhoon season, a temporary first anchorage was chosen in the lee or shadow-side of the Island, a location which offered good shelter from extreme winds. When this risk had passed, the *Seawise University* moved under her own steam one last time to an anchorage a few miles further north, at the entrance to the Rambler Channel, halfway between Tsing Yi and Stonecutters Islands.

15th July 1971: Almost there. Hong Kong's largest fire-fighting boat, *Alexander Grantham*, leads the *Seawise University* for the last couple of miles of a gruelling, 5-month trek half way around The World. The ship has just passed the fishing village of Aberdeen, with Lamma Island in the background. (Public Records Office Hong Kong)

Hong Kong: A 'Queen' Dies

The external reconversion work mostly involved hammering and sand blasting away the previous paint jobs dating back from 1946 – the last time the ship received a total makeover, from wartime grey to Cunard livery. (Hong Kong Govt. Information services)

The Commodore Bids Farewell

The time had come for Commodore Marr to bid a final goodbye to his beloved ship. With one last look into her eyes – the bridge windows, he turned away, resisting hard the temptation to look back for just one more glance. The long flight home to England offered the Commodore time to reflect. A major chapter in his life had finally come to an end. He felt overcome with emotion as he remembered the ship: "pushing forward with mighty power and effortlessly flinging the mighty Atlantic Ocean aside in great combers." This was his favourite description whenever he reminisced about the ship to his friends and fans around the world.

The Commodore felt an intense sadness because more than anybody, he understood the reality of the situation. The ageing *Queen Elizabeth* was a time capsule from the past which, whilst still lovely to behold, looked a mere shadow of her former self. She would continue to contrast more and more against the rapidly changing times and her machinery would not last forever. The risks of breakdowns or greater disasters were ever-increasing threats to her survival.

Seeing his former ship sitting so pitiably, idle in the midst of all that shipping traffic in one of the busiest harbours in the world, Marr feared the worst. Most likely the Commodore wasn't the only one in Hong Kong that day to have a gut feeling that, despite the impending refit that would see her emerge as a cruising university campus, her days may be numbered. Some persons, unknown to this day, would make sure of it.

Right: This is the first advertisement promoting cruising aboard the SS *Seawise University*. It was released in May 1971, two months before the ship even arrived into Hong Kong to begin her refit. The first voyage was to have been a four-month cruise slated for December 1971, departing from Los Angeles and terminating in New York. The second was a 75-day Circle Pacific Cruise, to have begun on April the 18th 1972 out of Vancouver and ending in Los Angeles. (Philpot Collection)

The Queen sails again!

You knew her as the R.M.S. Queen Elizabeth. Today, renamed S.S. Seawise University, the world's largest ocean liner sets out on a new career.

Winston Churchill sailed on her. So did Henry Ford, Charlie Chaplin, Vanderbilt, and a thousand other names that read like a Who's Who of the World.

The R.M.S. Queen Elizabeth was the toast of six continents . . . a magnificent ship with 13 decks, sumptuous public rooms, a 300-seat theater, and every luxury imaginable. During her 25 years of service, she carried 2.3 million passengers almost 3½ million miles.

But this will be the first time she sails around the world.

And you can join her on her new Inaugural Voyage.

You'll have the chance for an experience that once only the wealthy could afford. Saved from retirement, The Queen was recently rechristened the *S.S. Seawise University** and refurbished to accommodate over 700 first class passengers (plus an on-board university — World Campus Afloat — which will occupy separate areas of the ship).

* Registered in Bahamas

Travel first class at only $28 per day

Imagine traveling first class on The Queen! Her splendid accommodations are today modestly priced. The extra refinements that once cost so much have been put aside. And in their place you'll find a casual, relaxed style of cruising comfortable enough so that you don't feel you're "on view" all the time.

Here is a chance to sail the world in stately old world charm. The appointments are reminiscent of the best of a fabulous era. The ship has huge dining rooms, Turkish baths, beauty salons, libraries, gymnasiums, sumptuously paneled cabins (56 different kinds of wood were used) and a main lounge three decks high.

There'll be a full activities program on board. The dining room offers excellent Continental and Chinese cuisines. You'll love the personal, attentive service. And the informal atmosphere.

Extra long port stops

Another special benefit that former passengers on The Queen never enjoyed: With port stops averaging *three days apiece,* you'll have ample opportunity to really explore a city, to take side trips. To shop. To see a city at *your* pace, unpressured by a hurried schedule.

And with a university on board, passengers will be able to arrange for guest lectures on interesting historical or cultural topics by members of the university's faculty.

An exciting itinerary

The 4-month world cruise will give you up to 46 days on land to adventure in Honolulu, Pago Pago, Whangerei (New Zealand), Hobart (Tasmania), Fremantle (Australia), Bali, Singapore, Madras (India), Dar Es Salaam (Tanzania), Cape Town, Rio de Janeiro, Port of Spain (Trinidad), La Guaira (Venezuela). The ship returns to New York.

For all the captivating details, see your travel agent. Or write to Orient Overseas Line.

THRILLING 4-MONTH WORLD CRUISE LEAVES LOS ANGELES DECEMBER 1971. FIRST CLASS FARES BEGIN AT JUST $2,975.

MAIL COUPON TO: Orient Overseas Line, 311 California St., San Francisco, Calif. 94104. (415) 981-7340.

Yes, I'm excited about sailing on The Queen (now S.S. Seawise University). Please send me information on the following cruises:

- ☐ 4-month world cruise December 1971
- ☐ 4-month world cruise 1972

Name.....................................

Address..................................

City................ State........ Zip....

Other Offices in Los Angeles, New York, Miami, and Vancouver, B.C.

ORIENT OVERSEAS LINE
THE LEISURE LINE

MAY 1971

Hong Kong: A 'Queen' Dies

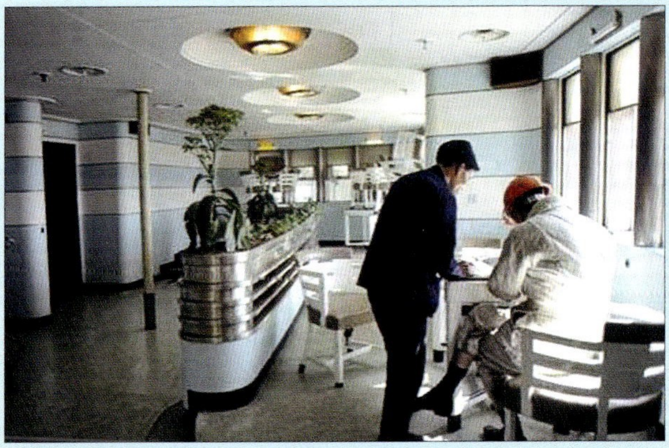

Inside the former Cabin Class Cocktail Bar, Seawise University's Refit Superintendent, CC Chou (seated), and one of the foremen, discuss an issue regarding the progress of the ship's conversion. Even after so many years this room, done in the Arte Moderne Style, continues to demonstrate an atmosphere of freshness and it has been left completely original. A jardinière is still contained in the streamlined silver-bronze balustrade which imparts a delightful air of Parisian street café to the terraced area. This is sadly the last image taken of this space before it and the rest of the ship, was consumed by fire in January 1972. (Michael Gallagher collection)

A very grimy First Class stairwell, just one week before the fire: A woman worker carries a stack of new life-vests to the various staterooms, replacing the older ones still on board. If, in fact, a no-smoking policy was in place during the refit - as is the norm on all ship conversions - it certainly wasn't respected on the Seawise University. Close inspection of the photo reveals a crushed cigarette packet, at least two stomped-out cigarette butts on the steps and a lit cigarette in the hand of the man walking down the stairs. (1st of January 1972 by Arthur Crook)

New steel was cut to cover pre-existing wooden bulkheads, thereby increasing fire-resistance in a specific area. The Chinese graffiti seen scribbled here was believed to be expressing anti-Tung sentiment, in a similar way that messages, perhaps from disgruntled workers, were painted on the ship's forward funnel which told C.Y. Tung to "Go Home" (Arthur Crook)

C.Y. Tung: Creating the World's Largest Cruising Campus Afloat

C.Y. Tung officially became the new owner of the RMS Queen Elizabeth on the 17th September 1970. In bestowing upon his latest acquisition the dual role of cruise ship and university at sea, the Hong Kong shipping magnate was hailed as the man who not only saved the retired former "Queen" from the scrap yard, but for reuniting the ship he so unequivocally loved with her natural habitat, the high seas.

Tung would at the same time be providing a unique location as the setting for his life's dream which was the nourishment of international friendships among students of differing nationalities, opening minds and hearts to cultural diversities. It was his wish that the cruising campus would become the breeding ground for the attainment of virtues such as respect, concord, goodwill, and humanity, in a place where positive energy would be passed from one individual to the other. The "Lizzie", with her courageous contribution to humanity during WWII, seemed to be the perfect choice.

By perpetuating the *RMS Queen Elizabeth* as the *SS Seawise University*, Mr. Tung's strong desire that people should be properly educated, along with his passion for establishing benevolence between people of all nations, would finally become a reality. The plan was as noble and enormous as the great ship herself and Tung's altruistic vision was avidly supported by the United Nations Secretary-General, Kurt Waldheim.

Mr. Tung's own Island Navigation Company would assume overall responsibility for the huge reconversion job. No less than 29 different sub-contractors were hired for the restoration or replacement of the ship's radio and safety equipment, the electrical system, lifts, telephone system and public address, joinery, and decoration. Meanwhile, many other contracted companies would provide a labour force for painting the hull and superstructure, refuse removal, machinery survey, cleaning and polishing all areas, especially the precious wood panelling and fire-watching. With an apparent abundance of enthusiasm, up to 2000 workers per day clamoured aboard through the R-Deck shell doors to carry out the *Queen Elizabeth's* conversion.

First and foremost, specific alterations would have to bring the ship into line with the latest Inter-Governmental Maritime Consultative Organization (IMCO) convention of SOLAS (Safety of Life at Sea). The last such convention was held in 1960 with the regulations activated in 1966. This was around the same time as the *Queen Elizabeth's* last major overhaul – a costly cruising-refit on the Clyde Estuary that was supposed to keep her going for another ten years. But alas, in her current state of repair, barely six years after that refit, she could not be insured to Lloyds highest class rating, and in any case, could not sail classed as a "Passenger Vessel".

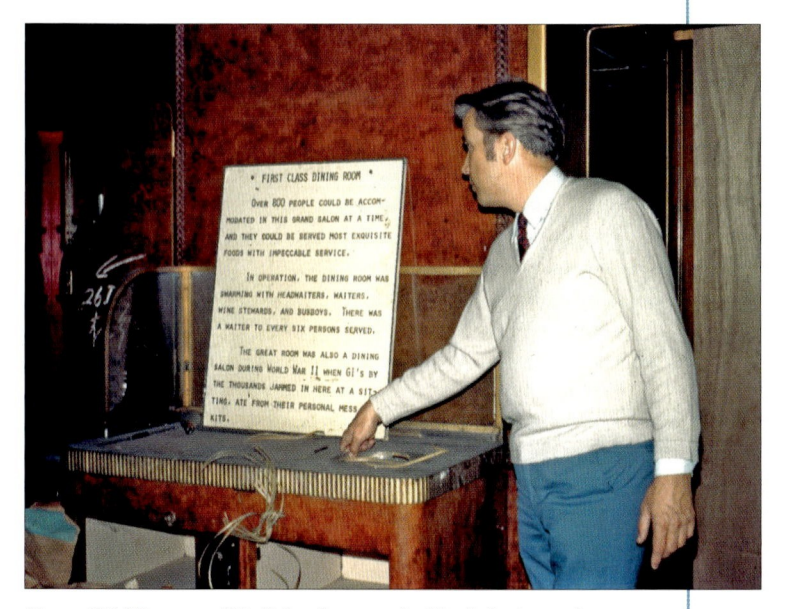

Above: Chief Passenger Ship Safety Surveyor for Lloyds Register of Shipping London, the Late Arthur Crook, was sent out to inspect the level of improvement made to *Seawise University's* fire safety. He is seen here in the former First Class Restaurant next to an original food heating station, on top of which is a sign left over from the liner's days as a tourist attraction. (Arthur Crook)

Below: Mrs. Elke Crook in the former First Class Lounge. Apart from the newly upholstered chairs, the room was left original at the wishes of C.Y. Tung. (Arthur Crook)

Hong Kong: A 'Queen' Dies

Top: Mrs. Elke Crook together with Refit Superintendent CC Chou, in front of the bronze sculpture Oceanides atop of the Promenade Deck Grand Lobby staircase - another area left intact and original. (Arthur Crook)

Above: The *Seawise University*, resembling a dazzle-painted liner from WWI, receives her final coat of white paint. To ensure that the funnels received a sufficient thickness of paint, C.Y. Tung had his workers apply different colours each day over several days -a clever tactic which ensured the work was carried out correctly. January 1972. (Arthur Crook)

Bringing the ship up to 1966 SOLAS requirements involved providing proper fire insulation between existing bulkheads and most of the fire-escape stairway enclosures. As well as ensuring the proper enclosure of her four main stairways with fireproof structural bulkheads, including the proper fire doors and fire dampers. The Lloyds Register of Shipping approved metal fire doors were made in Italy, and once installed they would raise fire safety to the level required. Other fundamental work saw the extension of the sprinkler system, the upgrading of many of her cabins, and providing suitable accommodation and work areas for 20 lecturers and about 800 students.

To the relief of the ship's loyal fans, C.Y. Tung had chosen to mostly preserve the liner's interior layout and décor, merely restoring and repairing wherever necessary, thus retaining the ship's British ambiance. Most of the original cabins had already been refurbished and modernized to some degree during various refits in the 1960s.

The Queen Elizabeth's engines, boilers and other machinery were to be reconditioned and returned to being fully operational. Electrical and safety wiring throughout the ship would be replaced using a much higher quality, fire resistant material.

The most noticeable external change would be the removal of her Cunard livery. Original paintwork, or what was left of it, would be hammered down to the bare metal. The "new" ship would have an all-white hull and superstructure with yellow stacks. Upon completion, her designated master, Commodore Chen Ching-yien, appointed on 15th November 1971 and taking over from Commodore Hsuan, would supposedly be standing at the helm of a totally rejuvenated ship which, in terms of fire-safety at least, would be at the highest level in her 32 year lifetime.

A Fond Reunion

On 8th January 1972, a musician named Bob Malinowski, who was visiting Hong Kong at the time, received a special invitation directly from the offices of the C.Y. Tung Group to tour the ship, after they discovered he was an ex-crew member. In 1965 and 1966, Malinowski was the bass player in "The Dougie Ward Trio", a popular act that played in the Mid-ships Bar, the former First Class Salon on Promenade Deck. It is likely that Malinowski had the double-distinction of being the very last Cunard employee to have been on the *Queen Elizabeth*, and shooting some of the final photographs from inside the ship before an "act" of a totally different kind would be performed onboard the very next morning.

In his own words:

"Both my wife and I were very keen to get onboard whilst we were in Hong Kong – me, to see how she looked after so many years and my wife, because having worked on the *QE2* with so many crew members that had previously been on board the "Lizzie", who had told her how great she was, she felt she wanted to see for herself.

RMS Queen Elizabeth: the Unruffled Cunarder

"Getting on board was not difficult for us once I had been to the offices of C Y Tung and explained about my time working on her. We were treated like royalty. We were both taken out to the ship on a tender accompanied by the Public Relations Officer who was very proud of the ship. After being provided with lunch we were given the run of the ship to explore. Much of the interior had been restored to its former glory (which had been allowed to deteriorate during her stay in America we were told). The beautiful wood panelling was all in place and we went into the "Queens Suite" and the "Winston Churchill Suite" which were finished and looking lovely.

"Much of the furniture in the public rooms had been reupholstered and I felt that before long she would have been as I had known her, although there did seem to be plenty more to do.

"It seemed strange to see all the makeshift bamboo scaffolding throughout the work areas – a bit like East meets West! Knowing that we were going back to work in Japan, the officer invited us to come on board again in Yokohama Japan, where she was due to go into dry-dock once all the internal work was finished. So obviously it was with great sadness that we witnessed her dying throes over the next two days, and when we returned to Hong Kong six months later, it was terrible to see the rusty, distorted hull on its side in the bay."

Below: The bamboo scaffolding is part of the restoration taking place in the former Mid-ship Bar space and is a visual reminder that the conversion of the former 'Queen' was truly a case of East meeting West. (Bob Malinowski)

Bottom: No matter what the colour scheme, the ship made for an imposing sight from all angles. (Arthur Crook)

Hong Kong: A 'Queen' Dies

8th January 1972: One last look at the iconic bridge of the former Cunard liner. The telegraphs have been stripped of their paint exposing the brass. Compare this with the image below taken a couple of years earlier in 1969. (Bob Malinowski/Kolman Rosenberg)

8th January 1972: The once lovely former Tourist Class winter garden, on Main-Deck, was also in a state of complete disarray this far into the conversion. But, in the end, it wouldn't matter, for in less than 24 hours it would be the end of this and all spaces in the ship. (Bob Malinowski)

RMS Queen Elizabeth: the Unruffled Cunarder

The day before the fire, the once tidy and immaculately-kept foredeck of the *Queen Elizabeth* now looks like a scrap metal yard. (Bob Malinowski)

A lacklustre name-sign was erected just before the forward funnel. (Bob Malinowski)

Hong Kong: A 'Queen' Dies

The Terrible Act

On that crisp morning of 9th January 1972, one of several large ships riding at anchor in Hong Kong Harbour clearly stood out from the rest. Instantly recognizable was the long, delightful contour of the twin-funnelled, ex Cunard "Queen", the *RMS Queen Elizabeth*.

Around mid-morning the occupants of one of the few pleasure boats underway in Victoria Harbour caught a glimpse of the majestic, statuesque liner to the north-east, only a few miles across the water. They were drawn to her like a magnet. Aboard the small craft were sightseers John Hudson, his fiancé, and her parents, all unanimously deciding to take a close-up look at the much talked about the *SS Seawise University*. In five days time she would begin her sea trials, her transformation almost complete.

At approximately 10:00, commodore Chen Chia-yien, onboard the *Seawise University*, went on a tour of inspection. He began along the Promenade Deck then walked to the bridge, where he would not stay long, instead heading for the crowded main restaurant on R-Deck for the regular Sunday morning progress meeting. The room was filling fast as many workmen had already started taking early lunchbreaks.

The other large public room aboard which saw a high concentration of people that morning, was the former First Class lounge, now renamed the Peacock Lounge. Here, catering staff were making preparations for a cocktail party and lunch for specially invited guests, an event being organized by C.H. Tung, the eldest son of C.Y. Tung.

Later that day, the wives and children of many workmen were being allowed on board for a sightseeing tour and by 11:00, many of them had arrived along with V.I.Ps for the cocktail party. This would be their last chance to inspect the ship before she began her new career in a few weeks time.

The scenario on board the liner that morning was thus a marked agglomeration of people in just a couple of areas, with the greater part of her long hull mostly void of souls. Being a Sunday, there were fewer workers than usual on board and by 11:00, many of them had already begun to pause work for their lunch, many going ashore.

The largest passenger vessel in the world provided miles of long, empty corridors, hundreds of unoccupied cabins and quiet out-of-the-way places. Along the ship's many cross-alleyways, numerous piles of neatly placed rubbish were to be found. The ship was dark, at best very dimly lit: perfect conditions for any mischievous "rats" to lurk about, doing as they pleased.

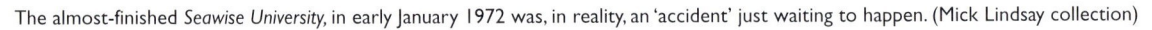

The almost-finished *Seawise University*, in early January 1972 was, in reality, an 'accident' just waiting to happen. (Mick Lindsay collection)

Up In Flames

Thousands of kilometres away in France, where C.Y. Tung was attending the launch of one of his new ship builds, it was around 04:00 local time. Soon, the sunlight which was heralding the dawn on his big, beautiful "baby" nearly 20,000 km to the East, gradually warming her decks, superstructure and hull, would reach him too. Also not far from reaching Tung, would be the shocking news which would literally bring him to tears.

Back in Hong Kong, the *Seawise University's* steelwork was gradually warming up, but the rise in temperature was not entirely the work of the still-weak, Sunday morning sun.

Inside the small boat, John Hudson, wielding a freshly-loaded camera, saw the *Seawise University* getting progressively larger before him. Just as anyone over the years who had spied this incomparable ship up close, the four sight-seers were entranced by the beauty and grandeur that lay before them. But fascination and admiration was soon replaced by worrisome curiosity when they noticed small puffs of white smoke coming from the ship's open portholes. As John Hudson recalls, from many of them along the port side:

"There wasn't a sign of any other problems with the ship, no fireboats alongside or added human activity aboard the ship. No sign of anything out of the ordinary – except this smoke blowing out of the portholes. Yes, it was alarming but at that early stage still all very fascinating."

Somewhere between 11:10 and 11:20, one of those very neat, small piles of flammable rubbish mysteriously and rapidly started to burn. Flames were seen emanating from the rubbish pile by three cabin boys who were about the duty of sweeping up rubbish from around the ship. The waste pile was about three feet in diameter and 20-30 inches high. The exact location of this fire, considered to be the first, was on a port-side cross alleyway of A-Deck at frame number 110. It burned several feet from an open shell door and the flames were clearly visible from outside the ship.

The Report published by the Marine Court in 1972 on the findings of the official enquiry into the loss of the *SS Seawise University*, shows that almost immediately after the initial outbreak of fire was discovered, an uncanny series of sudden and unrelated fire outbreaks took place in quick succession, spreading, as if by means of some ghostly phenomenon, over no less than five different decks.

Because these fires were so widely spaced apart from one another and mostly on different decks, all being reported within a very short time span, it meant that the likelihood of them being connected to one initial fire was not a feasible possibility.

What was actually occurring that morning aboard what C.Y. Tung referred to as "the last historic ship left", was a systematic torching of the *Seawise University*. It was pure arson on a grand scale, a coordinated act of terror at the hands saboteurs which, until today, have managed to escape punishment.

Fire Takes Hold

At least two independent fires were lit in the "Lizzie's" spacious foyers, near to or directly next to stairwells. Outbreaks in such places guaranteed the arsonists quick-spreading fire, as flames simultaneously climbed and descended the wood-enclosed stairwells that linked the various decks. It then spread with a vengeance horizontally in both directions along the wood-panelled and ventilated corridors of each deck, penetrating room

People are still gathered on the bow, too frightened to move aft into the burning hull. The smoke emanating from just under the bridge, is most likely from a new and separate fire, recently lit in the Tourist Class Stairwell between Promenade and Boat Deck deck. With the fires now out of control, frightened visitors still aboard had little time left to find their way to the R-Deck shell doors where boats were waiting to ferry them to safety. (Copyright John A. Hudson)

The liner is barely discernible under the billowing smoke. (Philpot collection from G.T. Marr)

after room in an unstoppable, destructive rampage.

The major blow to the ship's chances of fighting back was that the sprinkler systems were made inoperable after the main power supply generators, which they were connected to, were shut down in order to prevent more fires caused by short-circuiting. This was, in hindsight, a foolish decision because there was nothing to lose and everything to gain from having the sprinklers do what they were designed for – putting out fires.

Some of the fires on board were bravely fought by the ship's fire officers and other fire fighting groups rounded up by Commodore Chen Chia-yien and one of his Chief Officers. They used the ship's available fire hoses and extinguishers, but the enormous amount of thick smoke continually drove them back, and ultimately their efforts had to be abandoned. The flames proceeded unchecked, fanned by a steady airflow entering the ship from the shell doors and portholes which were nearly all open at the time.

The call for fireboats was made from a police launch which had moved to the vicinity of the *Seawise University* after noticing the smoke at around 11:45. Smoke was also observed around this time from signal towers on Hong Kong Island and Green Island, both of which also notified the Harbour's fire services.

At 12:30, the initial fire discovered aboard at the cross-alley at frame 110 on A-deck, had been fought for almost an hour. The tenacity of the fire-fighting group finally managed to extinguish it. Photos of the Port side of ship taken around this time, and which show the shell door in question, reveal an absence of both smoke and flame, indicating that the initial blaze onboard had successfully been put out. This solitary victory was but a temporary triumph, for no sooner had these flames been extinguished, than new and totally unconnected fires were raging uncontrollably elsewhere.

The first of these new fires was 80 yards aft and a deck below the initial blaze, at frame number 70. Another was at frame 48 on R-Deck portside, yet another some 150 yards forward on Boat-Deck at frame 255 and yet another still would ignite on the port side of Sun-Deck, in one of the unoccupied crew cabins, just aft of the after funnel at frame 140.

These fires burned unchecked and were of such size and ferocity that, just over one hour after being set alight, the *Seawise University* was virtually beyond saving, despite the faint hope given with the arrival of the first fireboat at 12:27.

By now the perpetrators of this terrible act had most likely strolled calmly towards the gangways to disembark the ship and have a nice lunch ashore at C.Y. Tung's expense, safe in the knowledge of a "job" well done, on a far-too-easy target. Mission complete. The "Lizzie" was dying and there was nothing anybody could do to save her.

Beauty Afire

About the time of the arrival of the first fireboats, the fire located at frame 205 in the main stairway on B-Deck, had reached the foyer on R-Deck which led to the entrance to one of the most loved rooms on the ship and one of the most beautiful rooms afloat: the elegant First Class restaurant.

Had anyone watched the destruction of that room, they would have witnessed a surreal and heart-wrenching scene, beginning with thousands of sparks cascading like glowing raindrops from the burning ceiling canopy, the falling cinders causing the carpet and tables below to ignite.

Flames would have clung eerily to the room's beautiful panelling of London Plane Tree Burr, bleached, according to early brochures, a delicate colour of "coffee and milk", the fire turning them a carbonised coffee black. The nightmare came to an abrupt end when the deck above came crashing down, flattening the whole space into oblivion.

Scenes like this one were repeated throughout the ship, obliterating in similar furious fashion, spaces containing important artworks, and beautiful furniture and fittings. Charming rooms full of memories that were admired by many thousands of people from all walks of life for nearly three decades – all gone within the blink of an eye.

John Hudson had now been circling the burning ship at a distance of about 20-30 feet for over two hours. He'd witnessed the initial puffs of smoke turn into several major fires.

Hudson, concerned for his passenger's safety, noticed that the volume of smoke and the intensity of the wind was quickly picking up, so he decided to slowly move away from the burning liner. He returned one more time to say his personal goodbye to the former "Queen" later that same year. It was a dark, cloudy afternoon and he took some very haunting images of the dead ship.

When one considers the fear and panic those trapped on board during the fire must have experienced, disoriented deep within an enormous and listing ship, in almost total darkness, its plain to see how miraculous it was that nobody died that day. At 15:27, the last person was evacuated. The *Seawise University* was now a ghost ship, inhabited only by the flames that were consuming her. For the first time in her 34 years of life, she was completely alone and without a single living soul onboard. It was at this moment one can say that her own soul left her and she truly died.

Hong Kong: A 'Queen' Dies

Above: By the late afternoon of the 9th of January 1972, the ship was completely burnt-out from forepeak to sternpost. Internally nothing was saved. All fireboats and otherwise, were removed from her vicinity, leaving her to die alone; a black day in maritime history. (Mike Cornwall collection)

Below: Flames exit the ship's superstructure high up on Sun Deck, behind the after funnel. This is an independent fire lit in or next to the officer's mess. At the bottom right of the picture, inside the open A-Deck shell door, the initial fire, lit in a small pile of rubbish, is still burning. It was eventually extinguished but in the meantime, other major fires had been lit in other parts of the ship. (Copyright John A. Hudson)

Aftermath and Inquiry

Dawn the following day confirmed to the world with stark clarity, what many people had wished was nothing but a horrible rumour. Alas, television and newspaper images of the still-smouldering, dead-in-the-water liner were very real.

Approximately 24 hours after the blaze started, the charred hulk made one final, gravity-induced movement and slowly rolled over. The *Seawise University* imbedded her bilge keel deep into the soft, muddy seabed, coming finally to rest in 40-50 feet of water with her huge funnels rising just above the surface. The 1972 Marine Court inquiry into the fire revealed a major finding. It highlighted the apparent negligent aloofness, indifference and suspicious disinterest displayed by most of the people in the vicinity of the very first fire outbreak:

"The earliest photographs ... bear testimony to the unconcern shown by everyone who was in the vicinity at the time of the first fire outbreak. The persons who are shown in the first few photographs leaving the vessel by launch, scarcely seem to be aware of any threat to the ship although one imagines that some of them at least must have seen some of the smoke coming from the shell door. This insouciance is echoed even in the behaviour of those workers who had heard the alarm aboard the ship, many of

Sunlight the next morning revealed both an eerie and tragic sight. The inferno had totally deformed and distorted the ship, her hull plates and entire deck sections twisting, buckling and caving in on themselves. The wreck has a pronounced starboard list, allowing sea water to enter the hull through open shell doors on 'D' Deck which would, with time, exacerbate the list. The liner's starboard bilge keel is only inches from touching the silty sludge of the harbour floor - a material which would not be able to support the ship's weight. (Philpot collection)

whom appear to have done nothing more than continue with their lunch. Indeed the three carpenters who had been working in a cabin just aft of the cross alleyway at 110 Frame and who saw smoke and flames as they left the cabin, neither raised the alarm nor joined in the fire-fighting, but simply proceeded, by a circuitous route to avoid the fire, to the restaurant for their meal."

"One may perhaps speculate that this reflected their confidence in the crew's ability to deal with fires which had been demonstrated on previous occasions during the course of the renovations, although it may simply have been that they were quite unaware of the effect that a serious fire could have on a ship in her situation."

That is one explanation, but perhaps there were more sympathisers who knew what was occurring than just the perpetrators themselves.

The Marine Court of Inquiry's investigation into the fire could only conclude that: "The most likely cause of the fires was a series of deliberate acts by a person or persons unknown." The case was then handed over to the criminal investigation department of Hong Kong Police but, even after so many years, nothing has ever been made public regarding what may or may not have been found.

According to *New York Times* writer Philip Bowling, in a December 2003 article titled "The Mysterious Demise of a Grand Ocean Liner" the police did receive an anonymous tip-off about an alleged mastermind plan to destroy the ship, but it was not acted upon. Bowling wrote:

"The public is still waiting to hear what they have found. There have been no arrests, no charges laid and there has been an almost total absence of follow-up discussion or press speculation. Historians and crime writers might hope that government archives would hold some clues. But if they do, they are still held too tightly to help."

Three likely hypotheses exist as to why the *Seawise University* was deliberately torched, these being political, business and insurance related. Speculation at the time suggested that communists set the ship alight to spite C.Y. Tung who was closely associated with the Nationalist Taiwanese Government. This was denied. If the motive was not political, a business dispute could have been behind the arson. However, C.Y. Tung would have, in this case, had an inkling of who was behind it, yet he remained tight lipped. The remaining theory suggests an "insurance fire" It was made public from early on that C.Y. Tung's latest acquisition would be an expensive one, even for the likes of

him. Headlines at the time asked: "Can even C.Y. Tung afford to keep it afloat?" It was also well known that the ship was in poor upkeep and very susceptible to destruction by fire should something go wrong during the refit. As such, a fire contingency plan had been set up. However, everyone who knew C.Y. Tung personally, including Commodore Geoffrey Marr, ruled this last theory out for the simple reason that Tung was so passionate about his famous ocean liner and his plans for her. He would never destroy something he loved so much.

Deduce what one will, nothing changes. Like the *New York Times* writer concluded in his piece, "the ship died, the mystery lives."

Wreck Removal: Butchering A Lifeless Hulk

For two years the gutted wreck of the *Seawise Univesity* rested on its side on the harbour floor, half-submerged in 50 feet of water. In that time, thousands of people were keen to get as close as possible to her remains for a good looking over. The world's largest ocean liner, even in her present condition, still had the ability to wow the crowd, only now in a most macabre way. A 'good' view was offered from aboard the Hong Kong to Macau, Hydrofoil Ferry and even from aeroplanes descending from the South, into the old Hong Kong International Airport.

So popular was the dead ship that, just like her earlier ocean liner consorts the *Normandie*, the *Queen Mary*, and the *Île de France*, to name a few, she scored a role as supporting actress in a Hollywood movie – the James Bond film *The Man with the Golden Gun*. The cameo role was brief, just three sombre scenes of her lying lifeless in the water for a total appearance of about 30 seconds. Following her movie debut, the curtains came down for good. After 35 years the show was finally over and it was time for this grand dame of the seas to make her last exit from the stage, piece by piece.

Subsequent to the loss of the *Seawise University*, tenders were called for and received from nine major salvage companies. A committee was formed to examine each one and it decided that not one single salvage company was capable of the work on its own and requested that the potential salvers form consortia and re-tender.

C.Y. Tung had all this time been in consultation with his underwriters and insurers, and in the end offered to accept the responsibility and pay for the wreck's removal in return for the sum of US$10,000,000 from Insurers P&I (Protection and Indemnity) Club. After many months, an agreement with harbour authorities was reached and C.Y. Tung immediately formed a partnership with Sir John Williams, a Welshman who migrated to Melbourne Australia, where he became a self-made-man. The newly-formed company was named JP Williams and Associates, Hong Kong.

Sir John's very good friend and partner Murdoch "Jock" Anderson, a gifted marine salvage expert with 30 years experience, was flown in from New Zealand where he'd been in charge of removing the sunken wreck of the *Wahine* from Wellington Harbour. Anderson would now be in command of the *Seawise University* wreck removal operation and he was very quick to point out that:

"Since the cost of this operation will exceed by very many times the proceeds from the sale of scrap metal recovered, I would make the point that it will be carried out solely with the object of removing a navigational hazard and certainly with no idea of salving (or body snatching) scrap metal for purely financial gain."

Captain Anderson wasn't joking when he said the one-thousand-foot-plus wreck posed a significant navigational hazard. The proximity of the wreck to a major shipping channel was cause for great concern. The *Seawise University* capsized and had sunk immediately next to the eastward approach channel to the Kwai Chung container terminals, in a body of water know as the Rambler Channel. The wreck's position was dangerously close to where vessels approaching that particular container complex are required to make a substantial turn to port.

Wreck Removal

The Hong Kong Government authorities had been patient, but after two years of waiting they were adamant – it was time for this massive obstruction to harbour movements and future port developments, to be rid of. The choices were two; refloating and towing away, or the less-attractive, more time-consuming and thus costlier piecemeal cutting.

When the *Seawise University* was still on an even keel and afloat, the distance between the ship's bottom and the harbour floor was merely ten feet. During the fire, as she started to fill with fire-extinguishing water and subsequently take on a list, her starboard bilge would have come into contact with the seabed when the ship was listing at only 15 degrees. Had the harbour floor been of firm material, at this amount of inclination, she would have merely filled with water through side doors, portholes and other openings on D-deck and she would have at least settled in an upright position. Unfortunately the natural seabed in that part of the Rambler Channel is covered with soft, anthropogenic mud comprising an admixture of natural silt and effluent. This offers little or no resistance with the result that, in an unstable condition, the ship continued to roll to a list of about 48 degrees. Aided by her massive tonnage, she continued to sink into the soft man-made sludge until her starboard bilge finally came into contact with a stratum of hard alluvium some 50 feet below the seabed.

A significant factor which influenced the choice of a

Overnight, the starboard list grew steadily and around Mid-day, the day after the fire, the ship finally came to rest at a 48 degree angle, burying her bilge-keel deep in the mud. Because the hulk was still smouldering in places, the *Alexander Gratham*, the fireboat which only six months earlier escorted the *Seawise University* into Hong Kong Harbour, continued spraying water. A solitary 'Red Duster', can be seen defiantly flying from dangling foremast rigging. Not long after this photo was taken, the flag fell onto the still scorching hot metal and almost completely shrivelled-up. It was recovered and a photo of this artefact can be seen in Chapter 7. (HKSAR Information Services Department)

Several months after the fire, on a dark and overcast day, John Hudson returned to say his personal goodbye to the ship lying dead in the water. (Copyright John A. Hudson)

167

Hong Kong: A 'Queen' Dies

An aerial view taken on the 10th January 1973, the first anniversary of the death of the 'Queen'. Oil seepage is being kept in check by the spraying of emulsifier on to it from a launch. (Philpot Collection)

wreck removal strategy was that this soft, silt-effluent concoction had flowed into the hull through the ship's numerous side openings so that the depth of mud within the hull was virtually the same as the depth of the external mud. Refloating the wreck would have involved a two-fold problem. First the need to remove the fine marine sediment that had oozed into all spaces within the hull, now 50 feet underneath the level of the harbour floor, and secondly the even more difficult task of having to remove at least 200,000 cubic yards of this smelly marine deposit from beneath the vessel's entire length, in order to create a reasonably firm and level bed on the harder alluvium base onto which she could be up-righted.

Also to consider was the condition of the wreck itself. Such was the intensity of the diabolic fires that they caused much of the superstructure, including the navigational bridge and structure abaft the after funnel, to collapse inwards to such an extent that the original height between the various decks had, in many places, been reduced to a matter of inches. Dewatering the hull for refloating would have involved ensuring the restoration of adequate structural strength to the hull, restoring watertight integrity to bulkheads, constructing cofferdams and so forth. Such work would have been extremely difficult, nigh on impossible, as the majority of transverse bulkheads within the hull had been either totally collapsed because of the fire, or were in a critically weakened state. Large areas port side and decks all the way down to the boiler room level had collapsed inwards. In short, the inside of the hull was virtually one single space, running the entire length of the ship. Even with the prior removal of the entire superstructure, regaining the required hull strength for refloating could never have been guaranteed.

Captain "Jock" Anderson and his colleagues explored every possible avenue in an attempt to find a means by which she could be refloated. While it was theoretically feasible to remove the wreck by refloating, to do so would have meant taking on such unacceptably high risks that failure to

complete the operation satisfactorily could have meant creating a situation far worse than the one already present.

Although piecemeal cutting is generally time-consuming, costly and is therefore usually only adopted as a last resort, under certain circumstances the costs involved are reasonably predictable and it can be considered as having a low risk factor. After first obtaining the green light from Hong Kong's harbour authorities, it was eventually decided a piecemeal removal of the wreck would get underway exactly where she lay.

A Long Task Begins

The first assignment for JP Williams and Associates was to contract the Fukada Salvage Company to undertake the removal of the thick, sticky ooze, known as bunker C-grade oil, that remained in the ship's deep tanks and which was already beginning to seep out of her belly and float to the surface. By method of pumping water into each tank, the sludgy oil was displaced and expelled into a barge lying alongside the sunken ship.

This work was completed in October 1972 after a dangerous manoeuvre in which divers removed manhole covers and entered each oil tank individually for inspection, with underwater television cameras and lights to confirm that no residual oil was left. Despite this, small amounts of oil leakage continued throughout the entire operation. Oil was also found to be lying within the upper portions of the submerged hull, along its entire high side, having escaped and floated there from fire-damaged fuel tanks and air pipes.

The above-water removal of the wreck was awarded to Universal Dockyards Ltd., a contractor with much experience in ship breaking. Work began on the 1st January 1974, and by the end of March that same year, much of the ship had vanished from above the water surface. What had become a very familiar landmark in Hong Kong for over two years disappeared in just over three months.

For the underwater part of the operations, the owners would form their own salvage company called The Far East Salvage Co. Ltd. The procurement of a sufficient number of experienced divers who could work under extreme conditions was of paramount importance. Eventually the Han Sung Salvage co. of South Korea was contracted and they provided a skilled team of some 25 divers. They were a close-knit group, highly self-disciplined and motivated. One diver was killed, not by a diving accident, rather by the frenetic keenness to get on with the job, leading to carelessness in handling an explosive charge on one of the barges. There was much good-spirited competition among the divers to see who could get the most work done in a day and this accident was the result of such competition.

Removal of the submerged part of the wreck began on the 7th July 1974. Precise coordination and absolute organization was needed throughout the entire underwater procedure, especially with regards to the familiarization of each group of four divers to that specific portion of the wreck they were assigned to. It was here that "Jock" Anderson's true worth as a gifted salvage expert would shine through. His attention to detail and conscientiousness was unparalleled.

Preparation meant taking into consideration the total lack of underwater visibility caused by the slightest amount

A rare image of a gesticulating C.Y. Tung next to the capsized, blistered hull of what was once was his pride and joy. (Courtesy of C Y Tung Archive, Hong Kong)

One year later: It is now January 1973 and the wreck has been untouched, only a single work hut has been erected atop the port side of the capsized hull. The large bulkhead, rising up out of the water, just forward and to the right of the men who are controlling the pumping of surface oil seepage, is the forward engine casing bulkhead that leads all the way down to the forward engine room - ten collapsed decks into the murk below. (Philpot Collection)

CHINESE JUNK TRIPS

SPECIAL ATTRACTION
Visit the Former Luxury
Queen Elizabeth
This magnificent ship, now laying on her side, is one of the sights we should all see. Our daily tours are routed to include
THIS SIGHT

Above: *Seawise University* theme park: Posing on the buckled hull plates of the once proud, former Cunard flagship, is a group of grinning students, risking life, or at least serious injury should they happen for a second take their eyes from where they tread. The numerous portholes, just centimetres from their feet, all lack their glass, providing for a deadly drop into dark, oily water strewn with jagged, twisted metal. (Courtesy of C Y Tung Archive Hong Kong)

Left: The title to this - the former *RMS Queen Elizabeth's* final brochure - says it all. The question is, was the pun intended? (Philpot Collection)

of movement of the mud within the wreck. This, in addition to the possible need for decompression, the use of explosives and cutting torches, and the difficulty of moving around in a confusing underwater labyrinth of mangled steel caused by the caved-in state of the superstructure and decks. The *Seawise University's* underwater configuration now rendered any remaining ship's plans and drawings, as guides for orientation within the wreck, virtually useless.

In early 1978, during the underwater operations, "Jock" stated in an English newspaper:

"There is still a challenging amount of work left because my divers have to do their thing in 90-feet of water and mud surrounded by rubbish like bedsprings, furniture, chunks of wood, china, ceramic, silverware, plumbing fixtures, remnants of carpet and curtains, etc. It's one big incredible, twisted, buckled mess down there."

After being severed from the wreck, sections weighing up to 250 tons were lifted out. Trapped within each section were unknown quantities of mud and debris, making it difficult at first to make sure that the weight being lifted from the wreck remained within the limits of the two cranes. It took about six months of cutting and lifting experience before estimated weights became more accurate so that very few sections had to be lowered back onto the seabed for re-cutting.

The recovered sections of the *Seawise University* were lifted from the water and placed onto flat-top barges. The larger portions of steel and debris were first cut up into standard sizes at scrap yards in Junk Bay, 11 miles away, and from there taken by overland route to China's steel rolling mills in Canton. The Queen Elizabeth's steel originally milled and forged at John Browns at Clydebank Scotland in the late 1930's, finally ended up in the construction of buildings within the fast-growing Chinese cities of Beijing (Peking) and Shanghai.

About a year into underwater operations, a decision had to be made whether to continue with piecemeal cutting, or try and refloat the entire amidships section of the wreck as a single unit. This unit incorporated the length of hull between frames 87 and 236, up to and including D-deck, which contained the forward and aft engine rooms, numbers 1, 2 and 3 boiler rooms, the turbo generator room, the water-softener and air conditioning plant. It was hoped that this could be done by utilising the potential buoyancy in the 87 wing tanks and double-bottom tanks found in this part of the vessel.

In order to achieve levity, all boilers and machinery, amounting to a total of 13,000 tons in weight, had to be removed. By October 1975, divers had access to parts of the boiler and engine rooms from where they could inspect the condition of the wing tanks. The inspection confirmed that some tanks were fire-damaged and would need repair to make them airtight prior to refloating the amidships section.

In the end, mainly for cost, time and risk factors, it was decided to continue with the piecemeal cutting of the remainder of the wreck.

Despite uncertainty regarding the weight of each of the 12 Yarrow water-tube boilers, a result of the complete lack of any original builders plans, it was obvious just from visual assessment that each complete boiler unit would be way beyond the lifting capability of the largest 250-ton floating Sheerleg Crane, and would therefore have to be cut into smaller pieces. It was found that the top section of the boilers, made up of boiler drums, air heaters and the upper half of the furnace, could be cut from the rest of the boiler unit relatively easily. However, even this section alone was too large to be lifted out of the water whole, so was carried underwater with the floating sheerlegs to Tsing Yi Island where they were beached at high tide and cut into smaller units that could finally be lifted onto the barges.

Now only the bottom part of each boiler furnace remained within the wreck, but their removal meant that diver safety would be compromised as it required the men to work in areas within the hull that were a considerable distance away from their means of access and escape from open water. Moreover, the divers had to work in tight spaces at a depth of around 90 feet, in total darkness, with the hull listing at 48 degrees, and with many overhead projections from which heavy debris could be dislodged by the movement of air hoses or supply lines from the surface.

Having been made aware of the critical safety issue, the Hong Kong Department of Marine showed complete sympathy to the divers, so much so that on the 13th September 1977, all wreck removal operations, once an unobstructed water depth of 60 feet had been reached over the rest of the wreck area, were terminated. This meant that only six of the ship's 12 boilers were totally removed – those on her port or high side, along with two of the main steam turbines. On the starboard or deepest side of the wreck, it was only necessary to sever the top part of the boilers. It was possible however, to remove much of the machinery from the fore and aft engine rooms. The minimum required water depth clearance above the wreck was achieved on the 15th March 1978 and on this day, the "butchering" of the hulk ceased, close to fifty months after it began.

Live and Let Die

In four years, some 8,000 tons of the ship was removed from above the water and a further 38,000 tons underwater. An approximate 15,000-ton, 140-metre-long piece of the former *RMS Queen Elizabeth* was abandoned. As this situation could have still presented an obstruction to vessels anchoring in the immediate vicinity, the excavation

Above: January 3rd, 1974 - A large and easily recognizable section of the *Queen Elizabeth's* forward superstructure has been cut free and is about to be placed on the waiting barge to the right. The shattered and fused glass of the windows, once upon a time allowed light into the First Class enclosed promenade which curved graciously around the First-Class Observation Lounge. (© South China Morning Post)

A portion of the house tops from the upper, forward superstructure has been removed and is being hoisted from the wreck by the large floating Sheerleg Crane. Late January 1974. (courtesy of HKSAR Information Services Department)

RMS Queen Elizabeth: the Unruffled Cunarder

Dwarfed by the sheer size of the job and from a tiny and unstable-looking boat, workmen from the Universal Dockyards Ltd. prepare a large piece of the former *Queen Elizabeth's* aft funnel to be raised out of the water after having been cut from its casing. Four workers can also be seen perched in the now-exposed funnel base with its six huge uptakes from her boilers. This image was taken soon after the above-water removal operations had begun, in January of 1974, two years after the fire. (© Corbis Photo)

173

Hong Kong: A 'Queen' Dies

Above: The *Queen Elizabeth*'s forward funnel was cut around its base and removed in one piece. It was towed on a flat barge 11 km away, to Junk Bay, where it was cut into standard-size pieces to be transported by train to China's steel mills in Canton. (Hong Kong Maritime Museum)

Below: By the beginning of February 1974, the steady cutting by blow torches and the removal of scrap steel by floating crane, has seen to the disappearance of the entire superstructure of the ship. (James Mackie)

was completely back-filled, covering what steel was left with 20-30 feet of mud.

The Queen Elizabeth's remains were casually interred in an unceremonious event that took place on the 19th April 1979. They lie, to this day, at the position of 22° 19'38.72" N and 114° 06'51.27" E.

If one looks closely at the first part of her grave's geographical coordinates (22° 19'38.72") an amazing coincidence is revealed. The Queen Elizabeth lived for 22 years as a transatlantic ocean liner; she was born (launched) in 1938 and died in 1972. It appears that, in some supernatural way, the "Lizzie" knew where the position of her own grave would be, integrating the site's geographical reference numbers into her personal epitaph.

Land reclamation on Tsing Yi Island has been prolific over the years, encroaching far out into the Rambler Channel. Since the termination of the wreck's removal, Container Terminal 9 has expanded so far out, that it now partially covers the *Seawise University*'s grave site. Nevertheless, most of the remains, although buried under the harbour floor, still lie in open water and many ships pass over them daily.

One large piece of the *RMS Queen Elizabeth* was unintentionally exhumed as the Rambler Channel was being dredged in 2004 to allow for the passage of ships with very deep draughts to berth alongside CT9. One of her four huge, manganese-bronze propellers, most likely the outermost starboard prop that was pressed deep into the soft seafloor as she rolled over on her side, was revealed. The historic relic was offered to the Government but they showed no interest in it. What became of the propeller after that is unknown, but most likely it was sold as scrap metal – almost 30 years after the wreck removal was terminated. It would have made the perfect commemorative piece for the Queen Elizabeth's grave site, placed atop CT9's seawall which runs directly over

RMS Queen Elizabeth: the Unruffled Cunarder

the wreck.

Sadly no inscribed plaque, nor memorial of any kind, can be found near the spot where, long ago, a wonderful ship was lost. There is however, something else nearby which, like the *Queen Elizabeth*, is also very big, beautiful and now teems with life. It stands long, tall and proud, just like the "Lizzie" did, and only a few feet away from her remains: Stonecutters Bridge, which opened to traffic in December 2009 – the second longest cable-stayed bridge in the world.

How fitting that such an impressive architectural and engineering feat, designed for the purpose of transporting life to and fro across a body of water, should be built almost directly above the grave of its maritime equivalent. The Stonecutters Bridge is therefore the unintentional marker which commemorates the spot where the *RMS Queen Elizabeth* died.

Above: March 1974 - Going… (Hong Kong Maritime Museum)
Below: …GONE! By mid-1974, Hong Kong had lost a major tourist attraction and the world had forever lost visual contact to a much-loved ocean liner. An oil boom and two wreck buoys are the only indicators to the wreck's now totally submerged position. (courtesy Karsten Petersen, photographer. global-mariner.com)

Hong Kong: A 'Queen' Dies

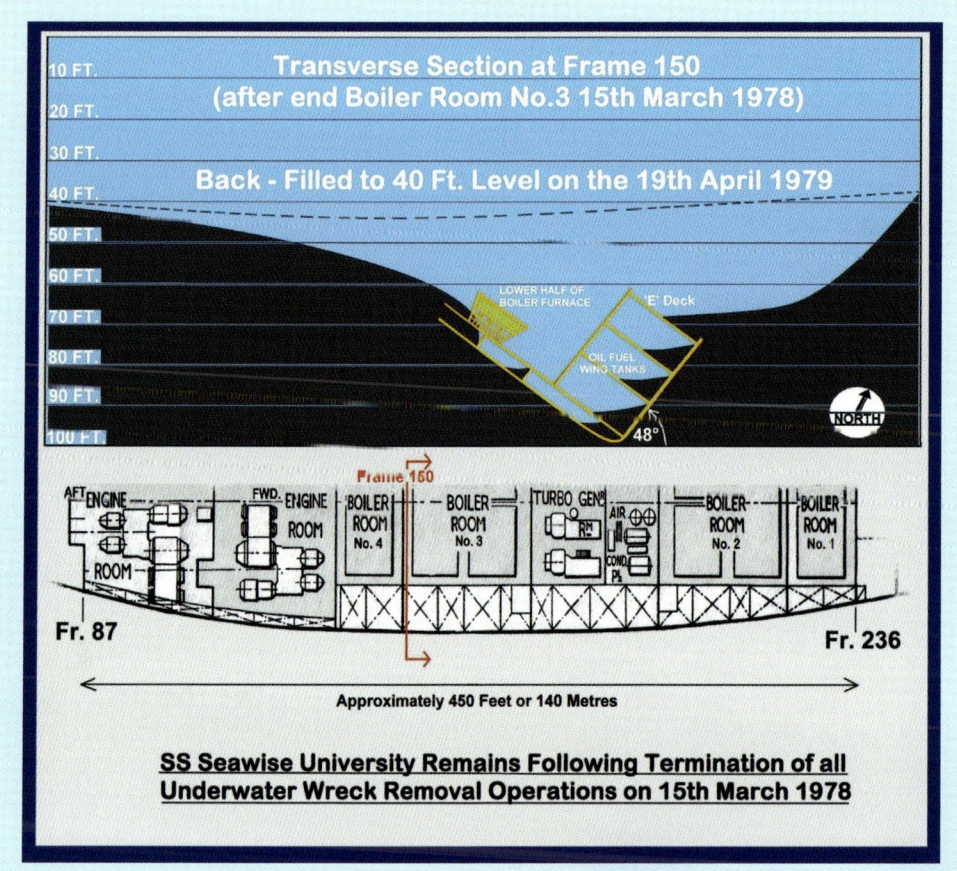

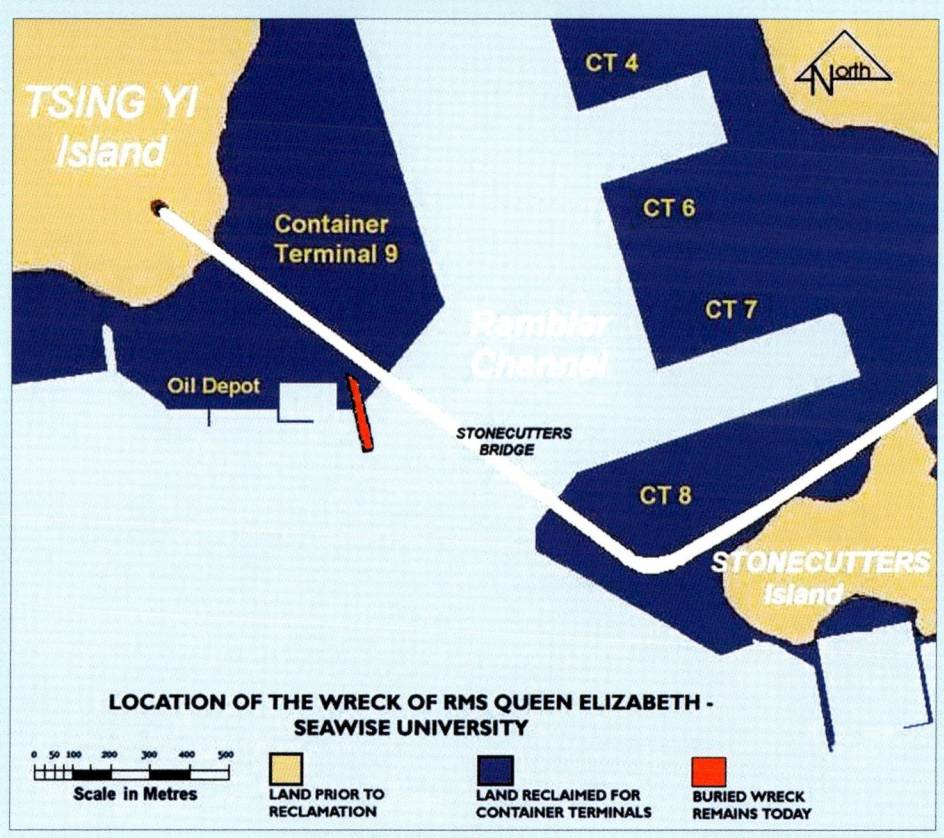

RMS Queen Elizabeth: the Unruffled Cunarder

A view of the Stonecutters Bridge and T9 Container Terminal taken from the peak of Tsing Yi Island. The superimposed red line indicates the present position of the *Seawise University*'s buried remains. (Ip Wan Lung)

SS *Seawise University*: What might have been. (Philpot collection)

Chapter 7

Preserved for Posterity

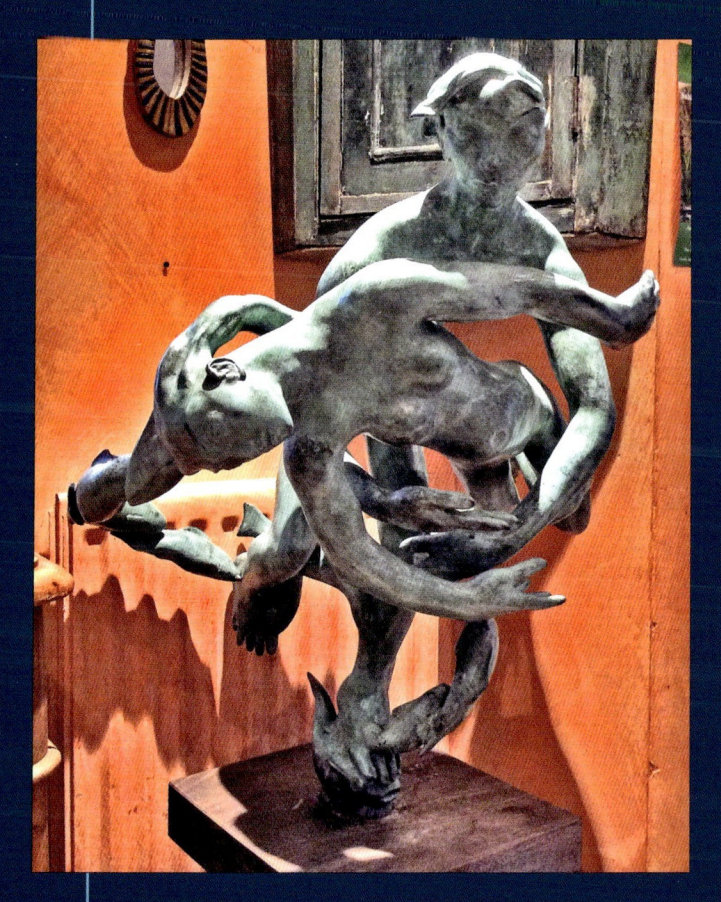

"It's hard for me to convey to you just why I am doing this;

I came over from Southampton on the *Queen Elizabeth* in 1950 and have since made three crossings on her and have grown to love this ship. Being somewhat horrified by the ignominious end to which she was subjected, I feel burdened to do something about her memory"

~ Harold Philpot, in his first letter to Commodore Geoffrey Thrippleton Marr, Feb 3rd 1982 ~

"For perfect proportion and beauty of line, the *Queen Elizabeth* must be the finest passenger liner the world has ever seen. Any effort to preserve that beauty for posterity, must be admired and worthwhile"

~ Commodore Geoffrey Thrippleton Marr to Harold Philpot, Feb 18 1982 ~

Harold Philpot: A Labour of Love

In a letter, dated 3rd February 1982, Harold Ernest Philpot confided to his new pen-friend, Commodore Geoffrey Marr that: "I have fallen in love with Queen Elizabeth! No, I have not been climbing drain pies at Buckingham Palace – that is not the right Queen Elizabeth. Mine is closer to my own age group. The Queen Mother, you ask? – also Queen Elizabeth, but no, not this one either. My heart-throb weighs 85,000 tons (British long tons) and is 1031 feet long – she is the *RMS Queen Elizabeth*."

It was during the flight to his native land England for a visit, in the summer of 1981, that Harold, a retired Automobile Body Designer for Chrysler in Detroit Michigan, was bitten by a bug – the *RMS Queen Elizabeth*

Replica of 'Oceanides': now in possession of the surviving members of the Wornum family. It was cast from the same mold as the original. (Reproduced with the kind permission of the family of Brigit Fletcher)

Harold Philpot poses on the landing of the First Class main entrance hall. Behind him is the stunning wood marquetry 'The Pilgrims Journey'. (Philpot Collection)

May 1950. The 34-year-old immigrant, on his way to America, poses next to number two cargo hatch. This was as far forward passengers were allowed to venture. (Philpot Collection)

Harold took this image on departure day - May 10th 1950. The ship is berthed at Docks 46/47 on the eastern side of Ocean Dock. (Philpot Collection)

Harold learning the ropes - on the *Queen Elizabeth's* Main Deck fore, or fo'c'sle, during his final voyage on the ship, in June 1964. (Philpot Collection)

New York, June 1964: Harold next to his ship, prior to boarding for the crossing back to visit his beloved homeland England. (Philpot Collection)

'When dealing with ships, one must expect to encounter sharks', commented Harold in reference to the steamship dealers. Yet even Harold found the temptation too great at times and occasionally spoilt himself with various non-work related memorabilia. In the picture are Cunard posters and photos, an original Perry life-ring and three of Commodore Marr's Uniforms. (Philpot Collection)

179

Making plans: The *Queen Elizabeth's* Breadth-Plan sheet during its creation. Drawn at ¼ inch to 1 foot or 1:48 scale, this particular drawing, emerged at over 21-foot -long and highly-detailed like the rest of the drawings. (Philpot/QEHS Collection)

A commemorative wooden builder's plaque was made by John Brown's Shipyard in 1938 and installed in the *Queen Elizabeth's* First-Class Stairwell. It is shown here, photographed in a heritage display cabinet aboard the now-decommissioned QE2. The graffiti carved into it by troops reads: 'Here we come Berlin' and 'It's all over now Hitler...run quick'. (QEHS Collection)

The *Queen Elizabeth's* final British master, Commodore Marr and Harold became close friends, both passing away within one year of each other. The Commodore generously donated, to the QEHS Museum, three of his bridge uniforms and the two flags seen here - the Cunard House Flag and his Commodore's Burgee. Both flags flew from the mainmast of the *Queen Elizabeth* from February 1966 to her final voyage in November 1968. Harold occasionally flew them from a mast attached to the roof of his home. (Philpot Collection)

Originally displayed on the street sidewalk, the bronze initials were relocated to the foyer of a bank at 88 Pine Street, Lower Manhattan - not far from their original position. The initials are set onto a chrome base plaque, inscribed with dedications to the ship. (Philpot Collection)

A monument to the *RMS Queen Elizabeth* was unveiled on September 20 1973. Weighing 7 tons, the monument contained the two and a half foot tall, bronze 'Q' and 'E' taken from the ship's bow name. It was set into the plaza next to what was once the Orient Overseas Building at 88 Pine Street, New York. Left to right in the picture are Mr Mori Chou of the C.Y. Tung Group in New York, C.Y Tung, New York Mayor John Lindsay and Commodore Marr. (Courtesy of C.Y Tung Archive Hong Kong)

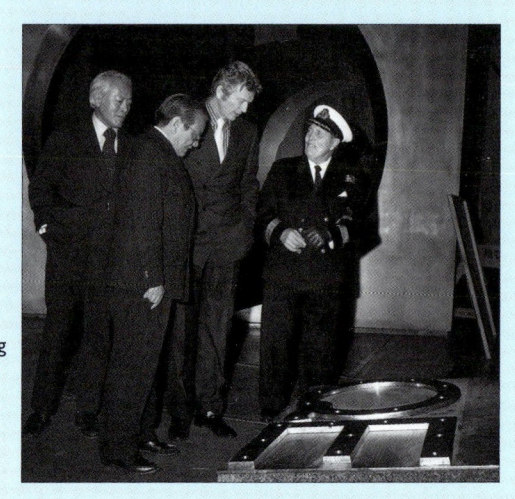

RMS Queen Elizabeth: the Unruffled Cunarder

"bug". Its effect caused him to devote the remainder of his life to the ship he had fallen in love with. Harold felt a strong and sudden urge to perpetuate the Lizzie's memory. It was, as he often put it, purely: "A labour of love".

Harold, born in 1916, in London England, migrated to the USA aboard the *Queen Elizabeth* in May 1950. In the latter part of his life he lived with his wife Beverley in Ararat, Virginia. This tiny village nestled near foothills of the Blue Ridge Mountains, is not too far from Mt. Airy in North Carolina, also known as Mayberry and made famous in the 1960's television sitcom, The Andy Griffith Show. Ararat is an idyllic spot and shares its name with a mountain in Turkey which is said to be the final resting place of another very famous ship – Noah's Ark. From 1982 until his death in 1996, Ararat provided Harold the peace and tranquillity needed to complete his burden.

Harold, "Chappie" to his friends, decided that he would use his skills as a qualified draughtsman to draw up a series of accurate, documentary scale-drawings, of the *RMS Queen Elizabeth*.

The *RMS Queen Elizabeth* Documentary Drawings

His first task was to transform the front of his house into a large drawing studio, museum, picture gallery and library, establishing the RMS Queen Elizabeth Historical Society. Then, daily, for more than ten years, Harold did what he loved to do – draw. His intention was to produce highly-detailed exterior views of the entire ship, along with equally-detailed, working deck-plans.

In order to acquire the plethora of information needed to produce such complicated drawings, Harold had to make two trips back to the Mother Land. Once back in England, he had copies made of hundreds of original Stewart Bale photographs, mostly of the ship's construction – which were kept at the Cunard Archives in both Glasgow and Liverpool – as well as official John Brown photographs, kept at the time in the University of Glasgow.

What both perplexed and frustrated Harold was the complete absence of any original builder's plans pertaining to the ship, although he had tried every avenue to locate them. It seemed that they had simply vanished. One possible explanation is that C.Y. Tung, upon purchasing the ship in 1971, managed to obtain the plans from John Brown, in which case they would have been destroyed in the fire, had they been kept aboard the *Seawise University* during her conversion.

Not being one to give up easily, and following a tip given to him from someone in Glasgow, Harold made a second reconnaissance trip to England. Success! On this occasion he managed to locate some 600 original John Brown drawings of the *Queen Elizabeth*, held in the Archives of Lloyds Register of Shipping in London, where they had been folded away for more than 40 years. He would quickly learn, however, that Archivists cannot be parted from their archives and that to have them all copied would cost him many hundreds of Pounds – much more than the cost of his airfare from the USA. The only option was to hand-trace as many of the drawings as he could in the time he was there, to gather all the relevant information he needed for his documentation.

Once back in Ararat, Harold began to accurately redraw the *Queen Elizabeth* at scales of 1:48 (¼ Inch = 1 foot) and 1:96 (1/8 Inch = 1 foot) – the same scale as the John Brown originals. Using such small scales meant that some of his drawings, like the full-length hull profiles and deck plans, reached a length of nearly 20-feet long, thus allowing for the incorporation an enormous amount of detail.

It is now established that the majority of original *Queen Elizabeth's* builder's plans no longer exist, never having reached their intended final destination: the University of Glasgow Archives. They were to be donated to these archives once John Brown's Shipbuilding Yard was liquidated in 1972. Harold's plans are therefore the most complete and accurate documentation of the *Queen Elizabeth* in existence. He had achieved what he set out to do – to perpetuate the memory of the *Queen Elizabeth* for future generations of ship lovers.

"Chappie's" unique and extraordinary drawings can be admired from the CD which accompanies this book. They have been scanned at high resolution from the original drawings and are thus suitable for enlarging and printing.

Pieces of the Past: *Queen Elizabeth* Artifacts

Given the completeness of destruction that the fires on the *Seawise University* caused, it stands to reason that, compared to other lost liners, far fewer artefacts originating from the "Lizzie" can be found today. Unlike the *SS Normandie*, a liner similarly consumed by fire, where the majority of her artwork, fittings and furniture were removed from the ship before the blaze, most of the *Queen Elizabeth's* interior paraphernalia, as far as can be discerned, were still on the ship that fateful day in 1972.

Had Cunard, instead of selling the *Queen Elizabeth* upon retirement, scrapped her, as was the fate of the *SS France/Norway* just a few years ago, then a great deal of her luxurious and beautiful trappings would have been saved and sold at auction to still be around and admired today.

Although a certain amount of liberation of items from the *Queen Elizabeth* must have taken place, there is no real way of knowing just what and how much was removed from the ship, especially during the two years she was in Florida when she was managed by "dubious owners", as quoted by Commodore Marr. Or, for that matter, during the six months the ship was in Hong Kong undergoing conversion as a floating university, when workmen of all sorts were coming and going in their hundreds. One only hopes that

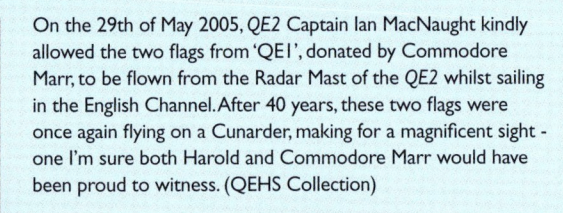

The *Queen Elizabeth's* 16-ton stem anchor, next to an identical monument to the one on Pine Street in Lower Manhattan New York, are displayed on a sidewalk lawn on Carson Street in Torrance, California. Currently, the protective plexi-glass cover to the bronze initials is split into two, becoming completely dislodged, with the elements, over the years, making it totally opaque. The building in the background was originally owned by C.Y. Tung. (QEHS Collection)

On the 29th of May 2005, *QE2* Captain Ian MacNaught kindly allowed the two flags from 'QE1', donated by Commodore Marr, to be flown from the Radar Mast of the *QE2* whilst sailing in the English Channel. After 40 years, these two flags were once again flying on a Cunarder, making for a magnificent sight - one I'm sure both Harold and Commodore Marr would have been proud to witness. (QEHS Collection)

After the *Queen Elizabeth* was decommissioned in 1968, the Bowes-Lyon's Royal Standard went on display in the Queen's Room aboard the *QE2*. The pennant now has a new, rightful home aboard the *M/V Queen Elizabeth*. (Richard Paul -photographer)

This four-inch-long countersunk or 'flush' rivet, was one of several recovered in 1972 by Captain Murdoch 'Jock' Anderson, the Salvage Master in charge of wreck removal operations. The inscription reads 'Queen Elizabeth – Hong Kong Harbour –May 1972' (QEHS Collection)

Left: In 1979, dredging of Hong Kong Harbour recovered two crumpled pieces of metal several hundred yards off Stonecutters Island. When they were cleaned-up and reshaped, it was discovered that the two copper plates were the original fire board panels from the bridge of the *RMS Queen Elizabeth*. (Philippe de Manny General Manager, Aberdeen Boat Club, Hong Kong)

Paint still adheres to this piece of steel shell plating cut from the *Queen Elizabeth's* hull at the time of her scrapping. The relic measures 310mm x 205mm x 30mm (12'x 8'x 1.2') and weighs 15kg (33 pounds) (From the collection of the Hong Kong Maritime Museum: Reproduced with permission)

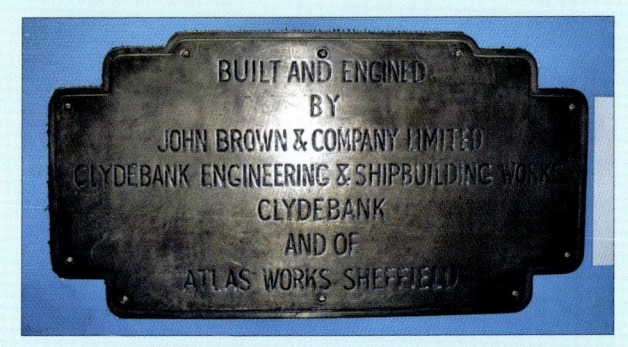

Another very significant, relic from *RMS Queen Elizabeth* is her brass builder's plate which was screwed to the forward superstructure. It is now displayed in Glasgow's Transport Museum, just a few miles up-river from Clydebank, where it was originally cast in 1938. (Robert Lightbody)

In the narrow hallway leading to the Mayors Office, at the Southampton Civic Centre, one can admire up close, the well-preserved glass mural created especially for the *Queen Elizabeth* by painter and muralist, Jan Juta. (QEHS Collection)

RMS Queen Elizabeth: the Unruffled Cunarder

items liberated are being treasured and well-preserved so that every now and then, some pieces may show up, giving others the chance to admire a piece of the "Lizzie".

A very significant relic from the *Queen Elizabeth* to have survived both the fire and the subsequent scrapping of the wreck, are two sets of bronze initials, "Q" and "E", from the ship's bow, which C.Y. Tung had removed after he purchased the former "Queen" in 1971. Today, one pair of these initials can be seen displayed inside the foyer of a bank at the Wall Street Plaza, located at 88 Pine Street in Lower Manhattan, New York, with the second set displayed on a sidewalk at the corner of Carson Street and Del Amo Circle East, in the Los Angeles suburb of Torrance, next to the ship's 16-ton bow anchor.

Unlike the pair in New York, the initials in California have been allowed to deteriorate over the years and are now in urgent need of restoration. Their protective plexi-glass cover has come apart completely, exposing them to both the elements and the threat of theft. Hopefully they will find their way to a more secure and worthy home, and none better exists than the nearby Queen Mary Hotel in Long Beach or aboard the latest *Queen Elizabeth*.

The most notable piece of artwork from the *Queen Elizabeth* to have survived to this day is the huge, decorated-glass mural (seen in detail in Chapter Four) designed and hand-painted by South African born artist Jan Juta and which was displayed in the ship's First Class Dance Salon. The mural was purchased from Cunard by a government surplus dealer in 1964 when the *Queen Elizabeth's* First Class salon was re-constructed to create a modern Mid-ships Bar and the fitting was no longer required aboard. Unfortunately, this historic mural is largely unbeknown to exist, currently well-hidden from the public eye, adorning a hallway leading to the Mayor's Office within the Southampton Civic Centre. It has been there, well-preserved since 1984.

A very important artwork from the *Queen Elizabeth* that survives to this day, aboard retired Cunarder the *QE2*, is the large portrait of the Queen Mother, Her Majesty Queen Elizabeth, painted by Sir Oswald Birley in 1948, which once hung prominently in the main First Class Lounge. A much smaller, printed replica of this painting has since been made and placed aboard the latest Cunard, the *Queen Elizabeth* but, not surprisingly, it has nowhere near the impact or value that the now-languishing original oil, in its ornately-carved wooden frame, does.

Two more "QE1" artifacts, apparently still aboard the *QE2* to this day, which could be displayed aboard the "QE3" are, firstly, a decorative wooden builders plaque which was originally installed on the "Lizzie's" main First Class Stairwell in 1938, which was later subjected to graffiti by American GI's on their way to war in Europe. While some tempting decorations from the ship were known to have gone "missing in action" during the war years, this relic managed to survive. Second, is the magnificent Queen Elizabeth Coat of Arms that was carved in lime wood by Bainbridge Copnall and so elegantly adorned the foyer to the *Queen Elizabeth's* First-Class Restaurant. The coat of arms can be seen in situ aboard the *Queen Elizabeth* in Chapter Four.

Thankfully, at least one original relic of the *RMS Queen Elizabeth*, formerly displayed aboard the *QE2*, has found its way onto "QE3" – the *M/V Queen Elizabeth*. This is the HM Queen Elizabeth Bowes-Lyon's Royal Standard, or banner of arms. The silk banner was presented in person by the then Queen, to the *RMS Queen Elizabeth* on the 28th July 1948 and was thereafter displayed in a glass case above the entrance to the First Class restaurant. Just recently, the banner has itself been reunited with its original wooden signage, a picture of which can also be seen in Chapter Four.

A handful of choice pieces from the *Queen Elizabeth* are also to be seen in Maritime Museums around the world. On display in the new Transport Museum of Glasgow, now a part of the Riverside Museum is the original John Brown and Co., brass builder's plate, which was originally welded on the forward superstructure of the ship. The plate was thoughtfully donated to the Museum by the Fire Master from Hong Kong's fire service, whose men salvaged it from the wreck.

In Shanghai, China, preserved in the C.Y. Tung Maritime Museum, is the *Queen Elizabeth's* large, brass fo'c'sle bell which was suspended from a metal arm at the ship's forepeak and was by far the largest bell aboard the ship. It now hangs, silently, adorning a small courtyard within the museum grounds.

In the autumn of 2012, a display dedicated to the memory of the *Queen Elizabeth* and the *Seawise University*, was set up in the new galleries of the Hong Kong Maritime Museum. Some of the items on display were six chrome-plated rivets taken from the wreck, a piece of steel plating, the bridge fire-alarm board recovered after harbour dredging, the Helmsman's Bell, which was located just outside the bridge door, and the burnt vestiges of the Red Ensign the ship was flying from the foremast the day she died in Hong Kong. (The flag can be seen still on the wreck in a photo in Chapter 6).

Captain Murdoch "Jock" Anderson, the Salvage Master in charge of wreck removal operations, collected a bucket-load of these steel rivets that had, due to the intensity of the fire, popped out of the plating in many areas of the ship. Jock, who was sufficiently undiplomatic to have, on occasion, bad-mouthed C.Y. Tung, had them chrome-plated and inscribed, then gave them away as presents to some of his closest friends and colleagues.

Word did eventually get back to the Tungs about Jock's discrediting of the wreck's owner and when Mr. Tung found out about the gifted rivets, he accused Jock of stealing his property. This infuriated the hot-tempered Scottish Salvage Master and, to put it mildly, much bad blood was generated between these two passionate men for the remainder of the time the *Queen Elizabeth* was being scrapped. An unfortunate but nonetheless riveting story – pun intended.

Preserved for Posterity

[The Last Mystery]

Mystery surrounds the fate of one iconic piece of the *RMS Queen Elizabeth's* artwork, which was well-remembered by those who travelled aboard the ship and often visible in many of her travel brochures and photographs. The colourful, five-metre wide and 4-metre high tapestry which hung in the First Class Restaurant – a splendid close-up picture of which can be seen in Chapter Four on page 81.

The tapestry was removed from the vessel when it reached New York at the beginning of WW2 and reinstated after the war was over. What's unclear is whether the tapestry was ever taken from the ship while it was in Florida, or if it made the trip to Hong Kong, in which case it would no longer exist today – unless, of course it was landed during the refit and survived the blaze which destroyed the ship and everything in it.

One person who would very much like to know the answer to this puzzle, is a gentleman whose parents were part of the team involved in the weaving of the tapestry. He still remembers, as a young boy, going with his parents to the disused farmhouse, in the South of England, where the tapestry was being created way back in 1938.

His father and a colleague went into the tapestry business in the 1930's at Aubusson in France – his father being Dutch. The two Dutchmen were given the contract from Cunard White Star to produce the tapestry on the condition it would be manufactured in Britain. In order to do so, all the machinery and workforce had to be sent over from France and the men then set up a UK Company. Most of the thread was spun and also dyed on-site to suit the colours chosen by the artists, but some had to be brought across from France – a fact which was well covered up back then so as not to cause any trouble with the unions. The tapestry was made in three parts and then sewn together.

If there is a chance the tapestry still exists somewhere today, and should anyone reading this happen to have a clue to its whereabouts, it could provide a happy end to the story, enabling one, now old Dutchman, to be reunited with an important work of art he saw being made as a young lad all those years ago.

The *Queen Elizabeth's* 'Noon' or Helmsman's Bell was displayed at the Hong Kong Maritime Museum's, 'Seawise University Exhibition'. Originally suspended outside the bridge, it was struck by the Helmsman at noon each day at sea - except during wartime when no hours were ever rung. It is significantly smaller than either the Crows Nest or Fo'c'sle bells. (From the collection of the Hong Kong Maritime Museum: Reproduced with permission)

Artist Bainbridge Copnall executed several carvings for the Queen Elizabeth, but The Queen's Royal Coat of Arms carved in Lime wood, was perhaps the most acclaimed of them all. In 1969, this magnificent carving was placed on display aboard the *QE2*, where, most likely, it remains to this day. (QEHS Collection)

The vestiges of the Red Ensign or Duster which flew from the *Seawise University's* foremast. The flag initially survived the fire but was reduced to this condition after falling onto the still-searing, foredeck. The flag was recovered by the Marine Branch of the Hong Kong Police and has been on display in their offices ever since. (Courtesy Hong Kong Marine Police and Hong Kong Maritime Museum)

A GE Co. ship-to-shore telephone from a First Class staterooms aboard the *Queen Elizabeth*. Often erroneously referred to as being made of Bakelite, (only black versions, which were not installed on the 'Queens', were made of Bakelite) these rare artefacts were in fact made of Urea-Formaldehyde, otherwise known as Roanoid Plastic. The *Queen Elizabeth* had 680 telephones on board, most of which were sold to the public when the ship was decommissioned. (Neil Carpenter of 'Antique Telephones')

Appendix 1: Chronology and Statistics

NOTABLE DATES

1935, JULY 29 — Government advance for building running mate to the *RMS Queen Mary* agreed.

1936, OCTOBER 6 — Contract placed with John Brown & Co. to build Hull "552".

1936, DECEMBER 4 — Keel plate laid.

1938, SEPTEMBER 3 — Britain declares war on Germany.

1938, SEPTEMBER 27 — Hull is named the *Queen Elizabeth* and launched.

1939, NOVEMBER 2 — Winston Churchill requisitions the *Queen Elizabeth* as troop ship.

1939, NOVEMBER 4 — The ship is painted in drab grey colour.

1940, NOVEMBER 19 — Certificate of registry dated.

1940, FEBRUARY 22 — First crew boards.

1940, FEBRUARY 26 — the HMS *Queen Elizabeth* leaves Clydebank to start maiden voyage.

1940, MARCH 2 — Leaves the Clyde's Tail O the Bank incognito for New York.

1940, MARCH 7 — Arrives in New York.

1940, NOVEMBER 12 — Leaves New York to start war duties as a troop ship.

1941, APRIL 9 — Encounters future running mate the *RMS Queen Mary* at sea for the first time off Sydney Heads Australia.

1946, MARCH 6 — Wartime duties end.

1946, MARCH 8 — While tied up at Berth 101 at New Dock Southampton, a serious fire ignites on Promenade Deck, in a space used as an isolation hospital during WWII and comes close to destroying the ship. The fire was started by a workers cigarette igniting volatile fumes from a broken bottle of spirits and took three hours to extinguish. The deck was pushed up into a blister.

1946, MARCH 31 — Anchors off Gourock to begin post-war refit.

1946, OCTOBER 8 — Official sea trials held in the Firth of Clyde.

1946, OCTOBER 16 — First commercial voyage as a passenger liner — Southampton to New York.

1946, DECEMBER 3 — Baby girl born on board, logically-named Elizabeth.

1947, APRIL 14 — Grounded for 26 hours on Brambles Bank.

1948, APRIL 7 — First call into Cherbourg.

1948, DECEMBER 8 — First and last time QE and QM docked together in New York wearing Cunard livery.

1953, JANUARY 30 — Potentially disastrous, unexplained fire ignites in the wardrobe of cabin M93 while the ship was in dry dock for winter overhaul.

1953, JANUARY 31 — Second potentially disastrous fire in less than 24 hours discovered in cabin C146 ignited in a pile of oil-soaked rags — another mystery, but like the previous one, probably linked to disgruntled militant Unionists.

1953, OCTOBER 22 — Dents hull after colliding with the pier at Cherbourg.

1954, OCTOBER — Her Majesty Queen Elizabeth, The Queen Mother, in her first voyage on the ship, travels to New York.

1955, FEBRUARY 23 — Stabilizers added.

1957, FEBRUARY 14 — First peace-time call at Halifax, NS.

1959, FEBRUARY 5 — Struck a submerged object in Cherbourg Roads — slight hull damage.

1959, JULY 29 — Collides with the freighter *American Hunter* in dense fog in Lower New York Harbour.

1960, SEPTEMBER 27 — Fire reported in cabins while ship in Southampton.

1961, FEBRUARY 2 — Fire in Galley.

1963, FEBRUARY 21 — Departs on her first cruise.

1963, MARCH — Victim of a bomb hoax in New York.

1964, JANUARY 11 — Fire in propeller tunnel while in dry dock.

1965, JANUARY 25 — Grounds on a sand bank approaching Cherbourg in dense fog.

1965, DECEMBER 11 — Enters the Firth of Clyde Dry Dock for a major cruising refit. Departs on 12 March 1966 with refit incomplete.

1966, JANUARY — Lido Deck and outdoor pool added.

1966, MAY 16 — Start of British Seaman's Strike. Ship laid-up until 2nd July — a total of 47 days.

1967, JANUARY 17 — Departs New York with just 70 passengers. Called the "Ghost-ship voyage".

1967, APRIL 26 — Decision made to retire the ship and put her up for sale.

1967, MAY 5 — First call into Cobh.

1967, SEPTEMBER 25 — 00:10 — The final mid-Atlantic meeting of QE and QM.

1967, OCTOBER 12 — QE and QM docked in Southampton. Last time they would ever be together.

1968, OCTOBER 30 — Last departure from New York.

1968, NOVEMBER 6 — The Queen Mother pays farewell visit to the ship.

1968, NOVEMBER 8 — Departs on her Farewell Cruise.

1968, NOVEMBER 28 — Last departure from Southampton bound for Port Everglades.

1968, DECEMBER 8 — Berths at Port Everglades, Florida.

1969, FEBRUARY 14 — *The Elizabeth* opens to the public for the first time.

1970, SEPTEMBER 17 — Purchased by C.Y. Tung and renamed *Seawise University*.

1971, FEBRUARY 10 — Departs Port Everglades for Hong Kong in what would be her final voyage.

1972, January 10 — Destroyed by fire in Hong Kong Harbour.

1974, JANUARY 1 — Scrapping of the wreck begins and terminates more than four years later, on the 15th March 1978.

1979, APRIL 19 — A submerged, 140-meter-long section of the hull containing the lower portion of a boiler and engine room is covered over with sediment.

2004 — Dredging of Hong Kong harbour uncovers one of her propellers.

Vital Statistics and Technical Data

BUILDERS — John Brown & Co. Ltd, Clydebank

OFFICIAL REGISTRATION NUMBER — 166290

OFFICIAL CALL SIGN — GBSS

OWNERS & PORT OF REGISTRY — Cunard S.S. Co., Liverpool (1940-1970), Seawise Foundation Ltd., Bahamas (1971-1974)

LENGTH OVERALL — 1,031 feet (314 Meters)

BREADTH — 118 feet (36 meters)

FREEBOARD — 35 feet (10.6 meters)

HEIGHT OF FUNNELS — Forward: 80 feet above Boat Deck (24.3 meters)

AFT: 78 feet above Boat Deck (23.7 meters)

HEIGHT OF MASTHEADS TO KEEL — 233 feet (71 meters)

HEIGHT OF MASTHEADS TO WATER LEVEL — 194 feet (59.13 meters)

DECKS — 14

PUBLIC ROOMS — 37

ELEVATORS — 35

WATERTIGHT COMPARTMENTS — 140

PORTHOLES AND WINDOWS — 2,000

RIVETS — More than 10 million

TONNAGES — Gross: 83,673 GRT (82,997,000gt after 1965/66 refit)

Nett: 41,260 NT

Deadweight: 15,856 DW

Total Metal in hull and machinery: 50,000 tons

DISPLACEMENT — 79,181 (loaded)

DRAFT — 39 feet (loaded) (11.8 meters)

PASSENGER CAPACITY — 2,288 (1946) 2,043 (1966) (subject to variation)

TOTAL NUMBER OF CREW — 1,296

TOTAL NUMBER OF LIFEBOATS — 26

CARRYING CAPACITY OF ALL BOATS — 3,492 souls

ANCHORS — Three, each weighing 16 tons with 990 feet of chain cable.

PROPELLERS — Four, four-bladed bronze-manganese screws, each weighing 32 tons and 18 feet in diameter.

WHISTLES — Three Tyfon whistles — two on forward stack and one on the aft stack. Each weighing one-ton, with the sound audible up to ten miles away.

RUDDER — 140 tons

TURBINE BLADES — 257,000

ENGINES — Four sets of single-reduction, geared, steam-driven turbines, developing 160,000 shaft horsepower and driving four screws.

BOILERS — Twelve water tubes, burning oil fuel, supplying steam to main engines at a pressure of 425 lb. per square inch and at a temperature of 750° F.

POWER STATIONS — Two stations producing a total 8,800KW of electricity.

OIL FUEL CAPACITY — 9,331.5 tons

SPEED — Maximum 30-32 Knots

Service speed 28.5 Knots

WAR SERVICE — February 26 1940 – March 6 1946, transporting 811,324 troops, travelling 500,000 sea miles world-wide.

TOTAL NUMBER OF NORTH ATLANTIC CROSSINGS — 896

PASSENGERS CARRIED IN PEACETIME — 2,300,000

TOTAL MILES STEAMED — 3,472,672

Appendix 2

Appendix 2 – Masters of The Queen Elizabeth

The following list of 29 mariners is a roll-call, in chronological order, of the elite group of men who were Masters of the *RMS Queen Elizabeth* throughout her lifetime – in war and in peace. Listed beside each name are the decorations and recognitions they achieved and the date from when they first took command.

Today, aboard Cunard's *M/v Queen Elizabeth*, a plaque, inscribed with the names of these Captains, is located outside of the port side entrance to the Commodore Club, on Deck 10 forward. At least four of the *Queen Elizabeth's* Masters have been buried at sea and three of the Lizzie's Masters – Commodore William Warwick, Captain Joseph Woolfenden and Captain William Law, have had the honour of captaining three Cunard "Queens" in their career, the *Queen Mary*, the *Queen Elizabeth* and the *Queen Elizabeth 2*.

Honours, Decorations and Medals – Definition of Acronyms
R.D. = The Decoration (medal) for Officers of the Royal Naval Reserve
R.N.R = Royal Navy Reserve (volunteer reserve force of the Royal Navy)
D.S.C = Distinguished Service Cross (third level military decoration awarded to Officers)
Kt. = Knight Bachelor
C.B.E. = Commander of the Most Excellent Order of the British Empire
O.B.E = Officer of the Most Excellent Order of the British Empire
LL.D. = Honorary Doctor of Laws

1. **Captain John C. Townley** (R.N.R) 19th February 1940.
2. **Captain Ernest M. Fall** (D.S.C., C.B.E, R.D., R.N.R.,) 28th August 1941.
3. **Commodore Sir James G.P. Bisset** (Kt., C.B.E., R.D., R.N.R., LL.D.) 7th September 1942.
4. **Commodore Sir Cyril Gordon Illingworth** (Kt., R.D., R.N.R.) 15th January 1943.
5. **Captain Roland Spencer** (R.D., R.N.R.) 9th November 1943.
6. **Commodore Charles Musgrave Ford** (C.B.E., R.D., R.N.R.) 27th April 1944.
7. **Captain John D. Snow** (R.D., R.N.R.) 9th September 1947.
8. **Captain John A. MacDonald** (R.D., R.N.R.) 24th November 1947.
9. **Commodore George Edward Cove** 13th August 1948.
10. **Commodore Harry Grattidge** (O.B.E) 14th December 1948.
11. **Captain Richard B. G. Woollatt** (R.D., R.N.R.) 25th August 1949.
12. **Captain Harry Dixon**, 15th August 1950.
13. **Commodore Sir Ivan Thompson** (Kt.) 14th June 1951.
14. **Commodore Robert G. Thelwell** (O.B.E., R.D., R.N.R.) 4th September 1951.
15. **Captain Donald W. Sorrell**, 31st March 1953.
16. **Commodore George H. G. Morris** (C.B.E) 22nd August 1956.
17. **Commodore Charles S. Williams,** 8th May 1957.
18. **Captain Alexander B. Fasting** (R.D., R.N.R.) 19th July 1957.
19. **Commodore John W. Caunce** (R.D., R.N.R) 21st July 1958.
20. **Commodore Donald M. MacLean** (D.S.C., R.D., R.N.R.) 5th August 1959.
21. **Commodore Fredrick George Watts** (R.D., R.N.R.) 14th July 1960.
22. **Captain Eric A. Divers** (O.B.E., R.D. R.N.R.) 25th July 1962.
23. **Captain Sidney A Jones** (R.D., R.N.R.) 15th November 1962.
24. **Commodore Geoffrey Thrippleton Marr** (D.S.C., R.D., R.N.R.) April 1964.
25. **Captain John Treasure Jones** (R.D., R.N.R.) 5th July 1965.
26. **Commodore William Eldon Warwick** (C.B.E., R.D., R.N.R.) 29th October 1965, (First Captain of the *QE2* in 1969).
27. **Captain George E. Smith** March 1966 (Captained the *QE2* in 1969).
28. **Captain Joseph Eric Woolfenden** (R.D., R.N.R., D.S.C.) 3rd May 1967, (Captained the *QE2* in 1970).
29. **Captain William James Law** (R.D., R.N.R.) 1st June 1967, (Captained the *QE2* in 1970).

Three Masters reunite: Pictured aboard *QE2*, on 4th of September 1995 are, from left to right, *QE2*'s Master, Commodore Ronald Warwick, his father Commodore Bil Warwick and Commodore Geoffrey Marr. The *QE2* was docked in the Port of Invergordon in Scotland. (Courtesy of Commodore Ron Warwick)

Commodore James G.P. Bisset: Commodore Bisset, knicknamed 'Jovial James', was one Cunard's cheeriest and amicable Masters. In retirement, he chose to live out the rest of his days in Sydney Australia.

RMS Queen Elizabeth: the Unruffled Cunarder

Commodore Sir Cyril Gordon Illingworth: Best remembered as the *Queen Mary's* Master during World War Two, Commodore Illingworth's pet hate were 'Irish Pennants' - loose or untidy ends of rope, dangling where they should not dangle.

Commodore Harry Grattidge: Commodore Harry Grattidge secured his Masters Certificate in 1913, joining Cunard as Fourth Officer on the *Carmania* and later on the *Carpathia*, the Cunarder which rescued passengers from the ill-fated *Titanic*. He survived brushes with death in both World Wars when the ship he was on was sunk. This included the *Lancastria*, one of the worst, single maritime horrors of WW2.

Commodore Charles Musgrave Ford: Although he stood over 6-foot tall, Captain Ford was affectionately known as 'tiny' by his Cunard colleagues. Upon retiring he stated: 'I dread the thought of the first time I will have to stand on the dock at Southampton and watch the *Queen Elizabeth*, hull down on the horizon, going away without me'.

Captain Richard B. G. Woollatt: During WW2, while serving aboard the Queen Elizabeth as 'Staffie' or Staff Captain, Woollatt had the reputation of being somewhat of a loudmouth. Daily, during forenoon inspections, he would lead a bullyish entourage, made up of the Master at Arms, Bosun and Bosun's Mates, around the ship, loudly bursting into crew quarters. Insubordinate crew and those who had been absent the day before, were summoned to the Bridge where he held court every morning, logging them a day's pay and an extra dollar to help pay for a Spitfire. His frequent logging of crew wages earned him the nickname of 'The Lumber Boss'.

Captain John D. Snow: Captained both 'Queens' between 1947 and 1948.

Commodore Ivan Thompson: In 1910, at fifteen years of age, Thompson first went to sea. 'Why? …God Knows!' he would say. 'In those days, the sea was romantic. Travel was a rare and inviting thing to a young fellow. Today, there's nothing to it! Everyone's been everywhere, and it's all so easy.' A fanatical supporter of Liverpool Football Club, as soon as the results came in over the radio, they were sent to the bridge. If the news was bad, officers knew to keep out of his way for the rest of the day.

Commodore George Edward Cove: Commodore Cove began his seagoing career in 1905 as a 15-year-old on a three-mast sailing vessel earning, as all cadets did at the time, the sum of one shilling per month. He served, throughout both World Wars, on many Cunarders.

Commodore Robert G. Thelwell: In his autobiography - *I captained the Big Ships*, Thelwell writes: 'To command a 'Queen' is the ambition of every Cunard officer and few can achieve it. The 'Queens' are magnificent ships, the world's best, and I love them both'. His impressive sea-going career spanned fifty years and it saw him serving in both World Wars.

Appendix 3

Captain Donald W. Sorrell: Joining Cunard in 1918, Sorrell was RMS *Caronia's* first Captain in 1949. In 1953 he became Relief Captain of the 'Lizzie' and in 1954 was appointed Master of the *RMS Queen Mary* until his retirement in 1956.

Commodore Geoffrey Thrippleton Marr: 'While I was away on one cruise, my seven-year-old wrote her first letter to me, It said: 'Dear Daddy, please come home soon, you have been away so long we feel as if we have no Daddy'.' Captain Marr was often torn between his terra firma home and the sea.

Commodore George H. G. Morris: Following a wild North Atlantic storm at the end of March 1959, which delayed the *Queen Elizabeth's* entry into New York by thirteen hours, Captain Morris sent word to newsmen meeting the ship: 'I'm sorry but I am too exhausted from the very, very rough crossing to be interviewed'.

Captain John Treasure Jones: Trevor Jones Captained the 'QE' for a single round-trip in 1965. In order for him to make this trip, he first had to discharge himself from hospital where he was recovering after having his tonsils removed. The day after bringing the *Queen Elizabeth* back to Southampton, he returned to his designated command - his beloved *RMS Queen Mary*. Captain Jones remained with the *Queen Mary* for the rest of her Cunard days.

Commodore William Eldon Warwick: 'My parents did not christen me 'Bil', I did that myself later. The world is full of Bills with two l's and I saw no reason why I should automatically fall into line.' Bil Warwick was relief Captain on the 'QE' for a return voyage in October 1965.

Commodore John W. Caunce: In an interview with local newspapers following his retirement, Captain Caunce revealed: 'I am entitled to unemployment pay but I never really thought it would come to this! Over 40 years with Cunard, in charge of the world's greatest liners and now… I'm on the dole'

Captain George E. Smith: A relief captain on the 'QE' in March 1966, Captain Law was one of only four Masters to Captain both the *RMS Queen Elizabeth* and the *QE2*. The other three were Warwick, Woolfenden and Law.

Commodore Donald M. MacLean: In 1916, the Chairman of the Cunard Line, Lord Inverclyde, sailed into Maclean's hometown of Stornoway in Scotland, in his yacht. MacLean was introduced to His Lordship who was favourably impressed by the young lad and duly instructed his father to apply to Cunard headquarters in Liverpool. The following year, Donald MacLean was an indentured apprentice with the Cunard Line. From that moment on, the only way was up. Maclean, who often referred to the *Queen Elizabeth* as 'the floating city' took command of Cunard's flagship on the 19th of May 1960.

RMS Queen Elizabeth: the Unruffled Cunarder

Captain Joseph Eric Woolfenden: Woolfenden captained the *Queen Elizabeth* for just one round trip, in 1967. It was on this voyage, with only 711 passengers aboard, that Captain Woolfenden received a radio message instructing him to open a sealed envelope which informed him and the crew of the pending retirement of both 'Queens'.

Captain William James Law: On the 15th of September 1967, the *Queen Elizabeth* passed the *Queen Mary* mid-Atlantic for the penultimate time. Captain Law, serving as substitute Captain for an ill Commodore Marr, sent a telegram to the bridge of the soon-to-be-retired *Queen Mary*: 'As we pass on your final Atlantic voyage we send you greetings and express our sadness that time is running out and that you will soon be leaving this Atlantic Ocean which you have crossed so many times - we salute the old Atlantic greyhound and the last of the Cape Horners.'

Commodore Marr, here welcoming passengers for pre-dinner-drinks in the *Queen Elizabeth's* First-Class Lounge, was always appreciative of the privileges and opportunities that came with his job, especially the chance to meet a wide variety of people. (Philpot Collection)

Commodore Geoffrey Thrippleton Marr – A Good Friend to all.

Geoffrey Marr, the final Captain of the *RMS Queen Elizabeth*, stood out among those who preceded him, not because of any notable superior navigational skills, but for his sensitivity, outspoken honesty, and genuine kindness. His good nature and approachability made him a much respected person – by his fellow crew and passengers alike. His love of poetry came second only to his love for the *Queen Elizabeth*.

Geoffrey Marr was born on the 8th of August 1908 in Pontefract, West Yorkshire. Since his childhood days the sea was such an irresistible attraction to him that he decided in 1922, against his parent's wishes, to put his name down for a cadetship aboard the *HMS Conway*, the Mercantile Marine Service Association's training ship for Royal Navy, Royal Navy Reserve and Merchant Navy officers.

Marr left Conway in 1924 and took up an apprenticeship on the banana boats of Elders and Fyffes Ltd., a subsidiary of the United Fruit Company of Boston, Massachusetts. His first appointed job was to polish the brass on the docking bridge – a simple task that ended up taking him much longer that it normally would have due the pronounced heaving of the vessel in the choppy sea and his frequent dashes to the ship's side to regurgitate.

In 1936 he joined Cunard as a Junior Third Officer in the *Andania* and as war broke out, he served as Watch-keeping Officer on the *HMS King George V*, the Flagship of the Home Fleet during the operations which led to the sinking of the dreaded German battleship the *Bismarck*.

During World War II, he served on various escort vessels as Navigator and Staff Officer and received his Distinguished Service Cross in 1946, the same year he returned to duties for Cunard as Junior First Officer on the Second *Mauretania*.

Marr boarded the *Queen Elizabeth* for the first time in 1947 when, as the first big liner to be returned to commercial service after The War, she was busy collecting the cream of transatlantic trade. He was made Staff Captain in 1953, first on the *Queen Mary* then followed by the *Caronia* in 1954 and the *Queen Elizabeth* in 1955. He also had brief spells as Relieving Captain in the *Ascania*, the *Franconia*, the *Parthia* and the *Samaria* in 1955.

In April 1957, Marr was finally given his own permanent command – the *RMS Scythia*. As this was his first ship, she was "a thing of beauty", as he put it. Regrettably, he would have to take the 37-year-old liner on her sad, final voyage to the breakers at Inverkeithing less than one year later.

From 1958 to 1962, Geoffrey Marr captained both the *Ivernia* and the *Carinthia*, on Cunard's Canadian Service, a job which tested nerves due to frequent sailings under dense fog and ice.

In 1962 he was relieved to be given the job of captaining the "Green Goddess", the *RMS Caronia*, travelling in warmer climates as

Appendix 2

Commodore's Table: To dine with the Captain was a hallmark of social eminence. For the social climbers aboard, some of whom would even go so far as bribing the Captain's Tiger and the purser's staff to secure their seat at the table, it was an almighty achievement to be seen rubbing elbows with the head of the ship. In the background is the huge woven tapestry which can be seen in detail on page 81. (Philpot Collection)

she circled the globe on her popular world cruises. But the appointment also meant he would spend a great deal of time away from home and his family ashore – something which ate away at him.

From November 1963 to October 1965, he had no ship of his own, acting instead as Relieving Captain of both "Queens" as well as taking over for the occasional cruise on the second *Mauretania*.

Between October 1965 and January 1966, he was the full-time commander of the *Queen Mary*.

Geoffrey Marr became Commodore of the Cunard Fleet on the 1st January 1966 and after bidding an emotional farewell to the *Queen Mary* that same month, he was appointed as Commodore Captain of the *RMS Queen Elizabeth*, joining the ship in March as her major cruising refit was nearing completion.

Commodore Marr was the one person who took it the hardest when news of the ship's retirement was announced. He felt deep empathy for the many hundreds of men and women, who would suddenly be without their means of livelihood, especially those who were not old enough for normal retirement. During a voyage in November 1967, he had the unenviable task of assembling his ship's company and reading to them the chairman's message that, in addition to the two "Queens", the *Caronia*, the *Sylvania* and the *Carinthia* were also to be withdrawn.

The Commodore was adamant that following positive signs of some solid bookings and the expensive cruising refit, the "Lizzie" should have remained in service for a few more years. The Commodore let it be known to the powers that be that he felt they were making a tactical mistake. Cunard's chiefs had waited too long to restructure and should have reacted much sooner to losses by cutting back on the company's many superfluous shore jobs, both in the UK and USA, instead.

It was very unlike the Commodore to ever openly criticise his employer and on this occasion his honesty was probably one of the reasons why he was not called to Captain the new liner *QE2*. When the "Lizzie" was decommissioned at the end of 1968, Commodore Marr, at 60 years of age, was still three years under Cunard's mandatory retirement age of 63; like his ship, he still had a few more good years of service left in him. Instead, as one of his colleagues aboard the *Queen Elizabeth* put it. "He was repaid for his loyalty over the years by having his job shot from under him".

After Geoffrey had brought the *Queen Elizabeth* to Port Everglades on the 8th of December 1968 he, along with a skeleton crew of about 150, had signed an agreement to 'stand-by' the ship for nine months. With sadness and great regret, Commodore Marr bid farewell to his ship on the 4th of August 1969. His official duties with Cunard ended on December 31st that year.

In retirement, Commodore Marr was still a very active man with

The Commodore in his day room with Beverley Martinez and baby son Ramon in 1968. Beverley, a Spanish dancer as part of act performing on the ship recalls: 'He was a wonderful man and a good friend to all'. (Philpot Collection)

A photo taken in 1990 showing the Commodore, by then in his 80's, at home in Salisbury, greeting Everette Hoard of Long Beach California, who'd travelled to England specifically to meet his hero. Today Everette is Honorary Commodore of The Queen Mary docked in Long Beach and still Commodore Marr's biggest fan. (Philpot Collection)

an excellent mind and memory. After writing his wonderful autobiography *The Queens and I* in 1973, he travelled and lectured on his life on the sea, captivating audiences with his vivid description of the *Bismarck's* sinking, and nostalgically talking about his great love – the big ships of the Cunard Line.

The Commodore always welcomed any opportunity offered to relive those wonderful days as master of the "Queens". He often received visitors from overseas to his cottage in the New Forest, where he would sit and chat with his adoring fans for hours. Deep down, he still yearned for the busier, more interesting days when he was in charge of the world's most luxurious ships.

His health became progressively more fragile in his later years, suffering a couple of very nasty falls due to a completely worn out knee and bad ankles which caused him excruciating pain, much frustration and misery.

Commodore Marr, one of Britain's most honoured seamen, much-loved and with many happy memories, died on March the 4th 1997 aged 88. His ashes were scattered on the North Atlantic from the *QE2* on April 14th, in position Lattitude 47 Deg 00 mins North, Longitiude 30 Deg 00 mins West.

"I have had a good life, one which has been satisfying in a professional sense. Learning and watching from other and better sailors doing their job in the days when standards of behaviour and excellence were higher than they are today. I have attempted to follow their flag and to pass on their standards." (Geoffrey Marr, *The Queens and I*)

Commodore Marr's ashes were committed to the deep on the 14th April 1997 from the *QE2*. Cunard announced publically at the time: 'His death marks an end of a seagoing era; a link with some of the most famous ships in Cunard's history has gone and will be greatly missed.' From left to right; John Duffy, Hotel Manager; Elaine McKay, Social Director; Terry Foskett, Hotel Officer; Ian McNaught, Chief Officer; Archdeacon R. Willing, Chaplain; Captain Hasell, Master; Jonathan Leavor, Purser; Ray Heath, Staff Captain, and Alan Parker, Security Officer. (Cunard Archive)

Appendix 3: R.M.S Queen Elizabeth Cruises

CRUISE VOYAGE 1. 21st – 26 Feb 1963 (New York—Nassau—New York)
CRUISE VOYAGE 2. 28th Feb -5th Mar 1963 (New York—Nassau—New York)
CRUISE VOYAGE 3. 6th – 11th Mar 1963 (New York—Nassau—New York)
CRUISE VOYAGE 4. 21st – 26th Nov 1963 (New York—Nassau—New York)
CRUISE VOYAGE 5. 27th Nov – 2nd Dec 1963 (New York—Nassau—New York)
CRUISE VOYAGE 6. 5th – 10th Feb 1964 (New York—Nassau—New York)
CRUISE VOYAGE 7. 12th – 17th Feb 1964 (New York—Nassau—New York)
CRUISE VOYAGE 8. 19th – 24th Feb 1964 (New York—Nassau—New York)
CRUISE VOYAGE 9. 27th Feb – 23rd Mar 1964 ("Med. Cruise") (New York—Las Palmas—Tangier—Piraeus—Naples—Cannes—Gibraltar—Lisbon—New York)
CRUISE VOYAGE 10. 26th – 31st Mar 1964 (New York—Nassau—New York)
CRUISE VOYAGE 11. 23rd – 28th Dec 1964 (New York—Nassau—New York)
CRUISE VOYAGE 12. 29th Dec 1964 – 3rd Jan 1965 (New York—Nassau—New York)
CRUISE VOYAGE 13. 18th Feb – 23rd Feb 1965 (New York—Nassau—New York)
CRUISE VOYAGE 14. 26th Feb – 23rd Mar 1965 ("Med. Cruise") (New York—Las Palmas—Tangier—Cannes—Naples—Piraeus—Gibraltar—Funchal—New York)
CRUISE VOYAGE 15. 6th – 12th Nov 1965 (New York—Bermuda—Nassau—New York)
CRUISE VOYAGE 16. 7th – 12th Apr 1966 (New York— Bermuda New York)
CRUISE VOYAGE 17. 28th Oct 1966 – 22nd Nov 1966 ("Indian Summer Cruise") (New York—Bermuda—Ponta Delgada—Lisbon—Gibraltar—Funchal—Las Palmas—Dakar—Barbados—Caracas Bay—St. Thomas—New York)
CRUISE VOYAGE 18. 22nd – 27th Dec 1966 (New York—Nassau—New York)
CRUISE VOYAGE 19. 28th Dec 1966 – 2nd Jan 1967 (New York—Nassau—New York)
CRUISE VOYAGE 20. 4th – 15th Jan 1967 ("West Indies Cruise") (New York—St. Thomas—Caracas Bay—La Guaira—Trinidad—New York)
CRUISE VOYAGE 21. 3rd – 18th Feb 1967 ("West Indies Cruise") (New York—Cristobal—La Guaira—Caracas Bay—Barbados—St. Thomas—Nassau—New York)
CRUISE VOYAGE 22. 21st Feb – 31st Mar 1967 ("Med. Cruise") (New York—Las Palmas—Gibraltar—Palma—Alexandria—Piraeus—Alexandria—Beirut—Haifa—Messina—Naples—Cannes—Barcelona—Lisbon—Madiera—New York)
CRUISE VOYAGE 23. 19th – 23rd Oct 1967 (New York—St. Thomas—Nassau—New York)
CRUISE VOYAGE 24. 21St – 26th Dec 1967 (New York—Nassau—New York)
CRUISE VOYAGE 25. 27th Dec 1967–3rd Jan 1968 (New York—St. Thomas—Nassau—New York)
CRUISE VOYAGE 26. 5th – 10th Jan 1968 (New York—Nassau—New York)
CRUISE VOYAGE 27. 26th Jan – 7th Feb 1968 ("West Indies Cruise") (New York—Cristobal—Caracas Bay—Barbados—Fort de France—St. Thomas—New York)
CRUISE VOYAGE 28. 21st – 26th Feb 1968 (New York—Nassau—New York)
CRUISE VOYAGE 29. 12th – 16th Apr 1968 (New York—Nassau—New York)
CRUISE VOYAGE 30. 8th – 15th Nov 1968 ("Farewell Cruise" – last scheduled voyage carrying passengers) (Southampton—Las Palmas—Gibraltar— Southampton)

Acknowledgements/Bibliography

Acknowledgements

First of all, I wish to express deep gratitude to Miles Cowsill of Lily Publications for having such a faith in my work and enabling it to become materialised into this wonderfully produced book. Thank you Miles!

There is also a large group of people who have, over the last few years, assisted me in preparing this book. They have lent me their precious time and resources – not to mention patience and encouragement. Their individual input – no matter what or how much, assisted in keeping my "fire" up, maintaining sufficient steam in my boilers, so to speak, in getting the job done.

To these kind hearted collaborators, who make up my world-wide-web of new and old friends I send a sincere thank you, good-on-ya mate, grazie, dankeschön, mercie, 唔該 (Mm Goy), 多謝 (do shia), dank je wel, and gracias. This book is also dedicated to you. I acknowledge specifically:

Beverley Philpot – generous soul and wife of the late Harold Philpot, Michael Gallagher – friend, Public Relations Manager and Historian at Cuanrd in London, Roz Stimpson - Copy Editor at Lily Publications, John Hendy, Ian Smith - book design, the late John Maxtone Graham, David Hutchings, John Duffy, Oswald Brett, the late Arthur Crook, The Estate of the late Biddy Fletcher, Anthony Wornum, Chris Mason, Stephen Davies, Everette Hoard, Scott Becker, David Boone, Commodore Ron Warwick, Captain Ian MacNaught, Holger Friese, John Dockray, Bill Lee, David Jones, Rob Craig Henderson, Douglas Ward, Rob Lightbody, Ian Johnston, Brian Newman, John Patrick Moldt, Philippe Conquer, Stephen Payne, Miles Wybourn, Cass Caswell, Juan and Beverley Martinez, Carolyn Jory, Louise Bloomfield, Josefina Cupido, Chris Konings, Nils Schwerdtner, Robert Lenzer, Russell Galbraith, Bob Malinowski, Gerry Freeman, Dave Hassell, Clark Lee Chi-pan, Peter Donnington, Philippe de Manny, Peter Truscott, John Hudson, Luis Miguel Correia, Charles Cotton, Simon Drake, Marc Piché, Christophe Walter, Neil Roger, Ray Hallett, John Hargreaves, Ed Kamuda (Titanic Historical Society), Heather Cole Kraft, Jon Archibald, Ed Richard, Warren Kendrick, Yvonne Thompson, Ross Goodman, Clement Chan, Geoff Whitmore, Phil G Forder, Ip Wan Lung, Graham Fitzjohn, Edwin J A Webb, Robert Edmiston, Ewart White, Allan Ryszka-Onions, Gerd Laschzok, Rob O'Brien, Edgar Hodges, Alan Richardson, Wayne Morris, James Mackie, Tony Bullock, George Mortimore, Captain Rex Cooper, Dave Beaumont, Geoff Eastwood, Mike Triplett, Neil Higgins, Tony Selman, Chris Howell, Robert Edmiston, Eden Cheung, Lynne Mulholland, Alan Colquhoun, Simon Fisher, H.S.Chan, Michael Cairns, Barry Dunnings, John Cameron Hong Kong Marine Police, Charles EB Shave.

Bibliography

ANDERSON, M.J. "Jock" – *Removal of the Wreck of the Seawise University from Hong Kong Harbor*, (Marine Technology Society Journal, Vol. 13, No. 4. – August-September 1979)

BISSET, Sir James – *Commodore: War, Peace and Big Ships*, (Angus and Robertson, 1961)

BUTLER, Daniel Allen – *Warrior Queens*, (Leo Cooper, 2002)

CASTLE, Colin M. – *Better by Yards*, (Murdock Carberry, 1988)

CONNERS, Michael and KING, Alice – *CY Tung: His Vision and Legacy*, (Format Limited Hong Kong, 1984)

CORNICAN, Frank – *This Noble Ship*, (Steamboat Bill, Number 109, spring 1969)

DAWSON, Philip and PETER, Bruce – *Ship Style: Modernism and Modernity at Sea in the 20th Century*, (Conway Maritime, 2010)

DEMPSEY, John – *I've Seen them all Naked*, (Waterfront Publications, 1992)

EISELE, Peter T. – *The Death of a Queen*, (Steamboat Bill, Number 122 summer 1972)

GALBRAITH, Russell – *Destiny's Daughter: The Tragedy of RMS Queen Elizabeth* (Mainstream Publishing Company Edinburgh, 1988)

GRATTIDGE, Harry – *Captain of the Queens*, (Oldbourne Press, 1956)

HARDING, Stephen – *Great Liners at War*, (Tempus 2007)

HARRIS, Kenny – *Geraldo's Navy*, (Woodland Press, 1998)

HARVEY, Clive – *RMS Queen Elizabeth: The Ultimate Ship*, (Carmania Press, 2008)

HOOD, A.G. (Editor) – *The Cunard White Star Quadruple-Screw Liner Queen Mary*, The Shipbuilder & Marine Engine Builder, June 1936 Reprint, Ocean Liners of the Past (Patrick Stephens Ltd 1972)

HUTCHINGS, David F. -*RMS Queen Elizabeth, From Victory to Valhalla* (Kingfisher Publications, 1990)

HUTCHINGS, David F. -*Southampton Shipping, with Portsmouth Poole & Weymouth* (Carmania Press, 2006)

JOHNMAN, Lewis & JOHNSTON, Ian – *Down the River*, (Argyll Publishing, 2001)

JOHNSTON, Ian – *Ships for a Nation*, (Westdunbartonshire Libraries and Museums, 2000)

KONINGS, Chris – *Queen Elizabeth at War: HMT 1939-1946*, (Patrick Stephens 1985)

MAENPAA, Sari – *Women Below Deck*, (Journal of Transport History; Sep2004, Vol. 25 Issue 2, p57)

MOODY, Bert – *A Pictorial History of Southampton Docks*, (Waterfont Publications, 1994)

MACLEAN, Donald – Queens' Company, (Hutchinson & Co. 1965)

MARR, Geoffrey Thrippleton, *The Queens and I*, (Northumberland Press Limited, 1973)

PLOWMAN, Peter – *Across the Sea to War*, (Rosenberg, 2003)

POTTER, Neil and FROST, Jack – *The Elizabeth*, (George G. Harrap and Co. Ltd. 1965)

REPORT of the Marine Court, *Loss of the s.s Seawise University*, The Marchant Shipping Ordinance Hong Kong, 1972

ROUSSEL, Mike – *Southampton Maritime City – Ocean Liners to Cruise Ships*, (The Derby Books Publishing Company, 2010)

SHIPBUILDING and Shipping Record, Volume 68, from July 4th to December 26, 1946, various articles

SMALLPEICE, Basil – *Of Comets and Queens*, (Airlife Publishing, 1980)

STEVENS, Leonard A. – *The Elizabeth: Passage of a Queen*, (Alfred A. Knopf Inc. 1968)

THELWELL, Robert G. and JACKSON, Robert – *I Captained the Big Ships*, (Arthur Barker Ltd. 1961)

WALKER, Colin – *Memory of a Queen: RMS Queen Elizabeth*, (Oxford Publishing Co. 1972)

WATT, D.S. and BIRT, Raymond – *The Queen Elizabeth*, (Winchester Publications, 1947)

WORNUM, Miriam – *Grey Matter* – (From the unpublished biography of Grey Wornum)